Lutheranism 101

General Editor: Scot A. Kinnaman

Assisting Editor: Laura L. Lane

Contributors:

Rose E. Adle

Charles P. Arand

Gary M. Arp

Ernest Bernet

Scott A. Bruzek

David J. Bueltmann

Kent J. Burreson

Allan R. Buss

Paul J Cain

Terry Cripe

Stewart D. Crown

H. R. Curtis

Rebekah Curtis

Randy Duncan

John G. Fleischmann

Dan Paul Gilbert

Jill Hasstedt

John Hellwege Jr.

Michael L. Keith

Shawn L. Kumm

Naomichi Masaki

Benjamin T. G. Mayes

Heather Melcher

Herbert C. Mueller Jr.

Scott R. Murray

Timothy Pauls

John T. Pless

Kurt Rolland

Douglas L. Rutt

Leopoldo A. Sánchez M.

Peter J. Scaer

Peter A. Speckhard

Scott Stiegemeyer

Cynda Strong

William H. Tucker

Gene Edward Veith Jr.

Larry M. Vogel

James Wetzstein

Roland Ziegler

CONCORDIA PUBLISHING HOUSE • SAINT LOUIS

Library of Congress Cataloging-in-Publication Data

Lutheranism 101 / general editor, Scot A. Kinnaman ; assisting editor, Laura L. Lane ; contributors, Charles P. Arand ... [et al.].
    p. cm.
  ISBN 978-0-7586-2505-2
  1. Lutheran Church. I. Kinnaman, Scot A. II. Lane, Laura L. III. Arand, Charles P. IV. Title.

  BX8011.A1L88 2010
  230'.41--dc22

2010025013

    4 5 6 7 8 9 10 11   19 18 17 16 15 14 13 12 11 10

Contents

Getting Started

Making a beginning is a crucial part of any journey; it can set you up for success or leave you scrambling to get on board. In this introductory section, you will learn about how this book is organized and some basics that will set a foundation for the parts that follow.

Quick Start Guide

When you are looking for primary material that quickly gives some of the fundamental teachings of Lutheranism, turn to the handy Quick Start Guide.

Part One: It's All about the Relationships

When God created mankind, it was His plan that we would have an everlasting relationship with Him. Sin destroyed that relationship. In sending Jesus Christ as the Savior of all mankind, God has done what we could never do to restore our relationship with Himself.

Part Two: Delivering the Gifts of God

The power of God and the grace of God are administered in the world for the benefit of all who have faith. God gives authority and power to the civil government to establish order and peace. God's Word establishes the Church. In the Church, God delivers the gifts of faith, forgiveness of sins, and everlasting life.

Part Three: The Means of Grace

God offers, bestows, and seals to people forgiveness of sins, life, and salvation through the Means of Grace. Lutherans recognize the Means of Grace as God's Word and the Sacraments, namely, Holy Baptism and the Lord's Supper.

Part Four: Lutherans at a Glance

Lutheranism arose out of a desire to reform the doctrine and practices of the Roman Catholic Church, but after being rejected by the Roman Church, has grown to be the fourth-largest Christian tradition in the world.

Part Five: Worship: The Blessings of God

People often think that worship is about what we do for or toward God. The reality is quite different. In the Divine Service, God comes to us and provides His service for us. The work we do in worship is to receive the gift of God's grace and respond.

Part Six: Living as Lutherans

Having received from God all good things for our body and for our soul, as Christians we live in relationship with not only God but also our neighbors. The love we have received becomes active in our faith. In this way the believer becomes the mouth confessing the Good News of Jesus Christ and the hands of God working for the good of the neighbor.

GETTING STARTED

The beginning is a crucial part of any journey; it can set you up for success or leave you scrambling to get on board. In this introductory section, you will learn how this book is organized and some basics that will set a foundation for the parts that follow.

Introduction

What Is This Book?

Lutheranism 101 gives you a quick, usable, and comprehensive overview of Lutheran faith and practice. While we have tried not to grind any axes, we would be less than living, breathing human beings if we told you that what you have here is totally impartial and neutral. First, we must acknowledge that we are writing about Lutheranism from an American perspective. So in discussions of customs, history, and missions, Lutherans in other parts of the world (and there are many!) will have a different perspective. We are also writing from within a tradition in the Lutheran Church that is identified as orthodox and confessional. The term *orthodox* simply means correct or right belief. The term *confessional* has come to mean different things to different people, but at its heart these two terms signify those who model what they believe, teach, and confess on God's Word and the historic teachings (Confessions) of the Lutheran Church as they are contained in the Book of Concord. Finally, we have to acknowledge that a book of this size is inadequate to cover the entire length and breadth of our subject. However, what you now hold in your hand is a good place to start your exploration of Lutheran belief and practice.

Who Are Those People?

Don't let the long list of contributors and titles intimidate you. People with many different backgrounds and positions contributed to *Lutheranism 101*—from presidents to pastors to professors to parents. Some of us have advanced degrees; some of us don't. Some of us are lifelong Lutherans; some of us aren't. Be assured that at some point all of us were once right where you are now: wondering about this thing called Lutheranism. We learned by attending worship services, asking questions of our pastors, and reading the Bible, among other things. You can do the same! If at any time you want to know more about a particular topic covered in *Lutheranism 101*, just ask your pastor or refer to the list of resources found in the Appendix.

Don't Be Afraid of the Latin

. . . or of the Hebrew, Greek, or German for that matter.

Every area of life has its own technical terms or jargon. Computers, car maintenance, a visit to the hardware store, and even cooking all have their own special words. It's no different for Lutheran Christians. We have many foreign words, or words taken into English from other languages. But why do we need them?

Unfortunately, the meanings of words change over time. This presents a danger: words that once communicated the Christian faith with perfect clarity are now no longer understood or have changed meanings. When this happens, those old words are often kept as technical terms, especially if our modern language doesn't have any words that still capture the full meaning of the old words. This sort of thing has been happening for centuries, especially as the Church has changed languages, and it's why we have so many technical terms. These words are like shorthand or abbreviations. They say something profound with just a few letters. These old terms, if explained, are lovely and meaningful. They are a way in which the wisdom, faith, and love of ages past are handed down to us.

Ultimately, since we desired to speak and write accurately about God, we could not avoid using some Lutheran-specific terms and the various languages of Scripture and theology used by the Church. However, we have inserted special icons, definitions, and translations to help you understand what is meant when these terms and words are used.

Abbreviations

AE   Luther, Martin. *Luther's Works.* American Edition. Volumes 1–30: Edited by Jaroslav Pelikan. St. Louis: Concordia, 1955–76. Volumes 31–55: Edited by Helmut Lehmann. Philadelphia/Minneapolis: Muhlenberg/Fortress, 1957–86. Volumes 56–75: Edited by Christopher Boyd Brown. St. Louis: Concordia, 2009–.

LW   Commission on Worship of The Lutheran Church—Missouri Synod. *Lutheran Worship.* St. Louis: Concordia, 1982.

TDP   *Treasury of Daily Prayer.* St. Louis: Concordia, 2008.

TLSB   *The Lutheran Study Bible.* St. Louis: Concordia, 2009.

Lutheran Confessions

You will see many quotations from the Lutheran Confessions as found in the Book of Concord. The following list provides abbreviations used, what they mean, and examples of how you would find the text.

AC   Augsburg Confession

Ap   Apology of the Augsburg Confession

BEC   A Brief Exhortation to Confession

Ep   Epitome of the Formula of Concord

FC   Formula of Concord

SA	Smalcald Articles
SC	Small Catechism
SD	Solid Declaration of the Formula of Concord
Tr	Treatise on the Power and Primacy of the Pope

Examples:

AC XX 4 (Augsburg Confession, Article XX, paragraph 4)

Ap IV 229 (Apology of the AC, Article IV, paragraph 229)

FC SD X 24 (Solid Declaration of the Formula of Concord, Article X, paragraph 24)

FC Ep V 8 (Epitome of the Formula of Concord, Article V, paragraph 8)

LC V 32, 37 (Large Catechism, Part 5, paragraphs 32 and 37)

SA III I 6 (Smalcald Articles, Part III, Article I, paragraph 6)

SC III 5 (Small Catechism, Part III, paragraph 5)

Tr 5 (Treatise, paragraph 5)

Navigating Lutheranism 101

WHAT DOES THIS MEAN?
Quotes from Martin Luther

MAKING CONNECTIONS
Connecting theology, faith, and life

NEED TO KNOW
Terms and phrases quickly defined

FROM THE BIBLE
Quotations from, well, the Bible

TECHNICAL STUFF
Big theological concepts in bite-size pieces

BELIEVE, TEACH, CONFESS
Quotations from the Lutheran Confessions

Reader's Guide to Scripture's Essential Teachings

These references are presented to encourage the study of, and the meditation on, the essential teachings of Scripture. This is by no means an exhaustive list, nor are all the great topics found in Scripture listed. In addition to inclusion in personal devotions, these references can serve as an outline for discussion or confession of the faith.

Creation and the Doctrine of Man

Genesis 1–2
Job 10:8–12; 38:8–9, 19–20
Genesis 3

Justification by Grace through Faith

Ephesians 2:16
Romans 8:6–8
Romans 3:23–24
2 Corinthians 5:21
Romans 4:25
1 Corinthians 15:20–23
1 Peter 1:3–4
John 3:17–18
Ephesians 2:8–9
Romans 6:3–4; 8:1–4

Sanctification

Philippians 4:4, 8
Romans 8:2–11

One God in Three Persons

Isaiah 44:6
Deuteronomy 4:35; 6:4–19
1 Corinthians 8:6

Genesis 1:26

Baptism of Jesus; Transfiguration of Jesus

John 14:9–10
Matthew 28:19
Ephesians 2:18
1 John 4:13
1 Corinthians 12:3
2 Corinthians 3:18

The Nature of God

Psalm 40:11, 51:1; 54:1; 85:7
Psalm 10:15; 59:5; 80:4
Psalm 53:2–3, 5
John 3:16
Psalm 85:4–7
Psalm 86:15
Romans 1:16–17
1 John 4:8–10

Jesus Christ: the God-man

John 1:1–4, 14, 16
Luke 2:1–20
Hebrews 2:14–18; 4:15
1 Peter 2:22–24; 3:18

The Means of Grace

2 Corinthians 5:19
Romans 3:21–28
Romans 1:16
Matthew 28:19
Ephesians 5:26
Titus 3:3–6
Romans 6:3–10
Colossians 2:12–13
1 Corinthians 12:12–13
Matthew 26:26–29
Mark 14:22–25
Luke 22:15–20
1 Corinthians 10:14–22; 11:17–34
Revelation 19:7–9

The Church of Jesus Christ

2 Timothy 1:9
Ephesians 1:18; 4:11
Colossians 1:12–20
1 Corinthians 6:11
Galatians 3:26–29
1 Peter 2:9–10
Hebrews 10:25
Ephesians 4:1–16
Ephesians 2:20

QUICK START GUIDE

What you'll learn about:

- Summary of the Christian faith
- The creeds
- Luther's seal
- The *Solas* of Lutheranism
- Common prayers for Lutherans

❶ Summary of the Christian Faith

These are the most important texts that every Christian should learn, know, and believe.

The Ten Commandments

The Ten Commandments show us our sin and our need for a Savior.

You shall have no other gods.

You shall not misuse the name of the Lord your God.

Remember the Sabbath day by keeping it holy.

Honor your father and your mother.

You shall not murder.

You shall not commit adultery.

You shall not steal.

You shall not give false testimony against your neighbor.

You shall not covet your neighbor's house.

You shall not covet your neighbor's wife, or his manservant or maidservant, his ox or donkey, or anything that belongs to your neighbor. (Deuteronomy 5:6–21)

I, the Lord your God, am a jealous God, punishing the children for the sin of the fathers to the third and the fourth generation of those who hate Me, but showing love to a thousand generations of those who love Me and keep My commandments. (Exodus 20:5–6)

The Apostles' Creed

The Apostles' Creed helps us confess the God who has done everything to save us from sin through Jesus Christ and to make us members of His Church.

I believe in God, the Father Almighty, Maker of heaven and earth.

And in Jesus Christ, His only Son, our Lord, who was conceived by the Holy Spirit, born of the Virgin Mary, suffered under Pontius Pilate, was crucified, died and was buried. He descended into hell. The third day He rose again from the dead. He ascended into heaven and sits at the right hand of God, the Father Almighty. From thence He will come to judge the living and the dead.

I believe in the Holy Spirit, the holy Christian church, the communion of saints, the forgiveness of sins, the resurrection of the body, and the life everlasting. Amen.

The Lord's Prayer

In the Lord's Prayer, we call upon God, the only source for all we need.

Our Father, who art in heaven, hallowed be Thy name, Thy kingdom come, Thy will be done on earth as it is in heaven. Give us this day our daily bread; and forgive us our trespasses as we forgive those who trespass against us; and lead us not into temptation, but deliver us from evil. For Thine is the kingdom and the power and the glory forever and ever. Amen. (See Matthew 6:9–13)

Holy Baptism

In Holy Baptism we are united with the life, death, and resurrection of Jesus Christ. Through Baptism the Holy Spirit gives to us the forgiveness of sins, life, and salvation.

Therefore go and make disciples of all nations, baptizing them in the name of the Father and of the Son and of the Holy Spirit. (Matthew 28:19)

Whoever believes and is baptized will be saved, but whoever does not believe will be condemned. (Mark 16:16)

He saved us through the washing of rebirth and renewal by the Holy Spirit, whom He poured out on us generously through Jesus Christ our Savior, so that having been justified by His grace, we might become heirs having the hope of eternal life. This is a trustworthy saying. (Titus 3:5–8)

We were therefore buried with Him through baptism into death in order that, just as Christ was raised from the dead through the glory of the Father, we too might walk in newness of life. (Romans 6:4)

Confession and Absolution

Confession and Absolution daily returns us to the promises and hope given to us in our Baptism.

Jesus breathed on His disciples and said, "Receive the Holy Spirit. If you forgive anyone his sins, they are forgiven; if you do not forgive them, they are not forgiven." (John 20:22–23)

The Lord's Supper

The Lord's Supper, also called the Sacrament of the Altar, is the true body and blood of our Lord Jesus Christ under the bread and wine, instituted by Christ Himself for us Christians to eat and to drink to strengthen faith against the temptations of the devil, the world, and our sinful flesh.

The holy Evangelists Matthew, Mark, Luke, and St. Paul write:

Our Lord Jesus Christ, on the night when He was betrayed, took bread, and when He had given thanks, He broke it and gave it to the disciples and said: "Take, eat; this is My body, which is given for you. This do in remembrance of Me."

In the same way also He took the cup after supper, and when He had given thanks, He gave it to them, saying: "Drink of it, all of you; this cup is the new testament in My blood, which is shed for you for the forgiveness of sins. This do, as often as you drink it, in remembrance of Me." (Matthew 26:26–28; Mark 14:22–24; Luke 22:19–20; 1 Corinthians 11:23–25)

❷The Creeds

A creed (from the Latin *credo*, "I believe") is a confession of faith used by individual Christians, congregations, and churches to give voice to what is believed, taught, and confessed about God. The Apostles' Creed is the oldest of the three Ecumenical Creeds (see pp. 236–38). The Apostles' Creed is often called the Baptismal Creed. It is commonly used in worship services where Holy Communion is not being celebrated, in small groups, and for individual prayer.

Apostles' Creed

I believe in God, the Father Almighty,
    Maker of heaven and earth.

And in Jesus Christ, His only Son, our Lord,
    who was conceived by the Holy Spirit,
    born of the virgin Mary,
    suffered under Pontius Pilate,
    was crucified, died and was buried.
    He descended into hell.
    The third day He rose again from the dead.
    He ascended into heaven
    and sits at the right hand of God, the Father Almighty.
    From thence He will come to judge the living and the dead.

I believe in the Holy Spirit,
    the holy Christian Church,
        the communion of saints,
    the forgiveness of sins,
    the resurrection of the body,
    and the life everlasting. Amen.

The Nicene Creed was developed to respond to controversies over the doctrine of the Trinity and the deity of Jesus Christ. As a result, the Nicene Creed talks more about Jesus and His relationship with the Father and the Holy Spirit. The Nicene Creed is used in worship services where Holy Communion is celebrated.

Nicene Creed

I believe in one God,
  the Father Almighty,
  maker of heaven and earth
    and of all things visible and invisible.

And in one Lord Jesus Christ,
  the only-begotten Son of God,
  begotten of His Father before all worlds,
  God of God, Light of Light,
  very God of very God,
  begotten, not made,
  being of one substance with the Father,
  by whom all things were made;
  who for us men and for our salvation came down from heaven
  and was incarnate by the Holy Spirit of the virgin Mary and was made man;
  and was crucified also for us under Pontius Pilate.
  He suffered and was buried.
  And the third day He rose again according to the Scriptures
    and ascended into heaven
  and sits at the right hand of the Father.
  And He will come again with glory to judge both the living and the dead,
  whose kingdom will have no end.

And I believe in the Holy Spirit,
  the Lord and giver of life,
  who proceeds from the Father and the Son,
  who with the Father and Son together is worshiped and glorified,
  who spoke by the prophets.
  And I believe in one holy Christian and apostolic Church,
  I acknowledge one Baptism for the remission of sins,
  and I look for the resurrection of the dead
  and the life of the world to come. Amen.

Although never officially adopted by the Church, the Athanasian Creed affirms Christian beliefs, especially Christ's divinity and His equality with the persons of the Trinity. The text of the Athanasian Creed can be found in *Lutheran Service Book*, pp. 319–20.

❸Luther's Seal

Martin Luther's seal is easily the most recognized symbol for Lutheranism, and for good reason. In Luther's day it was common practice for prominent members of the community to have a personal seal or coat of arms. The symbolism on the seal would tell others something about the person, what they did or believed. Through his bold preaching and teaching about the Word of God, Martin Luther had become well-known. So it was that while Luther was at Coburg Castle in 1530, Duke John Frederick, the Electoral Prince of Saxony, made an order for the creation of a seal that was meant to express Luther's theology. Luther's seal is rich with symbols and color. In a letter to a friend, Luther explained the symbolism of his seal.

WHAT DOES THIS MEAN?

Luther's seal clearly speaks what he believed about his salvation. He called it "my summary of theology."

The Meaning of Luther's Seal

"Grace and peace in Christ! Honorable, kind, gentleman and friend,

Since you are keen to know whether or not your example of my seal hit the mark, let me share with you in a friendly way some of my preliminary thoughts regarding the elements of my seal that I want to fashion as a kind of trademark for my theology.

The first element should be a cross, black within the heart. That is the color that it should naturally have, by which I can remind myself that faith in the Crucified One makes us into saved people. One becomes justified according to what one believes in the heart.

Now, about why it is a black cross, it should put the flesh to death; it should hurt. But leave the heart in its proper color [red]. This is because, through the cross, the human nature does not decay. The cross does not kill off the human nature altogether; rather, it preserves the human nature in new life. The just person shall live by faith, but only by faith in the Crucified One.

But this heart should be located in the middle of a white rose to show that faith gives joy, comfort, and peace. It immediately sets [the believer] into the midst of a white, joyful rose, not like the peace and joy that the world offers. That is why the rose should be white, not red. White is the color of the spirits and all angels.

This rose is set within a sky-colored field, because this joy that is comprehended in spirit and faith, this joy that is now grasped in hope but not yet openly revealed, is the beginning of the heavenly joy to come.

And around this field is a golden ring, because salvation in heaven endures forever; it has no end. It is more precious than all other kinds of joy and wealth, just as gold is the most noble, most precious of all ores.

May Christ our dear Lord be with your spirit, even unto that heavenly life to come. Amen!" (See AE 49:356-359)

❹ The *Solas* of Lutheranism

The Reformation rested upon three fundamental principles:

1. Our salvation is entirely a gift of grace from God and not our own doing.

2. We receive that grace through faith and not by any works we might do.

3. The sole norm and rule of all doctrine is the Holy Scriptures.

Although the word *sola* means "alone," the irony is that the three *solas* that follow are never alone! They are interconnected and woven together. These principles are referred to as the "three *solas*": **by grace alone, through faith alone, in Scripture alone**. To these many writers have added another *sola—to Christ alone*. Together these "Reformation *solas*" form a concise and useful outline of what Lutherans believe, teach, and confess.

Sola Scriptura: **Scripture Alone**

Lutherans believe that the Bible is the inspired Word of God and that it alone is the source and norm for what we believe and what we practice. Lutherans are not anti-reason or anti-tradition or anti-experience. We simply use the Scriptures to judge the validity of these things and not the other way around. We believe the Bible is God's perfect Word; therefore, we don't approach the Scriptures with a red pen!

NEED TO KNOW

Sola: The Latin word *sola* means "only" or "alone."

Sola Gratia: **Grace Alone**

At the center of what we believe is the assurance that salvation is based on the unearned free gift of God's grace. What is so amazing about grace is that though we are sinful by nature and deserve God's anger, we receive the riches of His love.

FROM THE BIBLE

For by grace you have been saved through faith. And this is not your own doing; it is the gift of God, not a result of works, so that no one may boast. (Ephesians 2:8–9)

WHAT DOES THIS MEAN?

We believe, as Luther says in his explanation of the Apostles' Creed, "that Jesus Christ, true God, begotten of the Father from eternity, and also true man, born of the Virgin Mary, is my Lord, who has redeemed me, a lost and condemned person, . . . not with gold or silver, but with His holy, precious blood and with His innocent suffering and death." (SC, Second Article)

Sola Fide: Faith Alone

God's gift of grace is received though faith in what Jesus has done for us. The good things we do flow out of being made right with God, but they have no power to make us right with God. This is what separates Christianity from all other world religions. Other religions point to what we have to do or what hoops we have to jump through to be made right with God. Christianity points to what Christ has done to make us right with God. Through God's Word, Baptism, and the Lord's Supper our faith is created and sustained.

Solo Christo: Christ Alone

Our sole basis and assurance of salvation is the life, death, and resurrection of God's Son, Jesus Christ. Christianity is inclusive in that Jesus died for the sins of the whole world. It is exclusive in that Jesus taught that there were not many ways to the Father. There is only one way: Himself! (See John 14:6.) And there is Good News: None of your sins have caught Jesus off guard. He knows you better than you know yourself. The One who knows you the most also loves you the most!

MAKING CONNECTIONS

Remember: It is not what we *do* but what God has *done* with what we *did* that counts!

❺ Common Prayers for Lutherans

Prayer at the Beginning of the Day

I thank You, my heavenly Father, through Jesus Christ, Your dear Son, that You have kept me this night from all harm and danger; and I pray that You would keep me this day also from sin and every evil, that all my doings and life may please You. For into Your hands I commend myself, my body and soul, and all things. Let Your holy angel be with me, that the evil foe may have no power over me. Amen.

Prayer at the End of the Day

I thank You, my heavenly Father, through Jesus Christ, Your dear Son, that You have graciously kept me this day; and I pray that You would forgive me all my sins where I have done wrong, and graciously keep me this night. For into Your hands I commend myself, my body and soul, and all things. Let Your holy angel be with me, that the evil foe may have no power over me. Amen.

Asking a Blessing before a Meal

The eyes of all look to You, [O Lord,] and You give them their food at the proper time. You open Your hand and satisfy the desires of every living thing. (Psalm 145:15–16)

Then shall be said the Lord's Prayer and the following:
Lord God, heavenly Father, bless us and these Your gifts which we receive from Your bountiful goodness, through Jesus Christ, our Lord. Amen.

Returning Thanks after a Meal

Give thanks to the Lord, for He is good. His love endures forever. [He] gives food to every creature. He provides food for the cattle and for the young ravens when they call. His pleasure is not in the strength of the horse, nor His delight in the legs of a man; the Lord delights in those who fear Him, who put their hope in His unfailing love. (Psalm 136:1, 25; 147:9–11)

Then shall be said the Lord's Prayer and the following:
We thank You, Lord God, heavenly Father, for all Your benefits, through Jesus Christ, our Lord, who lives and reigns with You and the Holy Spirit forever and ever. Amen.

PART ONE

What you'll learn about:

- God reveals Himself in three persons: Father, Son, and Holy Spirit.

- God has a fundamental problem with us called sin, and this problem has deadly consequences.

- While we cannot solve the problem of sin, God's plan of salvation redeems us from the consequences of sin and brings us into a relationship with Him.

- Only faith in Jesus Christ saves us.

- On the Last Day, Jesus will return and pass eternal judgment on all believers and unbelievers; the believers will begin to enjoy everlasting life with God, while unbelievers will be forever separated from God.

It's All about the Relationships

When God created mankind, it was His plan that we would have an everlasting relationship with Him. Sin destroyed that relationship. In sending Jesus Christ as the Savior of all mankind, God has done what we could never do to restore our relationship with Himself.

CHAPTER 1

Who Is God?

In This Chapter
- We know that God exists.
- God is three persons: Father, Son, and Holy Spirit.
- The doctrine of creation informs us what God is and who we are.
- We are different than the rest of creation.

What We Know

First, the bad news: there are many things about God that we cannot explain. Even theologians have to admit that they cannot answer every single God-related question. For example, if you want to know what kept God busy before the creation of the world, you will have to wait to ask the Source Himself. However, there are a great many things about God that we do know and that we can explain.

FROM THE BIBLE

For what can be known about God is plain to them, because God has shown it to them. For His invisible attributes, namely, His eternal power and divine nature, have been clearly perceived, ever since the creation of the world, in the things that have been made. So they are without excuse. (Romans 1:19–20)

We know that God exists. We know there is a God because of creation. Looking around, it is obvious the cosmos did not come into existence accidentally. We know there is a God because His Law is written in our hearts—morality is hardwired into us. Most of us feel, perhaps even without instruction, that it is not okay to murder or steal or lie. Deep down, at our core, we know right from wrong. We know there is a God because our heart says so. Call it a hunch; call it a deity-shaped hole.

But if we knew of God's existence only from nature and our own feeble tickers, that would not be a full knowledge of God. It would constitute only a natural knowledge or a conscience. That is not enough to enter a good relationship with this nebulous godlike thing that we think must exist.

We know the one and only true God through the way He has chosen to reveal Himself. And while God could have set up a difficult communication system, He used a medium with which we are all familiar: words.

1 + 1 + 1 = 1

In Scripture, God tells us about Himself, and we learn that while there is only one God, He is three persons: Father, Son, and Holy Spirit. Now this whole three-in-one and one-in-three business known as the Trinity is downright mind-boggling. We do not arrive at our understanding of God because it is reasonable or logical or mathematically sound, but because it has been revealed to us in Scripture.

Interestingly enough, the word *Trinity* never appears in Scripture. A long time ago a theologian took the liberty of assigning a name to this concept so that we do not talk in circles whenever we refer to the threeness of the one God.

Both the Old and New Testaments state that there is only one God. We also learn that the one true God consists of more than one person. Genesis 1:26 says, "Let Us make man in Our image." The three persons of the Trinity work together. A clear example of this is found at Jesus' Baptism, where we see

1. God the *Son* as an in-the-flesh human being,

2. God the *Holy Spirit* in the form of a dove, and

3. God the *Father's* voice coming down from heaven.

Also, when Jesus commands Holy Baptism in Matthew 28:19, He tells the apostles to baptize in the name of the Father, Son, and Holy Spirit. The one, singular name *God* includes all three persons of the Trinity.

Just to make sure we are all on the same page:

The Father is not the Son or the Holy Spirit.

The Son is not the Father or the Holy Spirit.

The Holy Spirit is not the Father or the Son.

They are all God—not three gods, but one God in three persons.

The three persons are all equally good and equally important. There are no inferiority complexes or power struggles within the Trinity.

All that being said, if you still do not completely understand who God is, you are in good company. The truth is that God has not revealed everything

TECHNICAL STUFF

In order to refer to the one true God of three persons, Tertullian (a theologian during the late second and early third centuries AD) coined the term *Trinity*. *Trinity* is now the shortcut we use to describe the fact that there is one God, and yet that one God is three persons. There are not three gods, nor is there only one person who appears to us in three different forms.

One God. Three persons. Three in One.

about Himself. Numerous errors and false teachings started because people wanted a God who fits their own limited human understanding. But Lutherans are most comfortable in confessing what God has revealed to us about Himself. No more, no less.

Creator, Creation, and Creatures

Scripture's narrative of creation does not just explain where everything came from. The account of creation defines what it means to be God. This may sound somewhat surprising and perhaps even a little bizarre. But ask yourself this question: what makes God *God*? What qualifies someone for the title of God? Often people provide an abstract and somewhat philosophical definition of God. It usually works something like this: "God is whatever we are not." In other words, since we are finite (that is, having limits and bounds), God must be infinite. Since we are limited in knowledge, God must be all-knowing (omniscient). Since we are confined in space, God must be present everywhere (omnipresent). Well, you get the idea. Or perhaps God might be defined as the Supreme Being—whatever that might mean.

> Lutherans confess what God has revealed to us. No more, no less.

Scripture takes a simpler and more obvious approach to the issue. It goes like this: "If you created everything that exists, then you are God. If you did not create everything that exists, then you are not God." Throughout the Old Testament (but especially in the Book of Isaiah), this is how idols or false gods are identified. They could not be God. Why? Because they were made with human hands. The very material from which these idols were constructed was made by the God, the creator of the heavens and the earth!

Creation also says something to us about the nature of God. When Scripture says that God created heaven and earth, it is saying that God created everything that exists. By mentioning two opposites, such as "heaven and earth," Scripture includes everything in between. It is like saying that God created everything from A to Z. The Early Church drew from these statements the teaching that God created everything *ex nihilo* (Latin, "out of nothing"). God did not depend on or use any preexisting materials for creation. This also means that He was not limited by any material in the way that a painter might be limited by the medium of watercolors or acrylics or oils.

There is a consistency to how God acts in creation and in salvation. He does both freely, that is, by grace.

An important consequence of the teaching that God created everything is that God created out of extravagant generosity. That is, nothing compelled God to create the world or us. As Martin Luther expressed it in his Small Catechism, God created us "out of fatherly, divine goodness and mercy, without any merit or worthiness in me." And so there is a consistency to how God acts in creation and in salvation. He does both freely, out of love for mankind.

God Is Good

If asked, "who is God?" the best answer is simply, "Father, Son, and Holy Spirit." That is who God is. The three Ecumenical Creeds explain each member of the triune God and describe how they work together (see pp. 236–38). The work of creation is given to God the Father. God the Son saves. God the Holy Spirit works faith in us.

We can also list some of God's characteristics, often referred to as His attributes. We know who God is by what He does and how He regards us. God is good. Luther pointed out that the words God and good are tied together—not only with regard to word origins but also with regard to God's very nature. Luther described God as "the Author and Source of good" (Pieper 1:433).

God the Father creates. God the Son saves. God the Holy Spirit works faith in us.

This good God is also merciful and just, not to mention all-knowing, all-powerful, and all-present. Another big bonus for us is that God is eternal and unchanging. In other words, He is who He is, and He stays that way. So all of those things listed above have been true of God for all time and will be true of God for all time. And these characteristics are true of each person of the Trinity. There is not one good guy and one bad guy—they are all good, and they all work together out of love for us.

Who Are We?

Now one final question: who are we? Or more specifically, who are we in relation to the triune God?

Through God's Word, our identity crisis is solved once and for all. Here is the

FROM THE BIBLE

For You formed my inward parts; You knitted me together in my mother's womb. I praise You, for I am fearfully and wonderfully made. Wonderful are Your works; my soul knows it very well. (Psalm 139:13–14)

FROM THE BIBLE

God's first act, the creation, is an act of grace. Even after the fall and the coming of sin, much of the goodness that God built into creation remains. Philosophers debate why evil exists, and people ask how a good God could allow bad things to happen. But it is not the existence of evil and suffering that requires an explanation; it is the existence of goodness and beauty and love that is most remarkable. A world without God cannot explain such things. The persistence of goodness reminds us of what we have lost, but it also offers us a glimpse of God's grace and the everlasting glory to which God has called us through Christ. (*TLSB*, p. 12)

truth: we are God's creatures, made by Him. We are not accidents. God Himself made us. We are unique from the rest of creation because we are created in the image of God Himself. When the Trinity created the world and everything in it, the grand finale was us. He saved the best for last.

That God is Creator gives us some important context. We are creatures! We are not gods. As creatures, we are not independent, autonomous, self-sufficient, self-determining beings. To the contrary, as creatures we are by definition dependent and contingent beings. Or to paraphrase the words of the apostle Paul, "What do we have that we have not received?" (see 1 Corinthians 4:7). As creatures, we are dependent upon God and His gifts.

But we also find ourselves as creatures among other creatures. The doctrine of creation shows that we are within a world in which we are interconnected and interdependent with God's creation and His other creatures. We are dependent upon the air we breathe, the water we drink, and the food we eat. Take these away, and we die. All of this suggests that we need to learn how to live as creatures rather than trying to live as if we were God. But then, that gets us into the next chapter.

CHAPTER 2

That's a Sin

In This Chapter

- Our fundamental distrust of God and His Word causes a problem in our relationship with God.
- Original sin is the desire that there be no God.
- Only God, in the Bible, truly shows and describes the depth of original sin and its consequences.
- Sin is a big deal and has deadly consequences.

Are Rules Really Made to Be Broken?

A lot of people, even Christians, think that too much has been made of sin. Sin is thought of as illicit fun, something just off the mark of some dumb rule made up by religion. And stupid rules, well, they are just meant to be broken. After all, life is about fun and happiness, joy and self-expression, freedom and self-fulfillment, isn't it?

There are others who discount sin, accepting that bad things happen. Or they plead, "How can I be responsible for my actions if my genes influence me? You expect me to act contrary to my nature?" They even ask, "Why should I be blamed if an evil force causes trouble? You know, the devil made me do it."

Underlying both of these positions is the belief that sin somehow doesn't apply. The problem with this line of thought is the assumption that human beings are the be-all and end-all and that morality is something that can be individually defined.

> **NEED TO KNOW**
>
> **Sin:** betraying God; rejecting His will and His ways; any thought, word, or deed that departs from the will of God.

The Bible, God's Word, turns that false thinking on its head. We don't define the reality in which we live; we don't create anything. "In the beginning, God created the heavens and the earth" (Genesis 1:1). This is the fundamental statement of Scripture. It gives us our context and defines our reality. We come into existence as part of reality that has already been defined, a world that is already created; values, morality—these have already been defined by the Creator who existed before anything else did. Genesis 1:1 asserts that all things are God's. He owns and has rights over everything. And one day, as a child of His creation, you will answer to Him for your every thought, word, and deed.

Identifying sin as personal and assigning the problem to ourselves causes us to fidget and squirm. Acknowledging an occasional white lie or admitting we do not always follow the Commandments is not too hard. Personally being accountable, accepting guilt, and submitting to God's judgment—that is when we find it far preferable to shift responsibility, find an excuse, and avoid confronting the real source of the bad and the wrong: sin.

A Damaged Relationship

There is a huge gap between our Creator and us, and it exceeds our ability to describe its extent. Guided by a compass that cannot point true north, we are unable to navigate toward God; our life and purposes are not aimed toward God. Sin is more than the individual bad things we do—let's call those words and deeds "fruit." Sin is the corrupt attitude and will of all humanity—let's name that "the root." The root of the problem is our fundamental desire that there not be a God so we can be the captains of our own souls, the self-determiners of what is good and right. That desire ultimately leads us to distrust God and His Word.

FROM THE BIBLE

The heart is deceitful above all things, and desperately sick; who can understand it? (Jeremiah 17:9)

By questioning the rights God has over us, Satan challenged the goodness of God as the giver of life and enticed Eve to rely on herself for the good. By rearranging God's words, Adam and Eve aspired to assume God's place, asserting themselves as the final determiners of what is good. This root sin, called original sin, is our desire and search for personal meaning and identity apart from what the Creator has bestowed. As punishment for this sin, Adam and Eve were limited at every point by death. They could not return themselves to a life of trust in God, and they would also experience this separation from God in their own bodies—they would return to the dust from which man is made. Man is by nature weak, ungodly, sinful, and an enemy of God (see Romans 5:6–10).

It Makes a Difference

Sin may be divided into original sin (the inherited corruption and its tendency to sin) and actual sin. Actual sin (every thought, emotion, word, or act conflicting with God's Law) may be involuntary or may be done ignorantly, and includes sins of commission and sins of omission. Sin gets only one reaction from God: His righteous wrath and punishment.

This original desire to be our own god and distrust the true God has affected every person's nature and all of our powers; even reason is corrupted.

> The root of the problem is our fundamental desire that there not be a God.

Sin is so deeply rooted in us that with all of our reason we cannot discern its depth; we can neither clearly see ourselves in relation to God nor rightly describe our circumstance before God.

Only God, in the Bible, truly shows and describes the depth of original sin and its consequences. Remember, God does not need anyone's permission to establish what is right and what is wrong. He is God. Everything belongs to Him.

The Ten Commandments identify, forbid, and condemn this root sin and its bad fruit: disbelief and false belief of God, defiance of parents, neglect of neighbors, slander, and selfish cravings. (See p. 15) We have lost all of our created goodness; we neither will nor can depend on God for anything. Our corruption is so deep and pervasive that the Bible declares us separated from God—dead. We cannot begin, maintain, or conclude a relationship with God. It doesn't matter if you don't think God's Commandments are important, and it doesn't matter if a majority of society feels something different. God is God, and the very fact that we even question this is the evidence of our corruption and of the brokenness of our relationship with God.

BELIEVE, TEACH, CONFESS

Original sin is also called hereditary sin, not that sin is encoded in human DNA, but because every person is as Adam, without actual trust in God.

Concupiscence *is another word for original sin; it includes not only sinful lusts and actions, and not just that human beings ignore and despise God, lack fear and trust in Him, hate His judgment and flee from it, are angry at Him, despair of His mercy, and trust in temporal things, but that human beings are actually incapable of doing otherwise.* (See Ap II 3, 6.)

Who Is Responsible?

To recognize our nature as sinful does not mean that God created mankind as disobedient or that our created essence is sinful. God created and declared all He created "very good" (Genesis 1:31). Original sin does not come from God. God is not sin's creator or author. Nor is original sin God's creation or work, but it is the devil's work.

In other situations, hard work, proper education, or having enough resources might rescue us. However, our attempts to escape God's judgment by redefining sin as educational deficiency or moral laziness or poor work ethic are nothing more than flimsy excuses for our real condition. Original sin is the inexpressible impairment and corruption of the human nature; nothing pure and good remains in our internal and external powers, and we can never produce anything good as judged by God.

Justice and Judgment

God's judgment on sin is that Adam and every person after him has lost the status of "very good" before God. With our disposition turned so wholly inward and completely away from God, our hostility toward God deserves only God's disfavor and judgment. And that judgment is a decree of death imposed on each person. This sentence includes physical death and eternal death and condemnation, which is hell and all the torments we associate with that place of destruction. No one in any way can ever free himself from that wrath of God.

The distresses and sorrows of this life—the miseries of body and spirit—daily remind us of our condition and the judgment of death. We are held captive to our own wretchedness and are subject to the present power of Satan, who continues to mislead us into false belief, wicked and shameful vices, despair, and pride. The Law does not make one a sinner. It seeks the sinner, and it unmistakably finds, judges, and kills the sinner it seeks.

And that makes sin a big deal.

FROM THE BIBLE

All have sinned and fall short of the glory of God. (Romans 3:23)

NEED TO KNOW

Hell: having our own way forever, separated from God.

Punishment for Sin

Even after we repent and seek forgiveness from others and from God, we will often suffer the effects of our sin. The effects do not take away or pay for our sins. We still deserve punishment. But we need not fear God's eternal punishment for sin. "God shows His love for us in that while we were still sinners, Christ died for us" (Romans 5:8).

What Do We Do with the Mess We're In?

Corrupted by original sin, we place ourselves at the center of our universe from the very moment of our birth. Because of this predilection to godlessness, we have stacked up crime after crime against God. We do what we do because we are what we are. We are in a world of trouble. If we are ever going to have the least hope of knowing God, let alone have a relationship with God, something will have to be done about who we are and what we have done.

It would be a sad state of existence if God just left us at this point, trapped in our self-made hell, separated from Him, our only future one of eternal torment. But God did not create us and then abandon us to our own failed devices. He did not thunder His Law at us and then turn away. God the Son came to earth as the one sinless human being, the one perfect person who kept God at the center and followed all the rules without breaking them. For the sake of Jesus, God does not count sin and its consequences against those baptized into Christ Jesus. And we would never hear this message as Good News if we did not understand the reality of sin.

FROM THE BIBLE

If you confess with your mouth that Jesus is Lord and believe in your heart that God raised Him from the dead, you will be saved. For with the heart one believes and is justified, and with the mouth one confesses and is saved. (Romans 10:9–10)

CHAPTER 3

It's All about Jesus, Part 1

In This Chapter

- Jesus is at the center of what we believe, how we worship, and what we do!
- The Second Article of the Apostles' Creed confesses Jesus Christ is the Son of God in the flesh for the salvation of the world.
- The Gospels are our primary sources for information about Jesus.

What is at the heart of the Lutheran faith? The better question is this: who is at the heart of the Lutheran faith? Martin Luther answered that question by searching the Bible. He discovered that "All the Scriptures point to Christ alone" (AE 35:132). Jesus, Himself, said, "You search the Scriptures because you think that in them you have eternal life; and it is they that bear witness about Me" (John 5:39).

> **NEED TO KNOW**
>
> **Christology** is the study of who Jesus is and what He did.

Take Jesus out of the message of the Church or out of a person's faith and it is no longer Christian! Christianity is solidly based on the saving work of Christ for the rescue of the world. Lutherans have a rich and exciting message about Jesus. He is at the center of what we believe, how we worship, and what we do!

What Do You Say?

We love to be asked our opinion and hear the word on the street. Who is popular and who is not? Jesus asked His disciples, "Who do people say that the Son of Man is?" They gave a variety of answers—all incorrect. Then He asked them the important question: "But who do you say I am?" Peter gave the answer that was commended: "You are the Christ, the Son of the living God" (Matthew 16:13, 15–16). Jesus reminded Peter that he did not come up with this confession on his own, but God gave Peter the words to say.

People today also have a variety of opinions of Jesus. He is considered a good man, a prophet, a figment of the imagination, a miracle worker, and many other things. Christians understand and believe that Jesus Christ is the Son of God, the

Second Person of the Holy Trinity. (See p. 27.) Jesus is not simply one holy man among many. He is God in the flesh for the salvation of the world.

While other religions teach that something must be done to earn God's favor and salvation, Christianity teaches that Jesus has already secured our salvation. God reaches out to people in Christ, rather than people reaching out to God. In fact, Peter, one of the apostles and leaders in the Early Church, said, "And there is salvation in no one else [Jesus], for there is no other name under heaven given among men by which we must be saved" (Acts 4:12).

God reaches out to people in Christ, rather than people reaching out to God.

BELIEVE, TEACH, CONFESS

Jesus Christ, our God and Lord, died for our sins and was raised again for our justification. He alone is the Lamb of God who takes away the sins of the world, and God has laid upon Him the iniquities of us all. (See Romans 4:24–25; John 1:29; and Isaiah 53:6.)

Guidance from the Creeds

The two creeds that are confessed regularly in Lutheran worship services, the Apostles' and Nicene Creeds, help us speak clearly about who God is based on God's Word. These creeds were born out of a desire to speak accurately what the Church confesses about God. See pp. 18–19 for their full text. As you read these creeds, one thing is clear: in both the second paragraph is the longest. Why? Many of the false teachings about Christianity have focused on Christ. If we do not get our teaching concerning Jesus right, we will ultimately not understand the Father, the Holy Spirit, and all of the other teachings God has revealed. False doctrines always diminish Christ and His saving work.

The Nicene Creed confesses Jesus as "God of God, Light of Light, very God of very God, begotten, not made, being of one substance with the Father" (see p. 19). These statements were articulated because a false teaching arose that said Jesus was not equal with God the Father. He was referred to as a smaller God, inferior to the Father and not eternal. But Church councils were gathered to deal with this and other false teachings about Jesus. Some of these false teachings, or heresies, denied Jesus' divinity, and others denied His full humanity. The creeds we use allow Christians and Christian congregations to speak together a clear confession of Jesus and protect us from having to repeatedly fight old battles against false teachings.

The Gospels

People look for God in many places. Some seek Him in the beauty of nature, in the bottom of a test tube, or in emotional experiences such as the birth of a child. While looking at any aspect of creation will certainly tell you something about the Creator, this natural knowledge of God falls short of revealing who God is. Only in Jesus, who is God in the flesh, can we find the ultimate revelation of who God is. In order to meet God, we encounter Jesus. When you know Jesus, you also know the Father, the Holy Spirit, and the relationship they have with one another.

We especially meet Jesus in the Gospels, the books of Matthew, Mark, Luke, and John (found in the New Testament). The Gospels are narratives of the life and work of Jesus. Eyewitnesses to the words and life of Jesus wrote Matthew and John. Two others—Mark and Luke—were written by those who spoke with eyewitnesses. The Holy Spirit uses these texts so that the reader sees, hears, experiences, and ponders the life of Jesus.

> **MAKING CONNECTIONS**
>
> With the inspiration of the Holy Spirit, the evangelists wrote the Gospels to persuade their readers that Jesus is the Christ, God's Son, who came to save sinners. . . . Although they focused on what happened, they wanted to illustrate *why* Jesus was born, lived, died, and rose again, even while they told the story. The evangelists commonly cited passages from the Old Testament to demonstrate how Jesus fulfilled the prophecies about the coming Messiah.
> (*TLSB*, p. 1572)

Who Was Jesus?

Like pillars that hold up a building, there are two pillars that uphold what Lutherans believe about Jesus. The first is the virgin birth of Christ, and the second is His life and death.

The First Pillar: One-of-a-Kind Birth

To speak of Jesus' birth is to speak of who He is. The Apostles' Creed confesses that Jesus was "conceived by the Holy Spirit, born of the virgin Mary" (see p. 18). Jesus was not conceived the natural way but through the action of the Holy Spirit in the womb of the Virgin Mary.

- Jesus is human because He was born of the Virgin Mary.
- He is God because He was conceived by the power of the Holy Spirit.

Jesus calls God "Father." Jesus is true man and true God because that was the only way God could accomplish His work of salvation.

In Jesus Christ, God put on "skin." Jesus is fully God, and He is fully man in the way God intended man to be: without sin and in full communion with God Himself. John 1:14 says, "And the Word became flesh and dwelt among us, and we have seen His glory, glory as of the only Son from the Father, full of grace and truth." Jesus Christ, who came from the Father, lived among us to do the saving work of God for a world destroyed by sin.

Why did Jesus have to be man? That is the only way He could take our place. We have not been obedient to God, but Jesus was perfectly obedient to God. Jesus was not guilty of any sin of thought, word, or deed. If He had committed a sin, He would no longer be the Savior because He would need to deal with His own sin. He is the ultimate substitute through all that He did.

Did Jesus face real temptations like we do? Was He tempted to not love God with His whole heart, to curse God, to hate His enemies, or to lust? The answer is a resounding "Yes!" We find great comfort in Hebrews 4:15: "For we do not have a high priest who is unable to sympathize with our weaknesses, but one who in every respect has been tempted as we are, yet without sin." Jesus, our Savior, is also our High Priest, and He does understand the spiritual struggles that we face on a daily basis. Because God became flesh in Jesus, we can be confident that He intimately knows our weaknesses and our problems.

That God would really become man and take on human flesh and blood has been a matter of debate since New Testament times. In fact, early in the history of the Church, people said, "The flesh is bad and the spirit is good." They did not believe that God would become man and take on flesh and blood. This heresy that has haunted the Church since ancient times is called "Gnosticism." The New Testament is quite clear that God did indeed take on a body in Christ as a fulfillment of the plan of salvation.

Pillar Two: One-of-a-Kind Life and Death

The second pillar that upholds our faith is what Jesus has done. He did miracles, taught the masses of people, mentored His disciples, and revealed the kingdom of God. He was willing to submit to the will of God, the cruel hand of His enemies, and the hatred of Satan. The climax was His suffering, death, burial, and resurrection. The greatest of His miracles was His resurrection from the dead. Jesus' work was validated, and He was vindicated as the resurrected Lord!

How could the death of one man be enough to pay for the sin of every person who ever lived or will live? Well, Jesus Christ is God. Only God could bear the burden and punishment for sin. Only God could pay the price for sin owed to God, who demands justice for sin. Only God could defeat the devil, and He did it by perfect obedience, suffering, death, and resurrection. In fact, "the reason the Son of God appeared was to destroy the works of the devil" (1 John 3:8b).

From God's perspective, this work of Jesus is necessary. Maybe this is not your plan or my plan, but it certainly is God's plan. And God would not and could not let death win. He saved our souls and our bodies. Jesus rose not only in "spirit" but also in body. Based on the clear testimony of Scripture, we believe in the bodily resurrection of Jesus. In fact, if Christ has not been raised from the dead, Christianity loses the core of its message because "you are still in your sins." (For more about this, see Chapter 4.)

FROM THE BIBLE

For I am not ashamed of the gospel, for it is the power of God for salvation to everyone who believes, to the Jew first and also to the Greek. For in it the righteousness of God is revealed from faith for faith, as it is written, "The righteous shall live by faith." (Romans 1:16–17)

True Son = True Salvation

The resurrection is the ultimate proof that Jesus is who He claimed to be all along. During Jesus' earthly ministry, the heavenly Father introduced Him to the world, saying, "This is My beloved Son, with whom I am well pleased" (Matthew 3:17). The Father showed His pleasure in and acceptance of Jesus' work by raising Him from the dead, thereby declaring to the world that this man from Nazareth was truly His Son. The way of salvation comes only through the Son. For knowing the Son is knowing His Father, and denying the Son is denying God the Father.

We are baptized into the name of the Father, Son, and Holy Spirit. Baptism establishes us in a new life and a new relationship with God. In this way we are drawn into the very life of God, and our life is caught up in this relationship, in which we are called children of God and can call God our Father. God sends His Son, and we in turn see the Father in His Son and pray everything in His name.

As we said before, the question of Jesus' identity is central to all that we as Christians believe. Our eternal salvation rests upon it. That is to say, on the cross, Jesus died as a sacrifice for the sins of the whole world. His death was a payment to God for all that we have done wrong. If He had died as an ordinary man, or even as a prophet, His death would not have been a sufficient payment. But, as God's Son, Jesus' death is surely sufficient. We can be sure that God's justice has been met and that God demands nothing more. God's own Son has paid for our sins.

Jesus died as a sacrifice for the sins of the whole world.

101 Biblical Names and Titles of Jesus

This list presents 101 biblical names and titles of Jesus and where they are located in Scripture. By studying the names and titles of Jesus, you can learn about His character, His nature, and how completely He cares for you. With 101 names of God represented, the list, though not exhaustive, is extensive.

- Advocate (1 John 2:1)
- Almighty (Matthew 28:18; Revelation 1:8)
- Alpha and Omega (Revelation 22:13)
- Amen (Revelation 3:14)
- Apostle and High Priest of our confession (Hebrews 3:1)
- Author of life (Acts 3:15)
- Beginning and End (Revelation 22:13)
- Beginning of God's creation (Revelation 3:14)
- Blessed and only Sovereign (1 Timothy 6:15)
- Bread of God (John 6:33)
- Bread of life (John 6:35, 48)
- Bridegroom (Matthew 25:1)
- Chief Shepherd (1 Peter 5:4)
- Christ (1 John 2:22)
- Cornerstone (Acts 4:11; Ephesians 2:20; 1 Peter 2:7)
- Creator (John 1:3)
- Deliverer (Romans 11:26)
- Descendant of David (Revelation 22:16)
- Door (John 10:9)
- Eternal Life (1 John 1:2; 5:20)
- Faithful and True (Revelation 19:11)
- Faithful and True Witness (Revelation 3:14)
- First and Last (Revelation 1:17; 2:8; 22:13)
- Firstborn of the dead (Revelation 1:5)
- Firstborn of all creation (Colossians 1:15)
- Founder and Perfecter of our faith (Hebrews 12:2)
- Founder of Salvation (Hebrews 2:10)
- God (John 1:1; Romans 9:5; 2 Peter 1:1; 1 John 5:20; etc.)
- Good Shepherd (John 10:11, 14)
- Great Shepherd (Hebrews 13:20)
- Great High Priest (Hebrews 4:14)
- Head of the Church (Ephesians 5:23)
- Heir of all things (Hebrews 1:2)
- High Priest (Hebrews 2:17)
- Holy and True (Revelation 3:7)
- Holy and Righteous (Acts 3:14)
- Hope (1 Timothy 1:1)
- Hope of glory (Colossians 1:27)
- Horn of salvation (Luke 1:69)
- I Am (John 8:58)
- Image of God (2 Corinthians 4:4)
- Immanuel (Matthew 1:23)
- Judge of the living and the dead (Acts 10:42)
- King of ages (1 Timothy 1:17)
- King of Israel (John 1:49)
- King of the Jews (Matthew 27:11)
- King of Kings (1 Timothy 6:15; Revelation 19:16)
- King of the nations (Revelation 15:3)
- Lamb (Revelation 13:8)

- Lamb of God (John 1:29)
- Lamb without blemish (1 Peter 1:19)
- Last Adam (1 Corinthians 15:45)
- Life (John 14:6; Colossians 3:4)
- Light of the world (John 8:12)
- Lion of the tribe of Judah (Revelation 5:5)
- Living One (Revelation 1:18)
- Living Stone (1 Peter 2:4)
- Lord (2 Peter 2:20)
- Lord of all (Acts 10:36)
- Lord of glory (1 Corinthians 2:8)
- Lord of lords (1 Timothy 6:15; Revelation 19:16)
- Man of heaven (1 Corinthians 15:48)
- Master (Luke 5:5; 8:24)
- Mediator of a new covenant (Hebrews 9:15)
- Mighty God (Isaiah 9:6)
- Morning Star (Revelation 22:16)
- Only Son of God (1 John 4:9)
- Our great God and Savior (Titus 2:13)
- Our Guard (2 Thessalonians 3:3)
- Our Husband (2 Corinthians 11:2)

- Our Passover Lamb (1 Corinthians 5:7)
- Our Redemption (1 Corinthians 1:30)
- Our Righteousness (1 Corinthians 1:30)
- Our Sanctification (1 Corinthians 1:30)
- Power of God (1 Corinthians 1:24)
- Precious Cornerstone (1 Peter 2:6)
- Prince of Peace (Isaiah 9:6)
- Prophet (Acts 3:22)
- Propitiation for our Sins (1 John 2:2)
- Rabbi (Matthew 26:25)
- Resurrection and Life (John 11:25)
- Righteous Branch (Jeremiah 23:5)
- Righteous One (Acts 7:52; 1 John 2:1)
- Rock (1 Corinthians 10:4)
- Root of David (Revelation 5:5; 22:16)
- Savior (Ephesians 5:23; Titus 1:4; 3:6; 2 Peter 2:20)
- Son of David (Luke 18:39)
- Son of God (John 1:49; Hebrews 4:14)
- Son of Man (Matthew 8:20)
- Son of the Most High (Luke 1:32)
- Source of eternal salvation to all who obey Him (Hebrews 5:9)
- The One Mediator (1 Timothy 2:5)
- The Stone the builders rejected (Acts 4:11)
- True Bread from heaven (John 6:32)
- True Light (John 1:9)
- True Vine (John 15:1)
- Truth (John 1:14; 14:6)
- Way (John 14:6)
- Wisdom of God (1 Corinthians 1:24)
- Word (John 1:1)
- Word of God (Revelation 19:13)

FROM THE BIBLE

For to us a child is born, to us a son is given;

and the government shall be upon His shoulder,

and His name shall be called Wonderful Counselor, Mighty God, Everlasting Father, Prince of Peace. (Isaiah 9:6)

CHAPTER 4

It's all About Jesus, Part 2

In This Chapter

- Sin corrupts us and would prevent us from having a relationship with God.
- We are justified by faith through Jesus Christ.

How deeply our human nature has fallen and been corrupted is not something we can ever know by reason and experience; Scripture must reveal it. (See p. 33.) Martin Luther described our condition as such: "[Original sin] shows us how very low our nature has fallen, how we have become utterly corrupted" (SA III II 4). There is no limit to our sinfulness. We will never know how sinful we really are in our lifetime!

Jesus came as the Lamb of God to bear the sins of the whole world. The sacrificial death of Jesus has paid the debt, satisfied God's justice, which includes the punishment required on account of our sin. Without the blood of Jesus, our sins have not been answered for and we must still bear them and pay their price. Left with our own sins, we are also left with the death that we chose by our sin, cutting ourselves off from God. In Christ, God reconciled the world to Himself. This is the fact of Calvary. To be justified is to be bought back, to have the account settled, to have the transaction closed.

Justification is all about Jesus, who bears our sin. It is a joyous proclamation that our sins are now located on our Savior, Jesus Christ—not only some of our sins, but all of our sins and sinfulness; not only small sins, but also sins of any size and magnitude. All that Christ did as our Savior counts for us; all the benefits Christ earned are given to us in faith. This does not mean that God overlooks our sins or ignores them as if they did not exist. This does not mean that Jesus merely performed what we were unable to do. Our sins are as real as Jesus, who suffered and shed His blood on the cross. Justification means that Jesus acted as our substitute both in His life and in His death. It means that in faith I am declared righteous because Jesus is righteous.

That we are justified by grace through faith in Jesus Christ is at the center of the Church's life and confession. When it is lost, the whole of Christian doctrine is undermined, and when it is not preserved, Jesus is diminished, and the comfort for sinners is taken away.

Justification is essentially Jesus answering for God's wrath over all our sins. Then, with His Spirit, He continues to deliver the forgiveness of sins through Baptism, Absolution, and the Lord's Supper.

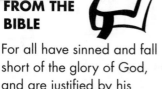

FROM THE BIBLE

For all have sinned and fall short of the glory of God, and are justified by his grace as a gift, through the redemption that is in Christ Jesus. (Romans 3:23–24)

BELIEVE, TEACH, CONFESS

Our churches teach that people cannot be justified before God by their own strength, merits, or works. People are freely justified for Christ's sake, through faith, when they believe that they are received into favor and that their sins are forgiven for Christ's sake. By His death, Christ made satisfaction for our sins. God counts this faith for righteousness in His sight. (AC IV 1–3)

Justification is forgiveness of sins. According to our Lord, forgiveness is our deepest need. If we are not sinners, justification is irrelevant!

Justification is before God. It is not before man or the world. To stand before God means to stand under His judgment, where I am responsible for my sinful actions. Because of my Baptism, though, God does not see me standing before Him, but see Jesus Christ, my substitute.

Justification is not by what we do or who we are. Before God all our achievements and fame in the world are vanity. We cannot prepare ourselves to be justified by Him.

Justification is a gift. We contribute nothing to our salvation at all. Martin Luther illustrates justification as rain, a heavenly gift from above.

Justification is Christ's doing. It is the office of Jesus alone to justify us. He bestows the forgiveness of sins in the ways that are most certain and true— by the water of Baptism, by words of Absolution, by the body and blood of Jesus to eat and to drink.

Justification is received through faith. As opposed to active righteousness, justification is passive righteousness. We receive—and only receive! Faith is nothing but receiving the Lord's gifts. If we are told that we must believe it and accept it to be saved, there is not much hope. Faith is not achieved by something that we do.

Getting Right with God

By Rev. Scott Bruzek

Yearning for What Once Was Ours

Scripture, the Holy Bible, is not a book about somebody else. Scripture is about you and me. Although it is an old book, it tells us the story of our lives right now. If you have ever wondered why you are here and what you are meant for, then the Holy Bible is the book for you.

It all starts as a love story. God made us to love us, and He wanted us to live with Him in His divine love forever. In the Garden of Eden, that wonderful place where the first humans walked, talked, and played with God as His own children, life was pure joy. In Eden, things were right.

What went wrong? In a word: sin. At some point along the way in Eden, Adam and Eve decided that they were better at being gods than God. With their first sin, Adam and Eve betrayed God's divine love, and the consequences have been devastating for us ever since. It was a terrible choice that shattered their relationship with Him and separated them from their Creator.

That same alienation has been felt by every one of us since Adam and Eve fell from grace. As human beings, we have a longing for more—for truth, wisdom, peace, beauty, holiness, happiness, safety, rest, justice, mercy, community, and all the other ancient blessings of Eden. But no matter how hard we try, we cannot make ourselves and our world right again.

The consequences of sin lie all around us. The damage is startling, broad, and harsh. The news each day is filled with stories of self-interest, hate, rebellion, chaos, violence, lust, theft, lies, and greed. Our world is especially good at victimizing the weak and the poor. But even if we do not make the news, this story is not about somebody else. Most of us don't have to go very far to feel the pain. Angry souls, tedious work, broken relationships, shattered families, fear, guilt, and shame are commonplace among us.

Our problem is that on account of sin we are dead to God, and there is nothing we can do about it. Yes, we get up in the morning and bump through our days, and sometimes we can even disguise our pain by piling up pleasures, but deep down something in us is just not right. We remain restless. Our hearts mislead us again and again, leaving us unsatisfied. The worst news is this: if we continue to walk "in the trespasses and sins . . . following the course of this world, following the prince of the power of the air" (Ephesians 2:1–2), we will end up having our own way forever—and that is a pretty good definition of hell.

We cannot fix the problem because we are the problem.

That original sin of Adam and Eve ruined us body and soul. But here is the Good News: The same triune God who made us and loved us never gave up on us. Instead, our God has returned to us in the person of Jesus Christ to make wrongs right.

Making Wrongs Right

Jesus' story is in Scripture, and it is rich beyond imagination. He has lived forever with the Father and the Holy Spirit as the only-begotten Son of God. When the fall came, God was so deeply grieved that the Father quickly promised His only Son would someday come to earth and make wrongs right.

FROM THE BIBLE

For God so loved the world, that He gave His only Son, that whoever believes in Him should not perish but have eternal life. (John 3:16)

To save us from eternal death, Jesus Christ became one of us, God in flesh and blood, born of the Virgin Mary. He came to be what we were always meant to be, the perfect child, and to do what we were always meant to do, live righteously according to the will and wisdom of our God. Jesus lived a perfect life and died a perfect death. Giving His life for the life of the world, His crucifixion atoned for the sins of every person everywhere. When Jesus hung on the cross and breathed out, "It is finished" (John 19:30), He announced that His sacrificial work was done. His death on earth had opened heaven to us once again.

This story of atonement—of one man's life given as a sacrifice and ransom to redeem all others—may sound odd to our postmodern ears, but it need not. Our world is still filled with glimpses of selfless love, such as firefighters climbing the burning stairs of the World Trade Center or a man plunging into a flooded river to save a drowning stranger. Sometimes treasuring others more than ourselves kills us.

This is why Scripture speaks of Jesus as our scapegoat. It is a term we still use today for somebody who takes the blame for the actions of another person. That is Jesus. Our heavenly Father takes our sins away from us and lays them all on His Son. "Greater love has no one than this, that someone lay down his life for his friends" (John 15:13).

NEED TO KNOW

Atonement: From an old French term for being "at one." Reconciliation between parties that were previously divided. One man's life given as a sacrifice and ransom to redeem all others.

Jesus dies for our sins as if they were His own, and we go free to live again. Jesus takes the punishment that we deserve as sinful rebels, and in return He gives us the life and joy that He deserves as the perfect child. Really, it is true: "In Christ God was reconciling the world to Himself, not counting their trespasses against them" (2 Corinthians 5:19).

God Is Working for Us, Not against Us

The story of Jesus is compelling, but it happened hundreds of years ago and thousands of miles away from us. How does that affect us today?

Since the Garden of Eden, the Holy Spirit has been at work in our world, easily moving through space and time. The Spirit's primary task is to make Jesus present, active, and known to us. He does this in a way that we can appreciate and understand. The Spirit speaks.

God's voice is a powerful thing. He has been speaking since the beginning of all things, creating the world, shaping history, bringing blessings, saving His people, inspiring awe, and promising never-ending good for us.

Like His Father's words, the Son's words also do what they say. When Jesus told the blind man to see, he saw. When Jesus told the demons to flee, they fled. When Jesus told the stormy sea to be still, it went calm. When Jesus told Lazarus to rise from the dead, he rose. Jesus speaks one miracle after another.

The Holy Spirit also speaks realities. When He puts words into the mouth of a prophet, the prophet's words come true. When He speaks love into the ears of His children, they believe what He says, and faith is born. The Spirit is the energy in divine words, the power in the preaching, and the miracle in the mysterious Means of Grace.

It is extraordinary Good News, therefore, when Scripture names the Holy Spirit as our Advocate, the one who calls, gathers, enlightens, and sanctifies us in true faith.

On our own, we stand ruined before God the Father. Proud and treacherous like Adam and Eve, we deserve to be scorned, separated, and damned. But then the Holy Spirit speaks to the Father on our behalf: "This child is one of Ours, Our creation. Christ died for this one too. Jesus took away her sins. She's clean. Consider her righteous. She's forgiven. Count her among the holy ones. Please bring her back home to Eden."

It is a miracle, really—the miracle of salvation. Despite all the evidence stacked up against us, the Spirit's words are taken as fact and win the day.

All of this is not without an echo in our world. You remember, perhaps, the old story about the baseball umpire. The pitcher throws, and the catcher catches, but the umpire is silent. Finally the batter says, "Was it a ball or a strike?" The umpire replies, "It's nothing until I say it's something."

That is how it is for you and me as we stand before our heavenly Father stained by our sins. When the Father looks at us, He sees Christ living in us. When He listens to us, He hears the Spirit speaking for us, sometimes "with groanings too deep for words" (Romans 8:26). Seeing no sins and hearing no ill, our heavenly Father judges us to be His own—clean, forgiven, holy, and new.

This is forensic justification: God declares us righteous. It is our ultimate reality. In the end, we are whatever God says we are, and the Father says that we are righteous. It is a miracle of divine love that takes us as its object. It is our resurrection from eternal death to eternal life. For the sake of Christ, God is for us and not against us.

Thy strong Word bespeaks us righteous;
    Bright with Thine own holiness,
Glorious now, we press toward glory,
    And our lives our hopes confess.
Alleluia, alleluia!
    Praise to Thee who light dost send!
Alleluia, alleluia!
    Alleluia without end!
        —"Thy Strong Word" (LSB 578:3)

As in any court of law, once we are found innocent, we go free. With His pardoning word, we are restored to our God, to our community, and to ourselves. Honored by the Holy Trinity, we are released from our guilt and shame. With our sins forgiven, we live this life on earth as those on the way to somewhere else, as disciples following Jesus home to Eden.

Jesus' Story Is Your Story

Every year on the night before Easter, the Church meets in vigil, awaiting the dawn. By reading one story of salvation after another throughout the night, the most important point of all is made: Jesus' story is your story.

From start to finish, Jesus did all this just for us. He made you and me, and when we fell from grace, He came as one of us, living and loving and dying and rising and ascending for our salvation. Scripture could not be more clear: "God shows His love for us in that while we were still sinners, Christ died for us. Since, therefore, we have now been justified by His blood, much more shall we be saved by Him from the wrath of God" (Romans 5:8–9).

This divine love is totally free. Justification is a perfect and complete gift from God to us. Jesus did everything necessary for salvation, so we cannot earn it or aid it or take credit for any of this. Because God is saving us, He will get it right and our salvation will be sure.

The Church's way of saying thanks is *Amen*. *Amen* means it is true, it is solid, and it is for me. This *Amen* is a living and an active thing. It is the joy of being on our way home again to Eden. Wearing the righteousness of Jesus Christ like new clothes, we spend our days looking for ways to love God and serve others.

FROM THE BIBLE

For if we have been united with Him in a death like His, we shall certainly be united with Him in a resurrection like His. We know that our old self was crucified with Him in order that the body of sin might be brought to nothing, so that we would no longer be enslaved to sin. For one who has died has been set free from sin. Now if we have died with Christ, we believe that we will also live with Him. We know that Christ, being raised from the dead, will never die again; death no longer has dominion over Him. For the death He died He died to sin, once for all, but the life He lives He lives to God. So you also must consider yourselves dead to sin and alive to God in Christ Jesus. (Romans 6:5–11)

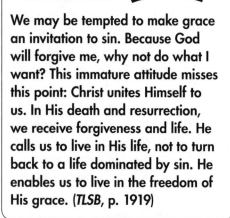

MAKING CONNECTIONS

Our best response to this Good News is the same one we offer for any spectacular gift: thank you very much! That is faith. Faith agrees with God. It's simple, really, to be saved. To be saved is to have the gifts of Christ. This is one reason that Jesus said His kingdom belongs to children. Children believe what we tell them, and in believing they receive the gifts. This is what the Church is thinking when it says that we are justified by grace through faith in Jesus Christ.

MAKING CONNECTIONS

We may be tempted to make grace an invitation to sin. Because God will forgive me, why not do what I want? This immature attitude misses this point: Christ unites Himself to us. In His death and resurrection, we receive forgiveness and life. He calls us to live in His life, not to turn back to a life dominated by sin. He enables us to live in the freedom of His grace. (*TLSB*, p. 1919)

Certainly we will get it wrong, stumbling and even falling down along the way. Old habits die hard. But if you are ever troubled by your sins, remember the words of a wise old friend of mine: "Jesus takes away your sins. The only way they can hurt you is if you take them back."

That is very Good News. When Christ's righteousness is our justification, making all our wrongs right, everything is different. We wake every day knowing that this world can be a hopeful place, filled with all the heavenly things we long for, because our story is winding its way back to where it all began. That is where we belong, and that is what we were always meant to be: children of our Creator, well-loved by Him in Eden.

CHAPTER 5

It's the End of the World as We Know It

In This Chapter

- While the end of the world is a popular topic, Christians are interested in the end times for a different reason: they want to be prepared for Christ's return and are eager to live with Him forever.
- Jesus Christ made it clear to us that no one, absolutely no one, knows when the last day will come.
- Ancient calendars, seers, and modern fiction all miss the truth and reality of the end times.
- Christians are encouraged to live each day in confidence, not fear, exercising themselves in the faith that works through love.

The Sky Is Falling

Or so you would think. There is an almost endless array of scenarios and speculations about how the world will end. Hollywood uses computer-generated special effects to paint frightening images of a catastrophic end to the planet if global warming is not halted. Along with earlier generations, many still fear that nuclear war will end life on earth. Others worry that overpopulation will bring down the final curtain. These speculations are interesting because they assume that we humans will be responsible for bringing an end to the earth.

Christians have also shown keen interest in this topic. The popular Left Behind series is only a recent addition to a long history of speculation about the end times. For instance, when the calendar turned from the year AD 999 to AD 1000, many Christians believed the end was near. Ancient calendars, seers, the convergence of planets and stars, and the writings and ravings of oracles have all been used to pinpoint exactly when the end times might start and what those last days will be. But Christians are interested in the end times for a different reason: Scripture tells us not just that Christ will return to His creation and bring an end to the world as we know it, but that He will come to judge us.

Tick . . . Tick . . . Tick . . .

The Book of Hebrews says that now we are in the last days (Hebrews 1:2). The last days began when the God sent His Son to be born as the God-man Jesus. And the Son made it clear to us that no one, absolutely no one (not even the angels!), knows the date of the very last day. The day, the hour, that last minute—only the Father knows when that will be (Matthew 24:36). Be suspicious of anyone who tries to pinpoint an exact date for Jesus' return. It has always been a waste of time trying to "decode" alleged messages hidden in Scripture that supposedly reveal the date of Christ's return.

Do not get anxious, but we are in the end times right now

When Is 1,000 Not 1,000?

Among Christians, the discussion of Jesus' return has been complicated by the idea that Christ's return is an event separate from His judgment. Some believe that before the world ends there will be a golden age of peace and prosperity lasting a thousand years. This teaching is called millennialism. It is based on the vision of St. John in Revelation 20, which speaks of a thousand-year rule of Christ before His final judgment.

Millennialists are further divided. Premillennialists say Jesus will return before this thousand-year period begins. Postmillennialists say Jesus will return after the thousand-year age of peace and prosperity ends.

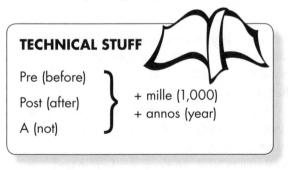

TECHNICAL STUFF

Pre (before)
Post (after)   } + mille (1,000)
                    + annos (year)
A (not)

Lutherans, on the other hand, are amillennialists. That is, together with the majority of Christians worldwide, they believe there will be no literal thousand-year reign of Christ on earth prior to His return for judgment. St. Paul writes that in heaven Christ now rules over all things for the sake of His Church. Why should He come back to establish an earthly kingdom when He steadfastly refused to do it on principle when He was here the first time?

"In Case of Rapture, This Car Will Be Unmanned"

Many Christians who believe in premillennialism also believe in what they call "the rapture." According to this teaching, Christ will return secretly to remove the Christians from the earth before He sets up a millennial earthly kingdom. Proponents of the rapture point to 1 Thessalonians 4:15–17, where Paul says that the believers will be "caught up" in the clouds to meet Jesus:

Yet the other events described in that same passage—the Lord's descent from heaven, the cry of command, the trumpet sound—are events Jesus associates with His return for judgment, not with a secret return. Proponents of the rapture think that Jesus' words "one will be taken and the other left," (Luke 17:34) are further proof that believers will be snatched off the earth before Jesus' earthly reign begins. But those verses only continue to develop the same topic Jesus has been talking about—His return to judge the world.

Popular View at Odds with Scripture

Unlike popular fictional views of the end times, St. John's vision of what will occur when Christ returns is not chiefly characterized by mass confusion, chaos, and hysteria. Certain people will not suddenly vanish into thin air while others are "left behind," holding the clothes, eyeglasses, and even the dental fillings of those "caught up" in the rapture. Airliners in flight will not suddenly become pilotless or city busses driverless, sending their passengers careening to their deaths. Spouses will not wake up next to an empty pair of pajamas. This sort of haunting imagery may sell books, but it is not what the Bible says.

John's Revelation, though certainly pertaining to the final judgment and the need for all people to be ever watchful and ready for it, is also about eternally joyful events. It is about heaven, which in Revelation is described as the "New Jerusalem," a beautiful place where all who trust in Christ will live eternally in the presence of God and their fellow redeemed. It is about the wedding of the Lamb, Jesus, to His Bride, the Church. It is about the roar of a great multitude in heaven shouting, "Hallelujah! Our Lord God Almighty reigns. Let us rejoice and be glad and give Him glory!"

How Will Jesus Judge?

Lutherans believe that on the Last Day Christ will return to judge all people, giving eternal life to the godly and condemning the ungodly to eternal punishment. The important question about the end times is not when it will happen. Instead, it is "How will you be judged?" Both in parable and plain speech, the New Testament

FROM THE BIBLE

For this we declare to you by a word from the Lord, that we who are alive, who are left until the coming of the Lord, will not precede those who have fallen asleep. For the Lord Himself will descend from heaven with a cry of command, with the voice of an archangel, and with the sound of the trumpet of God. And the dead in Christ will rise first. Then we who are alive, who are left, will be caught up together with them in the clouds to meet the Lord in the air, and so we will always be with the Lord. (1 Thessalonians 4:15–17)

BELIEVE, TEACH, CONFESS

In these last times it is certainly no less needful to encourage people to Christian discipline to the way of right and godly living and to do good works. We need to remind them of how necessary it is that they exercise themselves in good works as a declaration of their faith [Matthew 5:16] and gratitude to God [Hebrews 13:15–16]. But works should not be mingled in the article of justification. (FC Ep IV 18)

says that judgment will be based on how you lived your life. However, doing good is not the same as being godly. Suppose two children have cleaned their rooms. One did it because she loves her mom. The other did it so her mom would not ground her. Outwardly, both acts appear to be "good." But if mom knew what motivated each daughter, would she judge both to be godly? God sees behind how we live our lives. The Bible tells us what motivation is godly motivation when it says, "Without faith it is impossible to please [God]" (Hebrews 11:6). We might say that works are dead without faith. Faith in Christ is the key. The New Testament teaches that we are made right with God by faith in Jesus Christ and not by works (Romans 3:28; Galatians 3:11). On the Last Day, those who will be judged "godly" are those whose faith in Christ was genuine, producing acts of Christian love.

Because we know neither the day nor the hour of Christ's return for judgment, Christians are encouraged to live each day in confidence and not in fear, exercising themselves in the faith that works through love.

MAKING CONNECTIONS

Some people think they can predict when Jesus will come again. They study history and observe current events. Then they compare these events with information in the Bible that talks about the end of the world. By showing that certain wars have been fought and that governments have done certain things, they claim Jesus will come soon. However, Jesus clearly said that no one knows exactly when He will come again (Matthew 24:36).

Great Predictions of the End of the World as We Know It

Some Christians believe, despite what Jesus said about not being able to know when the Last Day will come (Matthew 24:36), it is possible for someone to be able to predict either the day or at least the events that would lead to that great Last Day—the End of the World as We Know It (TEOTWAWKI). Such predictions are not the exclusive property of bygone generations. Predictions of TEOTWAWKI and the events are still being talked about today. What follows here is a listing of only a few of the more well-known prophecies of TEOTWAWKI. The fact that you are reading this is ample witness that none have ever come true. Based upon past performance, there is every likelihood that the predictions of our day will not materialize either.

AD 992: Good Friday coincided with the Feast of the Annunciation; this had long been believed to be the event that would bring forth the Antichrist and thus the end-times events foretold in the Book of Revelation.

1000, January 1: Many Christians in Europe predicted the end of the world on this date. As the date approached, Christian armies waged war against some of the pagan countries in Northern Europe. The motivation was to convert them all to Christianity, by force if necessary, before Christ returned in the year 1000.

1033: Some believed this to be the thousandth anniversary of the death and resurrection of Jesus. His second coming was anticipated in this millennial reckoning. Jesus' actual date of crucifixion is unknown but is believed to be between AD 27 to 33.

1496: Said to be fifteen hundred years after the birth of Jesus, some fifteenth-century mystics predicted that the millennium would begin during this year.

1794: Charles Wesley, one of the founders of Methodism, predicted the end of the world would come in this year.

1843, March 21: William Miller, founder of the Millerite movement, predicted that Jesus would come on this date. A large number of Christians accepted his prophecy. When Jesus did not return, Miller revised his date to October 22, 1844.

1850–1856: Ellen White, founder of the Seventh-day Adventist movement, made many predictions of the timing of the end of the world.

1874, 1914, 1925, 1932, 1941, 1975, etc.: The Watchtower Society (Jehovah's Witnesses) has made many predictions of the end of the world since its founding in the 1870s. Prior to 1975, they predicted the end would occur in subsequent future dates; most notably they said the Christ arrived secretly in 1874 and would establish the kingdom of God on earth in October 1914. It was predicted that in 1925 Abraham, Isaac, Jacob, and other faithful prophets would return as a sign of the beginning of the new order; then that Christendom would be overthrown in 1932; followed by the prediction that in the fall of 1941 the world was in the last months before Armageddon; and then that 1975 was a promising year for the end of the world because of a supposed six thousandth anniversary of the creation of Adam and Eve. Obviously, all these dates came and went uneventfully. Since 1975, the Watchtower Society's predictions have been much less specific. Despite their failure in the past, the Watchtower Society still expects that the end may happen at any time in our immediate future. In December 1995, *Newsweek* quoted Witnesses spokesperson Bob Pevy as saying, "The end is still close. We just can't put numbers on Jesus' words." And with that, they ultimately get it right. (Kenneth Woodward, "Jehovah's Witnesses Decide the End Is Fluid," *Newsweek*, December 18, 1995).

1919, December 17: Meteorologist Albert Porta predicted that the conjunction of six planets on this date would generate a magnetic current that would cause the sun to explode and engulf the earth.

1936: Founder of the Worldwide Church of God, Herbert W. Armstrong, predicted that the Day of the Lord would happen sometime in 1936. When that prediction failed, he made a new prediction: 1975.

1948: Israel declared independence on May 14. Some Christians believed that this event was the final prerequisite for the second coming of Jesus.

1959, April 22: Leader of the Branch Davidian cult, Florence Houteff, prophesied that the 1,260 days mentioned in Revelation 11:3 would end and the Kingdom of David would be established on this day. Followers, expecting to die, to be resurrected, and to be transferred to heaven, sold their possessions and moved to Mt. Carmel, Texas, in anticipation of the end times. The failed prediction almost undid the group, and afterward only a few dozen members remained. However, seventy-six Branch Davidians did die on April 29, 1993, as a result of arson apparently ordered by their leader, David Koresh.

1962, October 15–28: Deemed the closest the world has ever come to nuclear war, the Cuban missile crisis spawned many predictions of the world's end.

1967: Israel again. During the Six-Day War, June 5–10, the Israeli army captured all of Jerusalem. Many Christians believed that the rapture would quickly occur. However, the supposed final biblical prerequisite for the second coming is that the Jews would resume ritual animal sacrifices in the temple at Jerusalem; that has not yet happened.

1970s: Moses David (aka David Berg), founder of the cult the Children of God (later know as the Family International and the Family), predicted that a comet would hit the earth, probably in the mid-1970s, and destroy all life in the United States.

1970: Hal Lindsey's best-selling book *The Late Great Planet Earth*, postulated that the then-current events will lead to a rapture of believers, tribulation, and second coming of Christ, which might play out in the 1980s. Lindsey later said that the "decade of the 1980s could very well be the last decade of history as we know it" (*The 1980s: Countdown to Armageddon* [New York: Bantam Books, 1983]).

1978: Chuck Smith, pastor of Calvary Chapel in Costa Mesa, California, predicted the rapture in 1981.

1981: Rev. Sun Myung Moon, founder of the Unification Church, predicted that the kingdom of heaven would be established this year.

1982: Pat Robertson predicted a few years in advance that the world would end in the fall of 1982.

1990, April 23: At least two thousand members of the Church Universal and Triumphant quit their jobs, amassed large debts, and traveled to Montana to take refuge in the CUT's fallout shelters after leader Elizabeth Clare Prophet predicted the start of nuclear war on this date. Later, church officials said the event was a drill.

1993, November 11: The July 20, 1993, issue of the *Weekly World News* contained an article titled "Doomsday Asteroids," in which "top scientists" allegedly wrote a top-secret document revealing that asteroid M-167 would hit the earth on November 11 and end all life. In the M series of astronomical objects, there is no object with a number higher than M-110.

1996, October 23: Since 1658, the calculations of James Ussher have been accepted by some Christians as a date for the end of the world. Ussher's calculations used millennial dating based on his theory that creation occurred on October 23, 4004 BC, and that 1996, the six-thousandth anniversary of creation, would usher in the end.

1997, March 26: Thirty-nine members of the Heaven's Gate cult are discovered to have committed suicide in order to evacuate Earth prior to its recycling. The Heaven's Gate members believed that the UFO traveling in the tail of the comet Hale-Bopp would take them to another level of existence above human.

1997, December 31: The July 29, 1997, issue of *Weekly World News* reported that a confidential Pentagon memo had been circulating in Washington and that President Clinton had called a secret meeting of Bible scholars on July 27. The memo outlined the details of cataclysmic worldwide events that would culminate in the shifting of the earth's crust on the last day of the year.

2000: There was widespread talk, among both the religous and the irreligous, the the world would end. The fact that it did not sent many experts back to the drawing board. Among the many predictions were those connected to the Y2K bug. It was thought that the resulting worldwide electronic failure would trigger global economic disaster and bring on the Antichrist.

2001: Jack Van Impe Ministries broadcast a program dedicated to laying out Van Impe's end-time prophecies detailed in his book *On the Edge of Eternity*. He said 2001 would see a beginning of global chaos that would lead to the seven-year period of tribulation, the Battle of Armageddon, and the second coming of Christ. Van Impe has since changed his predictions to some time in the future.

2006 June 6: Some believed that the number of the beast, "666," was really the date 06/06/06 and thus the start of the tribulation.

2006 July: Escalation of tensions in Lebanon led some Christian leaders to predict that the end of the world had already begun.

2011 May 21: *Family Radio* host Harold Camping spread the wordthat this day would be the End of Days, that is, Judgment Day.

PREDICTIONS FOR THE NOT-TOO-DISTANT FUTURE:

2012 December 21: The arrival of the winter solstice on this day is said to be the triggering event that will end the world as we know it. Many of these predictions are based on the calendar developed by the ancient Mayans, with this date being the last day to appear on the calendar.

CHAPTER 6

The Last Stop

In This Chapter
- Death separates our eternal souls from our physical bodies.
- Hell is existence away from God's presence.
- Heaven is life lived in the presence of God.

Until the day Christ returns, every person will experience death as the last event of his or her physical life. And no matter how strong the will to avoid death or how advanced the medicine, everybody ultimately dies. This is a tragic situation. Adam and Eve were not created to die. God imposed death as a penalty of sin in Genesis 2:17 and 3:19. This unnatural situation that we find ourselves in leads to fear and a horror of death. Christians bear this consequence of sin, just like everyone else. But for the Christian, death is deliverance, not punishment. Paul tells us that because we have been forgiven our sins in Christ, " 'Death is swallowed up in victory.' 'O death, where is your victory? O death, where is your sting?' The sting of death is sin, and the power of sin is the law. But thanks be to God, who gives us the victory through our Lord Jesus Christ" (1 Corinthians 15:54–57). For Christians, death is a change for the better. This is why a Christian can overcome the natural fear of death and depart in peace.

Where Have All the Souls Gone?

Death is not a total destruction or annihilation of a person. It is the loss of physical life that occurs when the body and the soul are separated. At the moment of death, the Christian soul enters the joy of heaven, while the spirit of the unbeliever is "in prison" (see 1 Peter 3:19). The soul then remains in heaven or hell until Judgment Day.

From childhood, our minds are filled with images of heaven and hell: halos and horns, harps and pitchforks, wings and pointed tails, floating among clouds and sitting in burning flames. Because these pictures live right next to those of a man in a red suit and a bunny carrying an egg-filled basket, we begin to ask ourselves, "Are heaven and hell real?"

The Hell It Is

St. Paul says that those who do not obey the Gospel of our Lord Jesus "will suffer the punishment of eternal destruction, away from the presence of the Lord and from the glory of His might" (2 Thessalonians 1:9).

The word *hell* is used to denote this eternal existence apart from God. Have you ever heard it said that people can experience hell on earth? They can't. In this life all people see God's creative hand every day in nature; every day and in countless ways all people receive the blessings of God through creation. And as long as a person remains in the world, he or she can hear the Gospel of forgiveness, repent, and be saved. Not so after the judgment. If you understand that hell is existence away from God's presence, you will understand why the Bible describes it so:

- "Down there" vs. God's presence "up" in heaven.
- "Weeping and gnashing of teeth" vs. God's presence of joy.
- "Outer darkness" vs. God's light.

TECHNICAL STUFF

Eternal destruction is not the same as annihilation. If your car is destroyed in a crash, it does not disappear. It no longer works as it was designed to function. Hell is an eternal existence where one is unable to function as God intended humans to live.

TECHNICAL STUFF

Gehenna (often interpreted as "hell" and as "hellfire") denotes the Valley of Hinnom, which purportedly was the fiery dumping ground outside of the city of Jerusalem for all the city's rubbish, including the bodies of dead animals, criminals, and the homeless. Sulfur was burned to keep the fires there going day and night. *Gehenna* became synonymous for the place of eternal punishment and is used in the Gospels to describe the opposite of life in the coming kingdom of God. This "hellfire" signifies that its inhabitants have trashed their lives by sin. They cannot function in the purpose for which they were created.

Heavenly Days

The word *heaven* is used to describe life lived eternally in the presence of God. This life is no longer corrupted by sin. Heaven's inhabitants will live as God intended humans to live—in *complete and perfect* fellowship and harmony with Him. As emperors and kings built their capitals to reflect their wealth and power, so the Bible pictures God's people living in a beautiful city lavished with precious jewels and gold-paved streets (Revelation 21:10–27). Beyond the picture language, the Bible describes this eternal life with God as "What no eye has seen, nor ear heard, nor the heart of man imagined, what God has prepared for those who love Him" (1 Corinthians 2:9). The Bible calls this the "new creation" (2 Corinthians 5:17) or "a new heaven and a new earth" (2 Peter 3:13; Revelation 21:1). As the creation was pure and uncorrupted before our first parents fell into sin, so will the new creation be when God establishes it on the Last Day.

FROM THE BIBLE

Therefore, if anyone is in Christ, he is a new creation. The old has passed away; behold, the new has come. (2 Corinthians 5:17)

But according to his promise we are waiting for new heavens and a new earth in which righteousness dwells. (2 Peter 3:13)

Then I saw a new heaven and a new earth, for the first heaven and the first earth had passed away, and the sea was no more. (Revelation 21:1)

Extreme Makeovers

Both the righteous and the unrighteous will enter their respective eternal lives with resurrected bodies. Why? Because God created humans to have bodies. We are not complete without them. While the Bible teaches that God will resurrect both the righteous and the unrighteous, it only describes the type of body with which the righteous shall live. Using an agricultural analogy of seeds and plants, the apostle Paul tells us in his first letter to the Corinthians that what goes into the ground does not look like what will come out of the ground:

So is it with the resurrection of the dead. What is sown is perishable; what is raised is imperishable. It is sown in dishonor; it is raised in glory. It is sown in weakness; it is raised in power. It is sown a natural body; it is raised a spiritual body. If there is a natural body, there is also a spiritual body. (1 Corinthians 15:42–44)

Paul further states that the Christian's resurrected body will be like the body of the resurrected Jesus. So if you turn to a description of the resurrected Jesus, say Luke 24:36–50, you see that His resurrected body has real substance, is human in appearance, and has recognizable features. And yet it is different—Jesus could enter a room and appear to His disciples even while they were behind locked doors.

What Scripture teaches concerning the death of the Christian is summarized as follows by Lutheran theologian Edward Koehler:

TECHNICAL STUFF

Do not confuse resurrection with reincarnation! Reincarnation is a belief that at death one's soul enters another body—perhaps that of an animal, insect, or human—and lives another cycle of life on earth.

In the moment of death the souls of the believers enter the joy of heaven. Jesus said to the thief: "Today you will be with Me in Paradise" (Luke 23:43). Stephen said in the hour of death, "Lord Jesus, receive my spirit" (Acts 7:59). Whoever dies in the Lord is blessed "from now on" (Revelation 14:13). Paul desires to "be with Christ" and adds that this is "far better" for him than to continue in the flesh (Philippians 1:23). For this reason we pray that finally, when our last hour comes, God would grant us a blessed end and graciously take us from this vale of tears to Himself in heaven. (Edward Koehler, *A Summary of Christian Doctrine*, 3rd rev. edition [St. Louis: Concordia, 2006], pp. 397–98)

MAKING CONNECTIONS

As we have begun to live with Christ here on earth in the Church through His Word and Sacraments, so we will continue to live with Him after we die. Death is not an interruption of this fellowship with our Lord. Our life with Christ continues, even after death, even before the resurrection. Our departed friends and family members who lived with Christ here below by faith in His cross for their forgiveness even now live with Him and are comforted. Because our life with Christ is not interrupted by death, death for the Christian may be sweet and joyful, even in the midst of tears. (*TLSB*, p. 1750)

On the day of the final judgment, the redeemed souls in heaven will be reunited with their own (now glorified) bodies, and will begin to enjoy the bliss of everlasting life in both body and soul. The Lutheran Church has always rejected as unscriptural the idea that the soul "sleeps" between death and Judgment Day in such a way that it is not conscious of heavenly bliss.

The Certainty of Faith

By Rev. Dr. Benjamin T. G. Mayes

Only those people who believe accept God's gift of salvation. But this leads to a serious question: Do I really believe? Many people ask themselves: "Did I really give my heart to Jesus?" People often have both certainty and uncertainty about God. In those cases, they are like the man in the Gospel who said to Jesus, "I believe; help my unbelief!" (Mark 9:24). If you want certainty, you should not look to any work or decision that you have made.

If you are uncertain about where you stand with God, don't think about yourself; instead, think about God and His gifts. As Lutherans, we direct people to Baptism, Absolution (the forgiveness spoken to us by the pastor), and the Lord's Supper for certainty, because they have God's promises. Our certainty of faith is not based on our faith. It is based on God's promises.

> If you want certainty, you should not look to any work or decision that you have made.

The Foundation of Christian Hope

Faith is not just historical knowledge about what God has done, and what Jesus did, but it is also and especially trust or certainty. The certainty of faith is connected with Christian hope—the God-given certainty that God will save me in the future, just as faith is the certainty that God, because of Jesus Christ, is my loving Father now. Faith is like the trust of a cancer patient toward his expert doctor before surgery. He trusts that the doctor knows how to heal him, even if it requires pain and cutting. He trusts that the doctor wants to help him, not harm him. Therefore, he gives his body to the doctor to be healed. We are like that cancer patient. We Christians trust Jesus our Physician to heal us. We trust that He wants to help us, not harm us. Having certainty of faith, we are then able to give our whole life to Him and trust Him for our salvation and future.

Now, certainty of faith is quite different from "hedging your bets" or "playing it safe." Hedging your bets may be the right way to act with many things in life, such as business or personal finance, when you have doubts about the future or doubts about the person with whom you are dealing. In a relationship of love, doubts can undermine the entire relationship and turn love into suspicion and fear. Since God has spoken to us through the prophets and apostles and revealed His heart to us, we have no need to doubt or "hedge our bets." Instead, we can trust God with certainty. When we deal with God, certainty is what we need, not doubt. If you believe, but you still have doubts, then pray, "Lord, I believe; help my unbelief!" (Mark 9:24). In His time, God will give you the certainty of faith.

Faith Informs Our Conscience

Have you ever had the feeling that God wanted you to do something? Often our heart or conscience speaks to us, telling us to do what is right or even to do something that is neither right nor wrong. Some people say that God speaks to them and tells them to do this or that, for example, to take a particular job or to live in a particular place. But this can be misleading. God only speaks to us with certainty through the Bible. If you hear a message in your heart, it might simply be your heart speaking, telling you something good or even something bad. Sometimes when people look back on their lives, they can see God at work—especially if the message in their heart led them to seek God in His Word and in His Church. But there is no certainty that God is the one speaking unless it is in His Word. It could just be your conscience speaking. Therefore, we do not say, "God laid it on my heart to do this," or "God told me to tell you this," unless we find it written in the Bible. After all, it would be a lie to say, "God told me" if He had not actually spoken. And we can only have certainty about His speaking when it is from His written Word.

Therefore, we make a distinction in how we pray. If God has made a promise to us in the Bible, then we pray with all boldness. For example, "God, You said that You do not desire the death of a sinner, but that he turn from his evil way and live (Ezekiel 33:11). Therefore, forgive my sins!" But if God has not made a promise to us, then we pray with an addition: "If it is Your will." For example, "Heavenly Father, if it is Your will, give me enough money to buy a new car. But let not my will but Your will be done."

Free to Choose

Certainty can help you find God's will for your life. His will for your life is clear: "Repent and believe in the gospel" (Mark 1:15). So many people are tormented, trying to figure out what God's will is. They doubt their decisions. If a decision turns out badly, they think that they have disobeyed God. But there is no need to be uncertain. God gives you His moral Law, which is written clearly in Scripture, and He gives you the Good News about Jesus. Beyond that, He gives you freedom. Do you want to be a plumber? You have freedom to do so or not to do so. Do you want to live in this city? You have freedom to do so or not to do so. To find God's will for your life, don't listen to your heart. In the Star Wars movies, Yoda tells people to trust their feelings. But here God says the opposite: "Don't trust your feelings. Trust God's Word." We know what usually

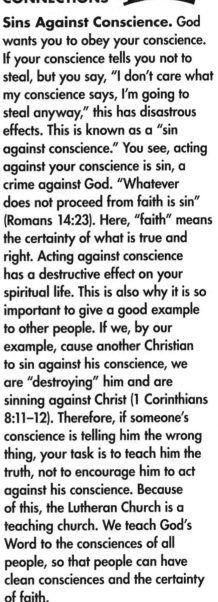

MAKING CONNECTIONS

Sins Against Conscience. God wants you to obey your conscience. If your conscience tells you not to steal, but you say, "I don't care what my conscience says, I'm going to steal anyway," this has disastrous effects. This is known as a "sin against conscience." You see, acting against your conscience is sin, a crime against God. "Whatever does not proceed from faith is sin" (Romans 14:23). Here, "faith" means the certainty of what is true and right. Acting against conscience has a destructive effect on your spiritual life. This is also why it is so important to give a good example to other people. If we, by our example, cause another Christian to sin against his conscience, we are "destroying" him and are sinning against Christ (1 Corinthians 8:11–12). Therefore, if someone's conscience is telling him the wrong thing, your task is to teach him the truth, not to encourage him to act against his conscience. Because of this, the Lutheran Church is a teaching church. We teach God's Word to the consciences of all people, so that people can have clean consciences and the certainty of faith.

comes out of the heart of man: evil thoughts (Mark 7:21). To find certainty about God's will for your life, don't look at your heart; look at His Word. Where He has not spoken, you have freedom. In those cases, use your reason. Then you can have certainty that what you are doing is acceptable to Him, even if your decisions go wrong.

The wrong view of certainty of faith can lead to what is called "security." "Security" is the view that once you are saved, you are always saved no matter what. "Secure" people look at Baptism and church membership as a ticket to heaven. They think once you've got the ticket, it doesn't matter whether you repent or believe. But security is much different than the certainty of faith. The certainty of faith belongs to people who are sorry for their sins and want to be forgiven. It belongs to those who seek forgiveness from God through the Word of the Gospel and through the Sacraments, having faith that God will be merciful for Jesus' sake.

> To find certainty about God's will for your life, don't look at your heart; look at His Word.

Certainty of faith is found in God and His Word of forgiveness. It is always a present reality. Are you sorry for your sins? Are you coming to the Church, where God gives out His forgiveness in the Gospel and Sacraments? Then you have the certainty that if you die today, you will enjoy God forever, with all your fellow believers in heaven.

WHAT DOES THIS MEAN?

One of the noblest and most precious virtues of faith is to close one's eyes to this, ingenuously to desist from exploring the why and the wherefore, and cheerfully to leave everything to God. Faith does not insist on knowing the reason for God's actions, but it still regards God as the greatest goodness and mercy. Faith holds to that against and beyond all reason, sense, and experience, when everything appears to be wrath and injustice. (AE 43:52)

How Should We Pray?

How we pray is as important to God as what we pray. He hopes that we will pray from the heart, that we will approach Him in prayer because we love and honor Him. He is not only our almighty God and Lord, He is also a loving and caring friend who is genuinely interested in us and in what we have to say. We approach Him confidently and comfortably because He is our friend, but also reverently and humbly because He is our God. We pray thoughtfully and attentively, relentlessly fighting the temptations to let our minds wander or merely to mouth words mechanically. We pray gratefully, fully aware of the fact that we need this time with God in prayer, even though we do not deserve the privilege of communicating with Him in prayer.

Posture can affect the quality of prayer. No special posture is commanded, but the Bible describes people praying in a variety of positions—standing, kneeling, with or without upraised hands, prostrate on the ground, even in bed during the long night hours when sleep will not come. The practice of closing eyes and folding hands for prayer began in later centuries. Normally, in Bible times people prayed with eyes open but downcast. This variety and openness indicates that the worshiper is free to adopt whatever practice is most meaningful. Kneeling may express humility and reverence; prostration, urgent need; upraised hands, expectation of outpoured blessings; closed eyes, intense concentration; standing, readiness to act obediently; sitting, comfort and security in God's presence. Except in church where worshipers are asked to share a common posture, each person should adopt the most meaningful position for him or her.

Should we use only prayers from a book, or should we always pray spontaneously? There is great value in both kinds of prayer. Prepared prayers are usually more elegant and complete. They remind us to think and pray about things that might otherwise have not occurred to us. They speak to God in ways far more beautiful than we might improvise. However, God does not require prayers that are literary masterpieces. No matter how simple the language or how many grammatical mistakes it has, God welcomes any prayer that comes to Him from a sincere and trusting heart. Prepared prayers can be very helpful in getting us started, but at some point it is important to move beyond someone else's words and thoughts to that which comes from your own heart and life.

—From Milton L. Rudnick, *Journey into Prayer* (St. Louis: Concordia, 2010), pp. 63–64.

PART TWO

What you'll learn about:

- God reveals Himself through human reason and through Scripture.

- Lutherans embrace the paradoxes of Scripture.

- The Church is a community of believers who are united in faith in Jesus Christ and has members in both heaven and on earth.

- The Church can be recognized through the marks of the Church.

- The Lutheran Church honors the saints as examples of faith and holy living.

- The government exercises the sword of God's power to establish order and peace.

- The Church's authority is the Office of the Keys, administered by her pastors.

- Christians are divided by not agreeing on what God's Word teaches.

- While all people have equal status in the Church, there are different roles.

Delivering the Gifts of God

The power of God and the grace of God are administered in the world for the benefit of all who have faith. God gives authority and power to the civil government to establish order and peace. God's Word establishes the Church. In the Church, God delivers the gifts of faith, forgiveness of sins, and everlasting life.

CHAPTER 7

The Conundrum of Faith

In This Chapter

- Our culture often pits faith against reason.
- While God employs human reason to reveal Himself to us, faith is necessary to grasp the fullness of His revelation through Scripture and move from proposition to belief.

Worthless Paper?

It is amazing how often people accept the reality of things on face value. Take paper money, for example. It looks like paper, wrinkles like paper, and even burns like paper. But everyone accepts that a $10 bill is worth $10 because the U.S. Treasury says that it is. We trust that if we take that bill to the bank, the bank will honor the face value of the bill. The bill has value because an authority says so. Now we can try to use reason to describe the workings of the Treasury department and economic theory to explain how the bill has value, and it may even make some sense, but at the end of the day, it takes trust to make the system work.

Faith works in a similar way. Our faith has a reasonable object, one that can be described in historical terms. We know that Jesus was born, lived, was crucified, and His body was missing from His tomb. All this is based on eyewitness accounts and external evidence. This all makes sense in a purely reasonable way. However, Jesus also claimed to be God, and demonstrated this through miracles and finally rising from the dead. These claims, while reasonable in the sense that only God could do miracles and rise from the dead, are not fully understandable but require trust in the final authority, God Himself.

Our faith has a reasonable object.

FROM THE BIBLE

Now faith is the assurance of things hoped for, the conviction of things not seen. (Hebrews 11:1)

Unfortunately, our culture often pits faith against reason, causing reason to appear more like rationalism, that is, reliance on reason as the best guide to all knowledge. This approach, however, falsely puts humans at the center of authority rather than God. Human reason after the fall was affected by sin, and as a result, is incapable of following God by itself. While God employs human reason to reveal Himself to us, faith is necessary to grasp the fullness of His revelation through Scripture and move from proposition to belief.

A Higher Authority

As Lutherans, we believe that the human authors of Scripture were inspired to write by the Holy Spirit. Scripture, then, because it is God-breathed, represents His revelation to man and man's highest authority. This is why Lutherans often call Scripture "God's Word." This requires reason to understand but faith to believe.

God reveals a portion of Himself through Scriptures that is just enough to create saving faith within us. However, in doing so, God does not reveal everything about Himself, for He is transcendently divine. Can a student be above his or her master, or a creature equal to the Creator? Some would argue that if we cannot know everything, then we cannot be sure of anything. This is surely inconsistent with what we experience in our daily lives. As with paper money, we do not have to completely understand something to acknowledge its existence.

This requires reason to understand, but faith to believe

Many mysteries we encounter in Scripture are about the character of God—who He is and ultimately how He works His plan of salvation and sanctification. These are, by their very nature, difficult concepts to understand, because heavenly or spiritual ideas are described in terms of earthly or physical ideas. There is bound to be a rationality (not *reason*) challenge trying to span this gap.

- God is described as Father, Son, and Holy Spirit (three persons), but He is also described as one God.
- Jesus described Himself as both God and man (two natures of Christ).
- This same physical Jesus also promised that He would always be with His Church and be present where the Gospel is preached and Sacraments administered.

We do not have to completely understand something to acknowledge its existence.

So, our faculties of reason allow us to understand what God has revealed to us, that which He authoritatively reveals in His Word. But we need faith to believe, and this is given to us by the Holy Spirit. Neither of these is in opposition to the other, as our faith needs an object or thing to be believed. We compromise or endanger our faith when we require rational (not reasonable) explanations to accompany our faith.

Faith Paradoxes

The Lutheran faith and doctrine is often referred to as paradoxical or operating within a tension. When two seemingly contradictory ideas are clearly taught from Scripture, it is necessary to accept and believe both. In striving to resolve the tension, we may end up rejecting one or the other doctrine.

Many early Christian heresies, for example, resulted from trying to resolve the paradox of the two natures of Christ. People just could not accept that Jesus was both fully human and fully God. When trying to understand the "real presence" of Christ in Word and Sacrament, people are again confused. Here an argument for or against Christ's physical or spiritual presence can contradict the paradox we find in Scripture when He says, "Take and eat; this is My body." (See p. 148.)

Martin Luther developed what he called the theology of the cross to aid in clarifying how we think about the mysteries of God. He wrote of both the revealed and hidden God. God is truly revealed only through Christ and His suffering and death. We cannot know God apart from His concealment in that revelation. God is hidden when we try to know or understand God apart from Christ. Seeking to explain something about which Scripture is silent, we gravitate toward a theology of glory, that is, trying to seek God apart from Christ.

Basically, we can define the terms in this way:

- Theology of glory: When we try to go up to God by our own reason and strength.

- Theology of the cross: God coming down to us through His Son, our Savior.

WHAT DOES THIS MEAN?

A theologian of the cross (that is, one who speaks of the crucified and hidden God), teaches that punishments, crosses, and death are the most precious treasury of all. . . . Indeed fortunate and blessed is he who is considered by God to be so worthy that these treasures of the relics of Christ should be given to him; rather, who understands that they are given to him. For to whom are they not offered? As St. James says, "Count it all joy, my brethren, when you meet various trials" (Jas. 1:2). For not all have this grace and glory to receive these treasures, but only the most elect of the children of God. (AE 31:225–26)

CHAPTER 8

What Is the Church?

In This Chapter

- The Church consists only of believers in Christ.
- The Church is not a building, not a club. The Church is God's creation.
- Human traditions and ideas must always be subjected to God's Word.

Which Meaning?

"Will you come to church with me?" You may have heard this invitation from friends or family members. What do they mean by that? Are they inviting you to the church building for a potluck? Are they inviting you to a worship service? Are they inviting you to become a part of the congregation? What does the word *church* mean?

In the Apostles' Creed, we confess "I believe in . . . the holy Christian church, the communion of saints, the forgiveness of sins." Here is the bedrock meaning: the Church (note the capital C) is the

WHAT DOES THIS MEAN?

Thank God, today a seven-year-old child knows what the Church is, namely, the holy believers and lambs who hear the voice of their Shepherd [John 10:11–16]. For the children pray, "I believe in one holy Christian Church." This holiness does not come from albs, tonsures, long gowns, and other ceremonies they made up without Holy Scripture, but from God's Word and true faith. (SA III XII 2–3)

FROM THE BIBLE

Christ loved the church and gave Himself up for her, that He might sanctify her, having cleansed her by the washing of water with the word, so that He might present the church to Himself in splendor, without spot or wrinkle or any such thing, that she might be holy and without blemish. (Ephesians 5:25–27)

TECHNICAL STUFF

The word in Greek for Church is *ekklesia*, which means "assembly," literally, "ones who are called out." The word *fellowship* in Greek means to have things in common. Those who have fellowship are sharing things together. *Holy* in the Bible means to be set apart for God.

fellowship of all those who are made holy by the forgiveness of sins through faith in Christ.

This then helps us sort out all the various uses of the word *church*:

- Worship services may be called "church" only because the Church (the believers) hears God's Word and praises His name.
- The building in which the congregation meets is a "church" because that is where the Church (the believers) gathers: St. Paul Lutheran Church on Main Street is "church" because it is a building where believers in Christ gather.
- The Lutheran "Church" is a grouping of believers who follow a certain confession.

These uses of the word *church* involve something believers in Jesus do. But at its heart, the Church is the sum total of all those who believe in Jesus Christ.

What Is the Church?

Every person, living or dead, who trusts in Jesus Christ as Lord and Savior is part of the Church. This is the biblical picture of the Church as the Body of Christ (note the capital *B*, referring not to Christ's physical body but to all believers). Everyone who is baptized into Christ and believes in Him is a member of Christ's Body. Jesus Christ is the Head of the Church, giving life and direction to the body of believers and connecting them to each other and to Him. Because the Church has one Head, we confess, "I believe in one holy Christian and apostolic Church" (Nicene Creed).

- **The Church is one** because there is one Christ. "Just as the body is one and has many members, and all the members of the body, though many, are one body, so it is with Christ. For in one Spirit we were all baptized into one body—Jews or Greeks, slaves or free—and all were made to drink of one Spirit" (1 Corinthians 12:12–13).

- **The Church is holy** because its members have the forgiveness of sins in Jesus Christ. With this Church "there is one body and one Spirit—just as you were called to the one hope that belongs to your call—one Lord, one faith, one baptism, one God and Father of all, who is over all and through all and in all" (Ephesians 4:4–6).

- **The Church is Christian.** Here the ancient text used the word *catholic*, a Greek word that means "universal" or "all over."

- **The Church is apostolic,** that is, founded on and drawing its life from the Word of God taught to us in the Scriptures by the apostles of Jesus. (See Chapter 31.) "And I tell you, you are Peter, and on this rock I will build My church, and the gates of hell shall not prevail against it" (Matthew 16:18).

The Church is not a building, not a club. The Church is God's creation. The Church is people called by the Spirit of God to believe in Jesus as Savior.

For just about two thousand years now, every Sunday, without fail, somewhere in the world, believers in Jesus Christ have gathered around their pastors to hear the Word of God and to worship the Father, Son, and Holy Spirit, receiving His gifts in faith. There are many languages, but they are united in one Word of the Lord. There are many cultures, but they are united in faith to Christ. On any given Sunday, when you approach the Table of the Lord, you do not come alone. You are joined by all those who in faith come to receive the Lord's Supper. But even more than that, you are joined with all the saints who have gone before us and all those yet to come.

TECHNICAL STUFF

The original word used in the creed is *catholic*. With the small "c," *catholic* means "universal," wherever believers are found, and is a helpful word. With a capital "C," *Catholic* refers to the "Roman Catholic Church," a particular denomination, not the whole Church.

MAKING CONNECTIONS

The Church's one foundation
Is Jesus Christ, her Lord;
She is His new creation
By water and the Word.
From heav'n He came and sought her
To be His holy bride;
With His own blood He bought her,
And for her life He died.

Elect from ev'ry nation,
Yet one o'er all the earth;
Her charter of salvation:
One Lord, one faith, one birth.
One holy name she blesses,
Partakes one holy food,
And to one hope she presses
With ev'ry grace endued.
(*LSB* 644:1–2)

- **The Church is universal.** Wherever there are believers in Christ, there is the Church, for the Church includes all those in every place and time who are connected by faith to Christ as the Head of His Body. "So then you are no longer strangers and aliens, but you are fellow citizens with the saints and members of the household of God, built on the foundation of the apostles and prophets, Christ Jesus Himself being the cornerstone, in whom the whole structure, being joined together, grows into a holy temple in the Lord. In Him you also are being built together into a dwelling place for God by the Spirit" (Ephesians 2:19–22).

BELIEVE, TEACH, CONFESS

Our churches teach that one holy Church is to remain forever. The Church is the congregation of saints [Psalm 149:1] in which the Gospel is purely taught and the Sacraments are correctly administered. . . . As Paul says, "One Lord, one faith, one baptism, one God and Father of all" (Ephesians 4:5–6). (AC VII 1, 4)

- **The Church is triumphant.** In one beautiful part of the Lutheran liturgy, the pastor states, "With angels and archangels and all the company of heaven we laud and magnify Your glorious name, evermore praising You" (*Divine Service*, Proper Preface). What a wonderful picture! We are united with all believers of the past and with all the angels of heaven as we praise God. How comforting to know we are singing not only with those near us in the pews but also with all the saints (believers) of all time now in heaven.

The Church Militant

There will always be struggles on earth within the Church. Sometimes it will be fighting the sin of the world. Sometimes it will be remaining steadfast in doctrine. But it will always be a struggle. All believers and all churches will struggle, but we fight the good fight as soldiers in His army.

FROM THE BIBLE

The Lord knows those who are His. (2 Timothy 2:19)

Narrow and Broad

Sometimes you will hear people define the Church in two ways: narrowly and broadly.

- **Narrow:** In the narrow sense, the Church includes only believers in Jesus. It is a fellowship of faith and of the Holy Spirit working in our hearts by the Word of God. Only God can see the heart.

- **Broad:** We cannot, like God, look into hearts to see who are the true believers. We can only go by what we hear people say they believe. That is why, broadly speaking, the Church includes all those who assemble around Word and Sacrament, that is, all who say they believe in Jesus Christ as our one and only Lord and Savior from sin because He died and rose for us. This is the Church we are able to see—the community of the baptized gathered around the Word of God and the Table of the Lord—everyone who participates outwardly in the life of the congregation. Here both believers and hypocrites are all mixed together.

What about Those Who Say They Are Christian But . . .

Perhaps you have heard the excuse, "I'll come to church when they get rid of all the hypocrites." Isn't the Church weakened by those who say they believe but really do not? Shouldn't we institute some sort of program to root out all the false believers? Actually, such a program can only fail because there is no way for us to know and judge what a person really believes—only God can do that. All we have is the outward confession a person makes.

Though both true believers and hypocrites are mixed together in the outward fellowship of the Church, we trust God to sort them out when Christ returns at the Last Day. In the meantime, we continue bringing God's Word to all people. For God's Word alone (spoken, written, given in Baptism and the Lord's Supper) leads us to repent of our hypocrisy, brings us to faith, and keeps us in the faith.

TECHNICAL STUFF

The phrase "Word and Sacrament" is Lutheran shorthand for the preaching and teaching of the Word of God, Holy Baptism, and the Lord's Supper. Through these activities God gives grace in Christ and calls people to faith. We also call Word and Sacrament the Means of Grace, that is, the channels by which God actually delivers to us all the benefits of Christ's death and resurrection.

NEED TO KNOW

Hypocrite seems like a harsh, judgmental word. The Greek word from which it is taken refers to someone who is wearing a mask. In other words, he is saying one thing about himself when really he is something else. A hypocrite is two-faced. A hypocrite is someone who says he believes when really he does not. Until the hypocrite is somehow exposed by his actions or words, we cannot tell. Only God can tell for sure.

Where Is the Church?

We cannot see it, but we believe the Church exists because God has promised His Word will not return to Him empty (Isaiah 55:11). The holiness of the Church does not come from the holy things we have done—all our works are tainted by sin (see Chapter 2)—but the Church is made holy each and every day by the cleansing blood of Christ (1 Peter 1:18–19) in the forgiveness of sins. At the end of time, Christ will raise to life all who believe in Him so that His Church will live with Him forever. Those who do not believe will be raised to eternal destruction. (See the parable of the sheep and goats in Matthew 25:31–46.) The fact that Christ establishes His Church is actually a very comforting teaching from Scripture. Even if your pastor, for instance, were to be exposed as a hypocrite, the Word he proclaims and the Sacraments he administers still do what God intends. Our Confessions explain, "Both the Sacraments and Word are effective because of Christ's institution and command, even if they are administered by evil men" (AC VIII 2). That is because the power is not in the pastor but in the Word of God and the promise of Christ. Pastors are called to live exemplary lives, but the Word of God is effective because it is the Word of God, not because of the one who speaks it. That way, everything depends on Christ and His Word. He is Lord. We are His Church, His Body. Give Him thanks and praise— He has called you to be a true member of His Church.

> Christ will raise to life all who believe in Him so that His Church will live with Him forever.

How Will We Find the Church?

God's Spirit uses the Word of God and the Sacraments to bring us to faith and to keep us in faith. Lutherans confess that we are justified, declared righteous before God, solely by God's grace for the sake of Christ alone, received through faith alone. Wherever this Gospel of Jesus is purely preached and the Sacraments are given in accordance with the Gospel, there you will find believers. There God will gather people around the preaching of His Word and the working of His Sacraments. There you will find holy believers who hear the voice of their shepherd.

Why Join a Church?

Within the walls of the building we call church, the local congregation of believers, is where you will see the "real action" of the Church commanded by God.

- Here God's Spirit comes to us with grace, mercy, and forgiveness.
- Here God is faithful to His promises.

- Here God's people, led by their pastor, worship, baptize, preach, teach, confess and forgive, gather at the Lord's Table, and reach others with the saving message of Christ.
- Here God's people have the privilege of associating with others who are faithful to the Word and linked to us through common beliefs.
- Here God's people build relationships with one another based on a strong foundation and linked to Christ.

Which One Do I Choose?

There are so many different churches—Baptist, Methodist, Roman Catholic, Orthodox, Presbyterian, Pentecostal, and Lutheran, not to mention the many cults. What are we do make of all this? Where is the truth in all this? Is there no such thing as universal truth? Our culture tells us that everyone's belief is equally valid.

Lutherans, however, know that Satan always tries to weaken the Church by dividing followers of Christ from one another. Divisions result when Satan leads people either to lose sight of Christ and His work for us or to make something more important than the Gospel. Divisions result when the Bible's focus on Christ is obscured or man-made traditions are mixed with the Gospel and the Sacraments.

What is the answer? Should the churches ignore their differences so that we can "all just get along"? (See Chapter 13.) Of course, we are called to love all people, particularly fellow believers in Jesus. The way to resolve differences in teaching is not to ignore our differences but to bring them together under the Word of God. Human traditions and ideas must always be subjected to God's Word. Scripture says, "Test the spirits to see whether they are from God" (1 John 4:1). "Keep a close watch on yourself and on the teaching" so that you do not depart from Christ or the true Gospel (1 Timothy 4:16). Only the Word of God in Christ gives life. This testing is an ongoing process in the Church because the unity of the Church is found only in the

WHAT DOES THIS MEAN?

Luther explains the Spirit's work of gathering the Church by the Gospel: "I believe that I cannot by my own reason or strength believe in Jesus Christ, my Lord, or come to Him; but the Holy Spirit has called me by the Gospel, enlightened me with His gifts, sanctified and kept me in the true faith. In the same way He calls, gathers, enlightens, and sanctifies the whole Christian church on earth, and keeps it with Jesus Christ in the one true faith. In this Christian church He daily and richly forgives all my sins and the sins of all believers. On the Last Day He will raise me and all the dead, and give eternal life to me and all believers in Christ. This is most certainly true." (SC, Third Article)

FROM THE BIBLE

St. Paul strongly warns: "I am astonished that you are so quickly deserting Him who called you in the grace of Christ and are turning to a different gospel—not that there is another one, but there are some who trouble you and want to distort the gospel of Christ." (Galatians 1:6–7)

The Truth we confess is Jesus Christ, who promises, "I am the way, and the truth, and the life. No one comes to the Father except through Me." (John 14:6)

BELIEVE, TEACH, CONFESS

But the Church is not only the fellowship of outward objects and rites, as other governments, but at its core, it is a fellowship of faith and of the Holy Spirit in hearts. Yet this fellowship has outward marks so that it can be recognized. These marks are the pure doctrine of the Gospel and the administration of the Sacraments in accordance with the Gospel of Christ. This Church alone is called Christ's body, which Christ renews, sanctifies, and governs by His Spirit. Paul testifies about this when he says, "And gave Him as head over all things to the Church, which is His body, the fullness of Him who fills all in all" (Ephesians 1:22–23). (Ap VII and VIII 5)

Gospel and the Sacraments.

This is why Lutherans are very serious about our confession of Christ and His Gospel—and why we do not have pulpit and altar fellowship without full agreement in the Gospel and the Sacraments. Church fellowship for believers is always around the preaching and teaching of the Gospel and the Sacraments as marks of the Church. To have fellowship is to have things in common, especially the pure Gospel and the rightly administered Sacraments.

Human traditions and ideas must always be subjected to God's Word.

Scripture tells us to mark and avoid false confessions (churches that teach apart from the Word of God) precisely because false teaching can and does lead people away from Christ. (See Romans 16:16–17; 2 Timothy 3:1–8; Titus 3:10–11.) Therefore, we have no church fellowship with those who teach in ways that cloud the clear witness to Christ and His work for us. This is not to say that those who hold a position contrary to the pure Gospel are thereby, of necessity, not Christian. Only God can see the faith in the heart. We, however, are called to compare both our teaching and the teaching of others with

Holy Scriptures, so that we remain faithful to the Word of God and call others to the same faithfulness. Remember, what saves is the faithful teaching of Christ! (See 1 Timothy 4:16; 6:3.) In the same way, differences and divisions within our churches can only be resolved as we seek our answers in the clear Word of God.

NEED TO KNOW

Catholic: (Greek: *katholikos*, "universal," or "general.") A term first applied to the Christian Church as a whole in a letter of Ignatius (ca. AD 110): "Where Christ is, there is the catholic Church." In Lutheran theology (as in early Christendom) the word is often used of the one, holy, catholic ("Christian"), and apostolic Church united to Christ by faith and transcending time, space, and all other barriers.

TECHNICAL STUFF

"Pulpit and altar fellowship" and "Church fellowship" are technical terms used to describe official relationships between churches and church bodies. When congregations agree in the Gospel and the right use of the Sacraments, they find themselves in "church fellowship." Pastors may preach in the pulpits of one another's congregations. Members are welcome at the altars of one another's churches. Church fellowship is always a fellowship or agreement in the Gospel. See Galatians 2:9. (See Chapter 13.)

The phrase "marks of the church" is used to describe the Gospel and the Sacraments. Where is the Church to be found? You look for the marks: where the Gospel is purely preached and the Sacraments are rightly administered according to Christ's institution.

CHAPTER 9

It's All about Jesus, Part 3

In This Chapter

- Unless and until a person believes in Jesus, he or she is dead to any kind of a relationship with God.
- The Bible calls conversion to faith in Jesus being "born again."
- The Holy Spirit calls people to faith when and where He chooses, and He uses the Gospel to make it happen.
- All those who believe in Jesus, even with doubts and fears and questions, can say with confidence that God has forgiven all their sins.

Have you ever tried to convert someone? Like maybe convert a Red Sox fan into a Yankees fan? That's pretty hard work. But let's say you succeed: who made it happen? You probably did lots of informing and responding to objections and making your case with personal stories and such. But in the end it came down to your friend deciding to make the change to become a Yankees fan. Your friend made a choice.

TECHNICAL STUFF

By *conversion* we mean the process by which a person is changed from someone who does not believe in Jesus to someone who does believe in Him.

What Can a Dead Person Do?

When a person changes from being someone who does not believe in Jesus as Lord and Savior to being someone who does, we say the person converted to Christianity. But there is a big difference between converting to Christianity and converting to another sports team. When someone converts to Christianity, when that person becomes a believer in Jesus, he or she did not decide to do it. It may seem like it, but it is just not so. Here's why.

A person who does not believe in Jesus is dead. Not dead in the normal physical sense, but dead in a very real spiritual sense. God says to people who are now believers, "You were dead in the trespasses and sins in which you once walked" (Ephesians 2:1–2). So unless and until a person believes in Jesus, he or she is dead to any kind of a relationship with God.

Imagine you are with a friend who suddenly grabs his chest, gasps, and falls down. You check for a pulse and listen for breathing. Nothing. Fortunately, you know CPR, so you shout "Call 911!" and you start resuscitation. Does your friend ask for help? Does he reach out and put your hands over his heart? Does he just decide not to have a heart attack? No. He is incapable of cooperating or even asking for help. And what if he dies? Can he choose not to be dead? Can he sit up and say, "Hey! How about a little help here, please"? Can he invite you to perform CPR? Nope.

And that is how God describes us before we believe: dead. We are unable to change or cooperate or even ask for help. Dead people are passive—as in totally passive.

That is why the Bible calls conversion to faith in Jesus being "born again." You might have heard that to be born again means to make a decision to ask Jesus to come into your heart. Consider the birth of a child: what did the child being born do? Nothing. It is the mom who does all the work in childbirth. Maybe others help, but that baby sure does not. The baby is completely passive. The baby cannot even ask to be born, let alone take an active part in the process. That is a good illustration of being changed from an unbeliever to a believer in Jesus: someone else does all that work. In conversion, that someone is the Holy Spirit. And that is a real comfort because it does not depend on us; God does it all for us.

What about Making a Decision for Christ?

When a mother gives birth, she uses her God-given physical strength to make it happen. When the Holy Spirit gives new birth, He uses words—a message. Specifically, the Holy Spirit uses the message of Scripture: that God gave His Son, Jesus, to die as payment for our sins and to come to life again to change death from something permanent to something temporary. That message—that God forgives us as a gift that is free to us and paid for completely by His Son—is called the Gospel, the Good News.

That is the message the Holy Spirit uses to bring a person to faith. The Bible says this Good News about Jesus is "the power of God for salvation" (Romans 1:16) and that "faith comes from hearing, and hearing through the word of Christ"

TECHNICAL STUFF

The word *Gospel* comes from the old English "god spel" or "good news." The Gospel is the Good News that Jesus payed for our sins by His death on the cross, defeated death for us by His resurrection, and that God gives the benefit of Jesus' death and resurrection as a free gift to everyone who confesses their sins and trusts in Him.

NEED TO KNOW

Regeneration: From a Latin word meaning "rebirth." The Holy Spirit gives new life through Baptism and God's Word.

Sanctification: The spiritual growth that follows justification by grace through faith in Christ. Sanctification is God's work through His Means of Grace: Word and Sacraments.

FROM THE BIBLE

But when the goodness and loving kindness of God our Savior appeared, He saved us, not because of works done by us in righteousness, but according to His own mercy, by the washing of regeneration and renewal of the Holy Spirit, whom He poured out on us richly through Jesus Christ our Savior, so that being justified by His grace we might become heirs according to the hope of eternal life. (Titus 3:4–7)

(Romans 10:17). Be sure to read the section on "The Means of Grace" for more about this (see Chapter 15). But for now, just know this:

- We don't choose to follow Jesus.
- We don't become a Christian by asking Him into our hearts.
- We don't make a decision for Jesus.

Unbelievers cannot do these things because unbelievers are dead to God. And the almighty God does not stand at the door of our hearts knocking but powerless to turn the doorknob and let Himself in. The Holy Spirit calls people to faith when and where He chooses, and He uses the Gospel to make it happen.

So, When Did You Know You Were Saved?

There are many Christians who claim that you need a born-again "experience" to be able to say when and where your salvation happened. Well, though some people can recall an exact moment and place when they first believed, many Christians cannot. Do you remember being born? Of course not. Does that mean you weren't born? Again, of course not. So how do you know if you have been born again? Simply ask yourself, "Do I trust in Jesus as my Lord and Savior, that He died and rose to life again for me?" If you answer "Yes," then even if your faith is new or weak, even if you haven't got all the details worked out, or even if you have some doubts, you are a believer, a child of God who has received God's gift of forgiveness and new life. You know this because God says, "No one can say 'Jesus is Lord' except in the Holy Spirit" (1 Corinthians 12:3) and "If you confess with your mouth that Jesus is Lord and believe in your heart that God raised Him from the dead, you will be saved" (Romans 10:9).

You also have God's promise in Baptism—or if you don't have it yet, it's available for you. Baptism is simply God's Good News applied to the individual. God promises that His message used together with water gives the gift of faith and forgiveness and new life, because "as many of you as were baptized into Christ have put on Christ" (Galatians 3:27). Since God makes promises like that, no one who believes in Jesus will delay being baptized; they will want the promises God gives in Baptism.

The Holy Spirit Calls You Out of Darkness

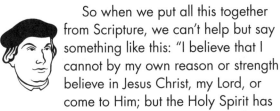

So when we put all this together from Scripture, we can't help but say something like this: "I believe that I cannot by my own reason or strength believe in Jesus Christ, my Lord, or come to Him; but the Holy Spirit has called me by the Gospel, enlightened me with His gifts, sanctified and kept me in the true faith" (SC, Third Article).

Some people who believe in Jesus have believed in Him for as long as they can remember. Some can remember a specific moment when the Holy Spirit called them out of darkness into light, like turning on a dime. Still others come to faith in a long process of hearing God's message, more like turning an aircraft carrier around than turning on a dime. Some have strong and mature faith; others have faith that is brand new and may be weak. But all those who believe in Jesus, even with doubts and fears and questions, can say with confidence that God has forgiven all their sins. He loves them as dear children, and they are already in a new life that will last forever. Christian confidence and hope is based upon this because they did not make it happen; the Holy Spirit did.

BELIEVE, TEACH, CONFESS

So that we may obtain this faith, the ministry of teaching the Gospel and administering the Sacraments was instituted. Through the Word and Sacraments, as through instruments, the Holy Spirit is given [John 20:22]. He works faith, when and where it pleases God [John 3:8], in those who hear the good news that God justifies those who believe that they are received into grace for Christ's sake. This happens not through our own merits, but for Christ's sake. (AC V 1–3)

FROM THE BIBLE

Blessed be the God and Father of our Lord Jesus Christ! According to His great mercy, He has caused us to be born again to a living hope through the resurrection of Jesus Christ from the dead, to an inheritance that is imperishable, undefiled, and unfading, kept in heaven for you, who by God's power are being guarded through faith for a salvation ready to be revealed in the last time. (1 Peter 1:3–5)

On Faith Alone

Certainty of faith, and this alone, is the way to receive forgiveness from God, the Judge, and to be healed by Christ, our Physician. "Faith alone" is a common phrase among Lutherans. (See Ephesians 2:8–9.) It means that I cannot save myself. My works cannot do it. God must be my Savior, and faith, which He gives me, is the way to receive this saving. When we say "faith alone," we're taking my good works out of the picture, but we are *not* taking God out of the picture. "Faith alone" goes right along with Christ's work, the Word, and the Sacraments. For example, a prisoner of war cannot be freed by any of his own works. But he can and must be freed by the works of his army or government. So also we cannot be saved by our works, but we are saved by Christ's works—His cross, resurrection, the Gospel, and the Sacraments. These are His works, not mine. If my salvation depended on my works, it would be uncertain. But because it depends on what God does, it is certain. I can trust that God is my Savior.

Lutheran Spirituality

By Rev. Ernest Bernet

"I'VE GOT SPIRIT, YES I DO! I'VE GOT SPIRIT, HOW 'BOUT YOU?"

Remember that old cheer at high school athletic games? There sure are a lot of spirits out there: school spirit, Christmas spirit, American spirit, and even distilled spirits. And each and every spirit has its own *spirituality*, its own way of talking about and relating to that spirit. One thing that you should realize now is this: Not all spirituality is Christian spirituality.

Holy Spirit Spirituality

You know the phrase "All that glitters isn't gold." Well, when it comes to spirituality, everything that sounds spiritual is not necessarily good or helpful. So the first thing we need to do is focus in from all spiritualities down to Christian spirituality. To do that, here is a quick trick to help us: Look at the word *spirituality* and the name "Holy Spirit." Notice anything? Well, of course, you can see the similarity in the word *spirit*. So here is the trick: say "Holy Spirit Spirituality" because that is what gets us right to the heart of the matter and takes us past all that other stuff that is not good or helpful. All we care about right now is talking about God's Spirit and how He relates to our spirit. Those are the only two spirits that concern us here. So now we know that we are talking about Christian spirituality.

As a Spiritual Embryo It's All about the Umbilical Cord

Lutherans speak very carefully about the intersection of God's action and human action in the life of the Christian. It is the distinctions that are drawn here that set Lutheran spirituality apart from other kinds of spirituality, even against some other Christian teachings on the subject. The trick here is to carefully distinguish whether we are talking about someone before conversion or after.

Let's begin by taking a look at this statement from the Book of Concord (which is the book containing our Lutheran Confessions of faith): "As soon as the Holy Spirit has begun His work of regeneration and renewal in us through the Word and holy Sacraments, we can and should cooperate through His power, although still in great weakness. This cooperation does not come from our fleshly natural powers, but from the new powers and gifts that the Holy Spirit has begun in us in conversion" (FC SD II 65).

There is no cooperation before conversion, but there is some cooperation after. That's what we mean by the limits of human cooperation after conversion—even after conversion we are now only spiritual infants. In fact, a better analogy might be an unborn baby still in the mother's womb, an embryo. This is a good picture of how we are in relation to the spiritual world beyond our perception. Like a baby in the mother's womb, we do not know about the real world outside the womb. All we see is the darkness of the womb and not the light and colors of the world beyond. Likewise, as spiritual embryos we do not perceive the true realties of the spiritual realm beyond our physical senses. How much then can we cooperate in spiritual matters? Answer: not much.

The most beautiful picture of how this works is in Jesus' own words: "I am the vine; you are the branches. Whoever abides in Me and I in him, he it is that bears much fruit, for apart from Me you can do nothing" (John 15:5).

Just as a branch draws its life from the vine, so also we draw our spiritual life from Jesus. His work was all about getting us reconnected to Him, reattaching that spiritual umbilical cord through the initial forgiveness of sin that happens at our conversion. And forgiveness of sin remains important to keep that spiritual umbilical cord open and flowing to us. Thus, Lutheran spirituality is very emphatic about the importance of Christ and continual forgiveness. As spiritual embryos, it's all about the umbilical cord!

How Does This Spiritual Umbilical Cord Work?

Now that we have covered the key dynamics that make Lutheran spirituality what it is, we can talk about the distinctive features of how it works in more practical terms.

1. CHRIST AND FORGIVENESS IS CENTRAL

We keep Christ and forgiveness central. While other Christian spiritualities might give the impression that forgiveness is a thing of the past, Lutherans see it as a continuing need in the life of a Christian, as the engine that drives the whole Christian life forward.

2. RECEPTIVE SPIRITUALITY

We place priority on God's action over our action. Ours is a receptive spirituality (not active spirituality) that rejoices in receiving all the gifts of God on God's terms. Like embryos at the end of the umbilical cord, it is all about living on the receiving end of God's grace in Christ.

3. THE WORD OF GOD AND UNRESOLVED TENSIONS

We stress God's Word and take things on God's terms, as revealed to us in the Bible. Specifically, Lutherans say that God's Word determines the reality but our faith determines the benefit. Lutherans prefer to take reality as it is, or better, as God's Word says it is; we do not speak of creating reality ourselves by our own perceptions. That's a God-thing. (See Chapter 15.) This relates to allowing unresolved tensions and paradoxes. For instance, Lutherans distinguish Law and Gospel but do not separate them, and ultimately the Gospel has priority. (See Chapter 16.) Or try this question: Are we physical beings seeking a spiritual experience, or are we spiritual beings having a physical experience? Lutheran answer: Yes! We feel both ways strongly. And we also believe in the resurrection of the body. We do not put a clean distinction between the spiritual and the physical. In fact, how you treat the material world is a deeply spiritual matter. In other words, matter matters spiritually! This means in matters of vocation we do not see the jobs of monks and nuns as somehow "more holy" than "ordinary jobs" like cleaning floors, waiting tables, or caring for children. For us, the ordinary is sacred too.

4. THE ROLE OF THE HOLY SPIRIT IN GENERAL

The Holy Spirit's role is to take the things that Christ won for us and apply them to our lives. He is the one through whom we are called to faith in Christ, and in the Christian life He goes on applying the benefits of Christ to us. That's how we are fed, are nurtured, grow, and mature.

5. THE ROLE OF THE HOLY SPIRIT IN DEVOTIONS

There is a close connection between the work of the Holy Spirit in the life of the Christian and the Word of God. Lutherans emphasize that God has chosen to tie His Spirit to His external Word. By that we mean that the Holy Spirit has chosen to limit Himself normally to operating through these external means, the things outside of us, which become the conduits of God getting into us—such as the preached Word from Scripture and the Sacraments. Also in our unique model for devotions—prayer, meditation, and struggle—the Holy Spirit is important.

- First, in prayer, we ask the Holy Spirit to be present in the Word we are about to read. He is the one who inspired it in the first place, and now we ask Him to help us understand it spiritually.
- Second, we meditate on the Word, again relying on the Holy Spirit to speak to us through that Word.
- Finally, we return to the world in our normal tasks. There we struggle with Satan, the things of the world, and ourselves.

Our spirits have been fed and nurtured through the Holy Spirit in the Word of God, and now we rely on that to carry us along, even as the Holy Spirit teaches us in our struggles. Thus, our devotions are done under the Holy Spirit's management, in the Holy Spirit's study of the Word, and out in the Holy Spirit's workshop of the world.

6. OUR ROLE IN DEVOTIONS

Read the above paragraph again and note how our role works in relation to the role of the Holy Spirit. We are not cloistered monks and nuns who withdraw from the world almost entirely. Instead, we retreat from the world for prayer and meditation on God's Word; then we come back out and engage the world in the strength of that Word. We withdraw only to be fed— it's a time for spiritually "going fetal." When we pray (think spiritual embryos), we close our eyes, fold our hands, and bow our heads.

7. GROWTH GOALS

We have different goals in mind for spiritual growth. We do not see ourselves as growing more and more spiritually independent from God but more and more aware of our spiritual dependence on God. Our growth is a growth in faith and trust, not in self-sufficiency. There is no goal of steady upward increase or perfectionism. We remain mere babes in relation to Christ—more like spiritual embryos.

8. LITURGICAL SPIRITUALITY

We live in the context of all other Christians in time and space. Whenever I pray, I pray as a part of the Body of Christ, even if I am physically alone, because of that spiritual connection that I have to Christ—the same connection that all other Christians have.

Lutheran Spirituality Is Distinctive

As seen above, Lutheran spirituality rejoices in two very distinctive features over and against other kinds of spirituality:

1. Focusing on the right spirit, the Holy Spirit
2. Focusing on the proper relation of God's action and human action

We might just be spiritual embryos, but we sure are thankful for that umbilical cord! For us it is all about living on the receiving end of God's grace in Christ through the Holy Spirit.

MAKING CONNECTIONS

When I speak about spirituality, I do not envisage something extraordinary—a superior way of being a Christian that is open only to a religious elite or a more advanced stage in the spiritual life. I have in mind what is given to every faithful person. Christian spirituality is, quite simply, following Jesus. It is the ordinary life of faith in which we receive Baptism, attend the Divine Service, participate in the Holy Supper, read the Scriptures, pray for ourselves and others, resist temptation, and work with Jesus in our given location here on earth. By our practice of spirituality we are not raised to a higher plane above the normal, everyday, bodily life, but we receive the Holy Spirit from Christ so that we can live in God's presence each day of our lives as we deal with people and work, sin and abuse, inconvenience and heartbreak, trouble and tragedy. We are not called to become more spiritual by disengaging from our earthly life, but simply to rely on Jesus as we do what is given for us to do, experience what is given for us to experience, and enjoy what is given for us to enjoy. Christian spirituality . . . deals with the whole life of those who have faith in Christ.

—**Dr. John W. Kleinig** *Grace Upon Grace: Spirituality for Today*

CHAPTER 10

Examples of Faith

In This Chapter

- There are saints in heaven and on earth.
- While we honor the saints of old, we do not pray to them.
- God makes holy. Saints do not make themselves so.

TECHNICAL STUFF

Saint is not a special designation for those "in the know" or who exhibit a higher or better piety than the rest.

BELIEVE, TEACH, CONFESS

Our churches teach that the history of saints may be set before us so that we may follow the example of their faith and good works, according to our calling.
(AC XXI 1)

"When the Saints Go Marching In"

Saint comes from the Latin word for "holy." The saints are the "holy ones." But who is in their company when the saints go marching in? Who should have the courage to put themselves in the company of the holy ones? The answer is simple: all those who trust Christ for their salvation are saints. We humans do not make ourselves saints any more than we make ourselves Christians. Just as salvation is by grace through faith, so is the title of saint. Just as the blood of Christ makes holy (Romans 5:9), it also makes saints. *Saint* is not a special designation for those "in the know" or who exhibit a higher or better piety than the rest. The New Testament letters are often addressed "to the saints" in a particular location (for example, Ephesians 1:1) as a designation for all the believers in that place. Nor are the saints only those who are in heaven, because the collections of alms was given for the saints (1 Corinthians 16:1), and the saints sent greetings to other churches in the New Testament (2 Corinthians 13:13). There are saints in heaven and on earth. On earth they are found among the people who gather around the things that count as holy: the Word and Sacraments.

No Longer Aliens

The apostle Paul calls those who are members of Christ, who is the cornerstone of the Church, saints: "So then you are no longer strangers and aliens, but you are fellow citizens with the saints and members of the household of God, built on the foundation of the apostles and prophets, Christ Jesus Himself being the cornerstone, in whom the whole structure, being joined together, grows into a holy temple in the Lord" (Ephesians 2:19–21). The New Testament never applies the word *saint* to any individual, but it is always plural, or a collective singular.

While we honor the saints of old, such as St. Paul and St. Augustine, we do not pray to them. Scripture includes no hint that they either hear our prayers or could rescue us from trouble if we did cry to them in time of need. Instead, God in His Word consistently portrays Christ as the one who desires to hear our prayers and answers them as our gracious Mediator before God. Only those who truly trust Christ and thus are among His holy ones will approach His throne of grace in eager and insistent prayer. All the saints have the faith to call on Christ as their only Mediator with God and Redeemer from sin.

God is the one who makes holy. Saints do not make themselves so. God Himself is the ultimate "thrice holy" (see Isaiah 6:3). Martin Luther called Christ Himself the "saint of saints" (AE 41:71). If we are to be among the saints, then we will need to be in care of the Saint of saints and partake of His generously distributed gifts. We have no holiness of our own but only what the Word of God and the Holy Sacraments give. This is why the gathering of the Church around the sacramental things that make holy is called the communion of saints. The saints possess by grace all God's gifts.

NEED TO KNOW

Saint: The word *saint* in Scripture refers to believers on earth (Acts 9:32; Romans 1:7) and in heaven (Matthew 27:52). Throughout Church history, it has been used to designate one set apart as especially holy (e.g., St. Paul, St. Francis of Assisi). The Lutheran Reformation rejected prayers and devotions to saints. In Lutheran usage, the formal title *saint* is not used for anyone except those who were called such before the Reformation.

FROM THE BIBLE

Call upon Me in the day of trouble; I will deliver you, and you shall glorify Me. (Psalm 50:15)

NEED TO KNOW

Commemorations:
Remembrances of the faithful dead who are set before the Church as an example.

A Community

The Church is the only true democracy in that when you die, you do not get removed from the Church's roll, but are translated to the community of saints who now see what you once believed. We honor the saints by imitating their faith and the life of good works that arose from their faith (Hebrews 13:7). Some in the community of saints receive the designation of martyr—those who died or who were put to death on account of their being Christians and confessing faith in Jesus Christ. We give thanks to God for these people who confessed so faithfully that they sometimes suffered death for their confession. This is why the Church celebrates these people with special days set aside to remember and commemorate the saints. We thank God for what He has worked through them. We use these days to glorify God for His sublime mercy and His gift of grace to our spiritual forefathers (Hebrews 12:1). The saints listed are listed for God's glory and not for the glory of their persons.

NEED TO KNOW

Feasts and Festivals:
Celebrations in the life of the Church that mark important events and commemorations, such as events in Jesus' life (The Circumcision and Name of Jesus), and celebrations of notable people (St. Timothy—January 24, St. Luke—October 18) and great events in the life of the Church (Reformation, Holy Cross Day).

"Oh, How I Want to Be in That Number!"

The Church Year designates November 1 as All Saints' Day. On this day we remember those who have confessed Christ with us and who have been taken by the holy angels to see Him face-to-face (1 Corinthians 13:12), like our faithful parents, children, and friends who have died before us. All Saints' Day is a bittersweet day for those of us left behind because we miss those who have died before us. But we smile through our tears because they live with Christ where there are no more tears for them, and they are in full possession of what we now only believe. We struggle forward in a life full of trial and trouble, honoring the saints by seeking to imitate their faith and good works. We are in that number because God our heavenly Father counts us with the saints.

CHAPTER 11

Who's Got the Power?

In This Chapter

- The state has the power of the sword, but the Church has the power of the Word.
- The Church remits sins to penitent sinners and retains the sins of unrepentant sinners.
- Pastors serve as God's representatives in their congregations, but all believers have a role in serving God.

BELIEVE, TEACH, CONFESS

The Church is the congregation of saints [Psalm 149:1] in which the Gospel is purely taught and the Sacraments are correctly administered. (AC VII 1)

The Source of All Authority

The Scriptures are the source of God's authority, be it in the Church or in the civil realm. The authority God gives to the Church and government are signs of His love for us, providing for our spiritual and temporal well-being.

The Church does not exercise secular, or civil, authority. She may not employ the power of the state to compel people to accept the teachings of the Gospel, to enforce Christian living, or to punish or imprison heretics. Lutherans teach that the state has the power of the sword, but the Church has the power of the Word. Christ gave His Word to His Church. The Word of the Gospel brings people to faith. Peter expresses this understanding when he speaks of the "ministry of the word" (Acts 6:4). Not by force or fines but by teaching

TECHNICAL STUFF

Some teach that the Church's authority comes from both the Scriptures and sacred tradition. Lutherans believe that the authority given by God is found in Scripture alone. A Roman Catholic, for example, asks the question, "What does the Church say?" A Lutheran asks, "What do the Scriptures say?" Therein lies a critical difference in understanding Church authority from a Lutheran point of view.

and the work of the Holy Spirit, the Church wins people for Christ and shepherds them to life under Christ in His kingdom.

The Authority of the Church: The Office of the Keys

The Office of the Keys is the term used to designate the power given by Christ to the Church on earth. Jesus said, "As the Father has sent Me, even so I am sending You. . . . Receive the Holy Spirit. If you forgive the sins of any, they are forgiven them; if you withhold forgiveness from any, it is withheld" (John 20:21–23). In the Book of Matthew, Jesus announced that He would give the disciples "the keys of the kingdom of heaven" (Matthew 16:19). This power was not exclusive to the apostles but transmitted successively by the Church to those whom the Church ordains and places in the Office of the Holy Ministry.

The Lutheran Confessions teach, "It must be recognized that the Keys belong not to the person of one particular man, but to the Church. . . . This is why it is first the Church that has the right of calling" (Tr 24). The Church exercises the Office of the Keys through her ministers, who, in the stead of Christ, and on behalf of the congregation, assure that the Means of Grace (see Part Three) are administered. Through these means the Holy Spirit imparts to people the blessings of Christ's redemption. Christ obtained the forgiveness of sins and salvation for all people. Through the Means of Grace, the Holy Spirit imparts these blessings to the people. Through her ministers, the Church administers these means.

The Releasing Key

The releasing key is the power to remit sins (to cancel the punishment of God against sin) and absolve the sinner (declare the sinner free from the guilt of sin). This power is not separate from or above the Gospel of Christ but is a specific application of the Gospel. The Lutheran Confessions hold that "the Power of the Keys administers and presents the Gospel through Absolution, which is the true voice of the Gospel" (Ap XIIA 39). In Christ, sinners are forgiven. In Absolution, the message

WHAT DOES THIS MEAN?

The Office of the Keys is that special authority which Christ has given to His church on earth to forgive the sins of repentant sinners, but to withhold forgiveness from the unrepentant as long as they do not repent. (SC, Confession)

BELIEVE, TEACH, CONFESS

Our churches teach that no one should publicly teach in the Church, or administer the Sacraments, without a rightly ordered call. (AC XIV)

of grace and forgiveness is applied to the individual in a more direct way.

The called ministers of Christ, who speak God's Word in the Christian congregation, have the power and authority to remit sins.

The Binding Key

The binding key is the power to retain sins. To retain sins, or bind them to someone, does not mean that these sins were not atoned for by Jesus or that they are not forgiven before God. Instead, it is the announcement that the unrepentant sinner, by desiring to remain in sin, has rejected the gift of grace offered by Christ for all those who have faith in Him. Forgiveness is received in no other way than by faith (Romans 3:28). The impenitent, because they refuse to believe it, have excluded themselves from the general amnesty proclaimed by God and hold themselves outside of God's forgiveness.

Using the Power of the Keys

The Church does not use the power of the keys lightly. Instead, she strictly follows the instructions of Christ. The Church remits sins to penitent sinners and retains the sins of impenitent sinners as long as they do not repent. Whenever the Church on earth through her ministers deals with sinners in this way, her actions are certain and sure also in heaven (Matthew 18:18).

So, What about the Rest of Us?

While it is given to pastors to serve in their particular way, all of God's people are given many opportunities to serve both God and others. There is a "flow" in every Christian's life. The flow is to receive God's gifts and then to serve God by serving others in daily vocations. The service of laypeople in the Church is referred to by Lutherans as "the priesthood of all believers."

MAKING CONNECTIONS

What happens to a congregation if a pastor turns out to be a nonbelieving imposter? Were they really forgiven during that time he was with them? Were the Sacraments they received during that time valid? Yes, absolutely! Praise God that the validity and efficacy of Word and Sacrament have nothing to do with the person delivering them to the congregation. God works in and through His Means of Grace despite those who are evil.

FROM THE BIBLE

But you are a chosen race, a royal priesthood, a holy nation, a people for His own possession, that you may proclaim the excellencies of Him who called you out of darkness into His marvelous light. (1 Peter 2:9)

Pastors serve as God's representatives in their congregations, but all believers have a role in serving God. Those who have received the gifts of God cannot help but thank and praise the Lord who gives them. As Christians live their daily lives fulfilling their vocations, they also have opportunities to tell those around them about the gifts they have received from Jesus.

All Christians have the responsibility to grow in their faith and understanding of God's love for them in Jesus Christ. All Christians have the privilege of serving as members of the "royal priesthood" by telling others about Jesus and pointing them to His gifts given in the Word and Sacraments in the Church.

There is no ranking of service among Lutherans. Lutherans do not view the service of pastors as more important or holy than that of laypeople. Pastors are given certain things to do, and laypeople are given certain things to do. Together as the Church, they work to the glory of God.

Authority Given to the Government

The Scriptures tell us that God has also given authority to the civil government. Instead of forgiving sin as the Church does, the government rules for the sake of order, safety, and peace in the world. God tells us to obey those who are in authority over us unless they command us to sin.

Civil power and authority to rule and govern originates with God. The apostle Paul writes: "Let every person be subject to the governing authorities. For there is no authority except from God, and those that exist have been instituted by God" (Romans 13:1). It is the will of God that there should be government, because anarchy is contrary to His will. This power of government is not invested in any particular person, family, or class but in God's Word. With this knowledge, you can understand that the vocation of governing is divinely instituted, and that through it, God works in the world.

Purpose of Government

Since the fall of Adam and Eve into sin, humanity's relationship with God has been disrupted. By means of civil government, God works to provide for security and peace. Governments, therefore, are to protect the lives, property, honor, and reputation of the people. Those in civil authority are to preserve order and discipline and are to safeguard the people as they pursue their occupations and enjoy their liberties. Government wields the sword of God's justice as "God's servant for your good" (Romans 13:4).

The government may also engage in other activities that promote and secure the general welfare of the people. This includes the education of its citizens, conservation and promotion of natural resources, the improvement of adverse conditions and suffering, combating those who threaten the peace from within and from without, and improving living conditions in general.

Rights of Government

To fulfill its purpose, the government has the right to enact suitable laws (1 Peter 2:13), to enforce these laws, to judge people in accordance with these laws (John 18:31), and to impose penalties on those who break these laws. To support these activities and other purposes, the government has the right to levy taxes (Matthew 22:17–21; Romans 13:7). The government has the right to wage war for the protection of its citizens.

Some churches teach that Christians should not be involved in politics or government. But not Lutherans! Our Confessions encourage us to be as involved as possible so that our Christian lives can witness to and shape society. The Lutheran Confessions hold that Christians who serve as government authorities may "impose just punishments . . . engage in just wars, [and] serve as soldiers" (AC XVI 2). Also, it is not sinful for Christians to take an oath when required to do so by the magistrates.

> **BELIEVE, TEACH, CONFESS**
>
> *Our churches teach that lawful civil regulations are good works of God. They teach that it is right for Christians to hold political office, to serve as judges, to judge matters by imperial laws and other existing laws, to impose just punishments, to engage in just wars, to serve as soldiers, to make legal contracts, to hold property, to take oaths when required by the magistrates, for a man to marry a wife, or a woman to be given in marriage.* (AC XVI 1–2)

The Basic Principle of Government

God appoints the governing authority, but this does not mean that the authority must govern according to the Scriptures or make the Bible the fundamental law book of the land. The Roman emperor Nero certainly did not rule according to the precepts of the Bible. However, the authority he represented was appointed by God. The Bible is the sole authority in the Church or the kingdom of grace. It is not the sole authority in those institutions that, like civil government, belong to the kingdom of power.

The basic principle in civil government is human reason, which turns natural knowledge of God into the organization and laws that promise and promote the achievement of the purpose of government. It is by the structures and laws that government rules, and government enforces these laws by the power of the sword.

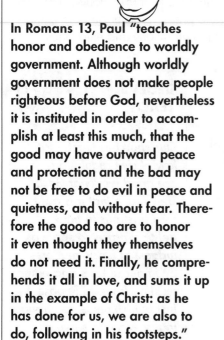

WHAT DOES THIS MEAN?

In Romans 13, Paul "teaches honor and obedience to worldly government. Although worldly government does not make people righteous before God, nevertheless it is instituted in order to accomplish at least this much, that the good may have outward peace and protection and the bad may not be free to do evil in peace and quietness, and without fear. Therefore the good too are to honor it even thought they themselves do not need it. Finally, he comprehends it all in love, and sums it up in the example of Christ: as he has done for us, we are also to do, following in his footsteps." (AE 35:379)

FROM THE BIBLE

Let every person be subject to the governing authorities. For there is no authority except from God, and those that exist have been instituted by God. Therefore whoever resists the authorities resists what God has appointed, and those who resist will incur judgment. (Romans 13:1–2)

CHAPTER 12

God's Deliverymen

In This Chapter
- Pastors are given the task of delivering God's gifts to His people.
- The Lord has established certain requirements for those who are pastors.
- Pastors are given the responsibility for the spiritual welfare of their congregations.

Many pizza restaurants offer home delivery. The restaurant manager hires people whose job it is to take the pizza to the customers' homes. The deliverymen don't make the pizza—that was made by others in the kitchen—but they deliver it. Without the deliverymen, you would not get your pizza. The essence of the Office of the Ministry is just that: the delivery of God's gifts to His people. You could say that pastors are God's deliverymen.

> **NEED TO KNOW**
>
> **Pastor:** Latin for "shepherd"; the title for the congregation's public minister who is ordained and called to be the spiritual supervisor of the "flock" that gathers around Word and Sacrament to receive God's good gifts.

Delivering the Gifts of God

Rather than pizza, pastors are given the task of delivering God's gifts to His people. God has "wrapped" these gifts in unique ways. He wrapped them in the Word and the Sacraments. It is through these Means of Grace that Christians receive the gifts of God. Through the waters of Holy Baptism, through the body and blood of Jesus given in Holy Communion, and through God's word of forgiveness in Holy Absolution, God is giving His gifts to His people.

Pastors are given the task to deliver God's gifts to His people.

What are the gifts given through the Means of Grace? For the sake of Jesus, Christians receive the gifts of the forgiveness of sins and eternal life. The forgiveness that Jesus earned for the world two thousand years ago is delivered today through the Means of Grace. It is through regularly receiving these gifts of God through the Means of Grace that the Lord keeps a Christian in

NEED TO KNOW ⚠️

You have likely heard the phrase "a means to an end." A means is how a result is achieved. Someone may ask you, "By what means did you travel here?" The means by which you travelled might be public transit, for example. When Lutherans talk about the Means of Grace, they are talking about the ways God gives us the grace that Jesus has earned by His life, death, and resurrection. Lutherans usually talk about the Word and the Sacraments. When Lutherans talk about the Sacraments, they are talking about at least two: Holy Baptism and Holy Communion. Holy Absolution is also often considered a Sacrament and thus a Means of Grace by Lutherans.

the faith. In the same way that our bodies need to be fed and nourished to remain strong, so we need to be fed and nourished to remain strong in the faith. The Lord feeds and nourishes Christians in the faith through the Means of Grace delivered in the Church by pastors. (See Part 3 for a full discussion on the Means of Grace.)

Who Are These Deliverymen?

To deliver a pizza, an applicant needs to meet certain requirements. For example, a valid driver's license, a reliable car, and the ability to follow directions could all be required for the position. In a similar way, the Lord of the Church has established certain requirements for those who are pastors.

This is quite a list! It is only by the grace of God that any man can fill this office. No man is sufficient to measure up to the requirements given.

FROM THE BIBLE

Therefore an overseer must be above reproach, the husband of one wife, sober-minded, self-controlled, respectable, hospitable, able to teach, not a drunkard, not violent but gentle, not quarrelsome, not a lover of money. He must manage his own household well. (1 Timothy 3:2–4)

He must not be arrogant or quick-tempered or a drunkard or violent or greedy for gain, but hospitable, a lover of good, self-controlled, upright, holy, and disciplined. (Titus 1:7–8)

TECHNICAL STUFF

What is an "office?" Not everyone can pull you over for speeding in your car and write you a ticket—only someone who has been given that office, such as a police officer. A police officer is one who has been given the office, which comes with the responsibility and authority to do certain things an officer of the law must do. If you have not been given this office, you will get into trouble if you try to do things that police officers are supposed to do. Impersonating a police officer is a serious offense! The Church has her own office—the Office of the Holy Ministry.

In the same way that a city gives the office of the law responsibilities and authority to act within the city, so God has given the Office of the Holy Ministry responsibilities and authority within the Church. Pastors have been called by God into the Office of the Holy Ministry. The Lord of the Church has given the Office of the Holy Ministry the responsibility and authority to preach, teach, and distribute His gifts through the Means of Grace. A pastor carries out his duties because he has been given the office to do so by God through his call and ordination.

The Lutheran Church recognizes that God calls men to serve as pastors. In God's Word we see that it is not given to women to serve as pastors. Only men have been called to fill the Office of the Holy Ministry. While it may seem very strange in our day and age to maintain a distinction between men and women, Lutherans base their beliefs solely upon the Word of God in the Bible. The Bible teaches that there are different roles and responsibilities given to men and women. Lutherans do not change their teaching because of changes in the culture. We will talk more about the different roles of men and women later in this chapter when we discuss the priesthood of all believers.

NEED TO KNOW

Ordination: The rite through which a man's call into the Office of the Holy Ministry is formally and publicly acknowledged. According to biblical custom, the "laying on of hands" is associated with this rite where pastors place their hands upon the head of the one to be ordained.

The Location of God's Gifts

Lutherans teach that only those who are called and ordained into the ministry are to publicly preach and teach in the Church. This is because only those who have been given the Office of the Holy Ministry have been authorized by God to carry out the responsibilities of the office. This preserves order in the Church and assures that God's people know where God's gifts are to be found: in the Word and Sacraments in the Church delivered by God's appointed deliverymen—pastors. This leaves no uncertainty and provides the Christian peace and comfort in the knowledge that where God has promised to be with His gifts He will certainly be! When Christians follow God's Word and command and seek His gifts in His Word and Sacraments in the Church delivered by pastors, they can be certain of what they are receiving: forgiveness, life, and salvation for the sake of Jesus.

Pastors Are Normal People, Really!

Are pastors more holy than everyone else? Are they closer to God? Are they removed from everyday life? Certainly not! Pastors are no more holy than anyone else and are no closer to God than anyone else. Pastors are sinners like everyone else and are forgiven for Jesus' sake like all Christians. In fact, many people are rather surprised to find that pastors are normal people with normal lives like everyone else! Lutheran pastors often are married and have children. They have many of the same joys and face many of the same challenges that everyone does. They cheer for their favorite sports teams, take out the garbage, and mow the lawn like everyone else.

What Does a Pastor Do?

Does a pastor work only on Sundays? What does a pastor do the rest of the week? There is a lot that a pastor does between Sundays. Much time is set aside to prepare the sermon for the coming Sunday. The pastor teaches Bible studies throughout the week. The pastor visits the homebound members of the parish to bring them the Word of God and Holy Communion. The pastor visits those who are sick, injured, or hospitalized. Pastors meet with engaged couples to discuss marriage and plan for the service. When a member of the church dies, a pastor is called to bring God's Word to comfort the family and prepare and officiate at the funeral.

In many circumstances throughout the week, pastors are called upon to bring the Word of God to people. This can take place in a formal setting or just as often in informal conversations. A pastor has been given the responsibility for the spiritual welfare of the people in his congregation. He cares for them and seeks to give them spiritual guidance and comfort whenever called upon and needed. In all that a pastor does, his focus is on delivering the gifts of God to people.

MAKING CONNECTIONS

The Making of a Pastor: Pastors are trained at a seminary, which is a school for theological education. While studying at the seminary, the future pastor studies many subjects, such as how to interpret the Bible, preaching, teaching, how to lead a service, and how to give biblical counsel. The program is usually a four-year period of study.

The Pastor's Uniform

Lutheran pastors often wear a clerical collar. This is usually a black shirt with some sort of white collar or tab in the front. This could be considered the pastor's uniform. Just as a police officer wears a uniform to identify him or her as an officer of the law, so a pastor wears a clerical collar to identify him as one who holds the Office of the Holy Ministry.

When a pastor is leading the Divine Service, he will often wear some garments called "vestments." Vestments look like robes or gowns. They are worn while conducting the Divine Service to identify the pastor as one called by God to the ministry. However, vestments also serve another very important purpose: they "hide" the man. The man behind the vestments is not important—the Word of God that is proclaimed is! Whether the pastor has a sparkling personality or lacks fashion sense (as seen by his choice of suit) is irrelevant during the service. The focus during the Divine Service is not to be on the pastor but upon the Word of the Lord and His gifts.

So, what is the ministry about? It is about the gifts of God. It is about distributing that which Jesus earned by His life, death, and resurrection to the world. Those in the Office of the Public Ministry have the privilege of serving God's people with His gifts. God's people, fed and nourished through Word and Sacraments delivered by pastors in the Church, serve God by serving others.

On Justification

When you have the certainty of faith that God loves you and forgives your sins because of Christ's death on the cross, that is what we call justification. It's as if you had an enormous debt to God that you could never hope to pay. But Jesus made an infinite payment to God by His death, and He defeated your enemies (death and the devil) by His resurrection. By faith, God counts that payment as being made by you. You are free. Because this depends on God's works, it is totally certain.

CHAPTER 13

Can't We All Get Along?

In This Chapter

- Early on, the concern for Church unity went hand in hand with the need for discerning between true and false teaching.
- What unites Christians to one another is faith in Christ.
- What divides Christians is lack of agreement on what God's Word teaches.

Christian Unity

Why are so many Christians divided today? After all, Jesus prayed to His Father in heaven, asking that all generations of believers would have spiritual unity (John 17:20–21). So why can't we just get along? Is there any way Christians can have unity and fellowship in Christ?

Division in the Church is nothing new. When Jesus sent His apostles into the world to proclaim His Gospel, they dealt with divisive issues between Jewish Christians and new Gentile converts to the Christian faith—in particular, whether it was necessary to be circumcised to be a Christian. Christian leaders even had a council in the city of Jerusalem to settle the matter. The answer: no way! Christians are accepted by a gracious God because they trust in Christ as their Savior, not because they follow certain laws. The Gospel of God's forgiving grace in Christ won the day.

As the mission of the Church expanded from Jerusalem, the message of the apostles (based on Jesus' own words) was the unifying norm for Christian faith everywhere the Gospel of God's grace in Christ reached hearts and minds. Teachings or writings that did not jive with the apostolic message set boundaries between faithful Christians and those

> **NEED TO KNOW**
>
> **Unity:** The spiritual bond all Christians share with one another as a gift from God because of their faith in Christ.
>
> **Ecumenics:** The field of Christian theology that deals with the study and objectives of unity and fellowship between Christian churches.
>
> **Council:** A solemn meeting of bishops often called to settle doctrinal matters that threaten the unity of the Church.

NEED TO KNOW

Concord: The public manifestation of agreement in doctrine among Christian churches. Concord can be seen as the taskto promote external unity through dialogue leading to altar and pulpit fellowship.

who did not hold the same beliefs. The concern for Church unity went hand in hand with the need for discerning between true and false teaching.

In the sixteenth century, Martin Luther claimed that the Roman Catholic Church, under the leadership of the pope, was moving away from the Gospel by teaching that people must cooperate with God's grace by performing good works in order to be a Christian. This sounds similar to the problem Jewish and Gentile Christians went through back in apostolic times. Luther sought to have the Roman Church reform their teaching to proclaim the apostolic message, God's Word, for the sake of comforting consciences with the Gospel. Sadly, the powerful Roman Catholic Church did not heed the call to reform and insisted that those who did not submit to the authority of the pope were no longer members of the Church. Ouch!

Both the apostles and Luther had to deal with the challenges of church fellowship among Christians. Despite their distinct historical circumstances, we can still gather two lessons from their dealings with Christians who did not see eye to eye.

LESSON 1

What unites Christians to one another is faith in Christ. This means that even when sincere Christians of different churches disagree with one another on the teachings of God's Word, they are still united because of their faith in Christ, who is the Head of the Church. This unity in Christ is a gift from God, and it is present even when we do not see such unity in the form of a visible Church on earth.

LESSON 2

What divides Christians is lack of agreement on what God's Word teaches. This means that we must admit the reality of division in the Church but not admit defeat. We must work toward achieving fellowship between all Christian churches.

HOW THEN DO WE PROMOTE PUBLIC HARMONY, CONCORD, OR FELLOWSHIP IN THE CHURCH?

1. By drawing the line between true and false teaching any time we see serious errors creeping into the Church. Practically speaking, this means not giving the impression that you agree with a particular teaching when you really do not. For example, an orthodox Lutheran pastor would not preach in a Baptist church because doing so would indicate that he agreed with their teachings. Similarly, an orthodox Lutheran would not take Holy Communion in a Catholic church because doing so would indicate that person agreed with their teachings.

2. By dialoguing on divisive issues. With God's help, these dialogues could lead to a common public confession of such agreement. This confession would also lead to pastors sharing pulpits (that is, preaching in one another's churches) and Christians having Holy Communion at the same altar. This is the unity that all Christians should pray for.

Admittedly, the task of promoting unity and fellowship among the many different Christian denominations is easier said than done. Yet it is still God's will. Jesus' prayer to His Father that His disciples be one is also our prayer and task today.

FROM THE BIBLE

Let love be genuine. Abhor what is evil; hold fast to what is good. Love one another with brotherly affection. Outdo one another in showing honor. Do not be slothful in zeal, be fervent in spirit, serve the Lord. Rejoice in hope, be patient in tribulation, be constant in prayer. Contribute to the needs of the saints and seek to show hospitality.

Bless those who persecute you; bless and do not curse them. Rejoice with those who rejoice, weep with those who weep. Live in harmony with one another. Do not be haughty, but associate with the lowly. Never be wise in your own sight. Repay no one evil for evil, but give thought to do what is honorable in the sight of all. If possible, so far as it depends on you, live peaceably with all. Beloved, never avenge yourselves, but leave it to the wrath of God, for it is written, "Vengeance is mine, I will repay, says the Lord." To the contrary, "if your enemy is hungry, feed him; if he is thirsty, give him something to drink; for by so doing you will heap burning coals on his head." Do not be overcome by evil, but overcome evil with good. (Romans 12:9–21)

Christian Denominations

Christian denominations can be divided into three main categories based on their beliefs about the Sacraments. There can be a lot of variation within a specific denomination.

1. Denominations that have seven sacraments, baptize babies, and believe that the bread and wine of Holy Communion *become* Jesus' body and blood

   Orthodox (Eastern, Greek, etc.)**:** They treat some traditions as being just as valid as Scripture.

   Roman Catholic: The pope and certain traditions shape their beliefs with as much authority as the Bible.

   Church of England (Anglican & Episcopal)**:** While largely a Reformed Church, there are factions among the Anglicans and Episcopalians who lean in sacraments and tradition decidedly toward Roman Catholic beliefs.

2. **Lutherans** have two sacraments, baptize babies, and believes that Jesus' body and blood are "in, with, and under" the bread and wine of Holy Communion.

   Presbyterian: have two sacraments. Baptism seals the believers in covenant grace and marks them for service; the Lord's Supper remembers the covenant promises of God and they pledge their obedience anew.

3. Denominations that have no sacraments baptize only at an "age of reason" when a person chooses Jesus, and celebrate the Lord's Supper as a memorial meal.

   Baptist: They deny that any human can have spiritual authority over another and avoid creeds or other human statements of faith.

   Anabaptist: (Mennonite, Hutterite, Amish) Many people in these denominations strive for a simple life.

   Charismatic/Wesleyan: (Four Square, Holiness, Pentecostal, Church of the Nazarene, Assemblies of God) They often emphasize the importance of spiritual gifts and good works to prove a person is saved. They believe that we need to be baptized by the Holy Spirit in addition to water baptism.

There are also various independent congregations whose beliefs are not consistent with the categories above; for example, there is a denomination of Baptists that believe that the Lord's Supper is a sacrament for the forgiveness of sins and that Christ's body and blood are present in the bread and the wine of the Supper.

CHRISTIAN OR CULT?

All Christian denominations believe that every part of the Apostles' Creed is true. If a group claims that Jesus was just a good man or an angel or a prophet, it is not a Christian church body. Some groups who sound Christian but are not:
-Christadelphian
-Christian Science
-Church of Jesus Christ of Latter-day Saints (Mormons)
-Jehovah's Witnesses

CHAPTER 14

What about Women?

In This Chapter

- The highest honor ever given to any human being was given to a woman.
- The influence that Christian mothers and teachers have upon the spiritual development of children and youth is enormous.
- Submitting does not indicate inferiority.

The relationship between men and women is the subject of countless jokes and endless debate. Women have been the brunt of many of the jokes and badly discriminated against in workforce. So what about in the Church? How are women treated in the Church? Because the Bible is God's inspired Word, the real question is "What does the Bible say about women in the Church?"

What God Has to Say—No Joke

While there is some disagreement in practice among Lutherans, Paul gives us God's intended relationship. In the New Testament, women are in every way granted equal status with men. God says through the apostle Paul, "For as many of you as were baptized into Christ have put on Christ. There is neither Jew nor Greek, there is neither slave nor free, there is no male and female, for you are all one in Christ Jesus" (Galatians 3:27–28).

The highest honor ever given to any human being was given to a woman. The Virgin Mary gave birth to Jesus. Jesus was and is God's only-begotten Son. He was born into this world to be the Savior of all people. During Jesus' ministry, women were among His closest followers. After Jesus was crucified and buried, it was the women disciples who went to the tomb to prepare His body for a proper burial. The first person to see and speak with Jesus after He rose from the dead was Mary Magdalene. Jesus gave her the assignment of informing the men, who were hiding behind locked doors for fear of their lives, that He had risen from the dead!

The New Testament Book of Acts notes the charity work of a woman named Dorcas. A woman by the name of Priscilla and her husband Aquila were active members of the Church in Ephesus. The two of them instructed a Jew named Apollos in the Christian faith. And of course, just like men, women could cause trouble in the Church! In the congregation at Philippi, two ladies named Euodia and Syntyche were fussing with each other. The apostle Paul wrote: "I entreat Euodia and I entreat Syntyche to agree in the Lord. Yes, I ask you also, true companion, help these women, who have labored side by side with me in the gospel together with Clement and the rest of my fellow workers, whose names are in the book of life" (Philippians 4:2–3).

Women Are Really Pretty Important

Throughout the history of the New Testament Church, women have served side by side with the men. It is impossible to calculate the contributions made by women. How many famous pastors and theologians were brought to Christ through the tireless, patient efforts of a Christian mother or grandmother? Monica (AD 333–387), a native of North Africa, is one example that we know of. She was the mother of St. Augustine. Augustine was a wayward son. "Throughout her life, she sought the spiritual welfare of her children, especially that of her brilliant son Augustine." She finally "had the joy of witnessing her son's conversion to the Christian faith" (*TDP*, p. 663). Augustine extols his mother's Christian love and witness.

The importance of the traditional role of women in the family life of God's people cannot be over emphasized. In the Book of Proverbs, King Solomon wrote, "Train up a child in the way he should go; even when he is old he will not depart from it" (Proverbs 22:6). Women have been and continue to be the primary educators and caregivers of children.

Women are the authors of some of the best-loved hymns. Anna Laetitia Barbauld wrote "Praise to God, Immortal Praise," among many others. Charlotte Elliot wrote about 150 hymns, including "Just as I Am." Sarah Adams wrote "Nearer, My God to Thee." Cecil Frances Alexander wrote some 400 hymns, among them "There Is a Green Hill Far Away," and "Once in Royal David's City." Frances R. Havergal composed over 50 hymns, including "Take My Life and Let It Be" and "I Am Trusting You, Lord Jesus."

MAKING CONNECTIONS

He came down to earth from heaven,
Who is God and Lord of all,
And His shelter was a stable,
And His cradle was a stall;
With the poor and mean and lowly
Lived on earth our Savior holy.

And our eyes at last shall see Him,
Through His own redeeming love;
For that child so dear and gentle
Is our Lord in heav'n above;
And He leads His children on
To the place where He is gone.

—"Once in Royal David's City"
(*LSB* 376:2, 4)

In many Lutheran congregations, the majority of Sunday School teachers, Christian Day School teachers, and directors of Christian education are women. Deaconesses assist pastors in carrying out their ministry to the sick, the suffering, and the women in the congregation. The influence that Christian mothers and teachers have upon the spiritual development of children and youth is enormous.

Equal Status but Different Roles

In the apostle Paul's Letter to the Christians in Ephesus, God had him write: "Wives, submit to your own husbands, as to the Lord. . . . Husbands, love your wives, as Christ loved the church and gave Himself up for her" (Ephesians 5:22, 25). In our modern society, this passage from God's Word raises some eyebrows! At first glance it seems to put women down. However, note that God does not tell the husband to "rule" his wife. The husband is to love his wife "as Christ loved the church and gave Himself up for her." Christ died for His Bride, the Church, in order to save her. Submitting to someone who shows that kind of love is not a burden. All relationships among Christians are to be governed by love—Christ's love for us and His love flowing through us to all those around us.

It should also be noted that submitting does not indicate inferiority. If you are driving down the road and a female police officer turns on the siren and red lights, it is a good idea to submit! Doing so does not mean you are inferior.

The only restriction God places on women serving in the Church is that the Office of the Ministry is not given to them. Paul wrote, "I desire then that in every place the men should pray, lifting holy hands without anger or quarreling. . . . I do not permit a woman to teach or to exercise authority over a man; rather, she is to remain quiet" (1 Timothy 2:8, 12). Paul is talking here about the role of pastor. God calls qualified men to teach and preach the Scriptures and to administer the Sacraments in the Church's public services. Women may actively teach the Scriptures to other women, to children, and in private conversations with other believers and unbelievers.

PART THREE

What you'll learn about:

- The Scriptures are God's holy, inspired Word by which He creates and sustains faith.

- God's Word is divided into two great doctrines: Law and Gospel.

- The distinction between Law and Gospel is vital for correctly understanding Scripture.

- God gives the Sacraments to His people for their forgiveness, life, and salvation.

- When one is baptized, he or she is joined to the death and resurrection of Jesus Christ.

- Repentance defines the Christian life and occurs in the very concrete practice of Confession and Absolution.

- Jesus is really present in His body and blood in the bread and wine of the Lord's Supper.

The Means of Grace

God offers, bestows, and seals to people forgiveness of sins, life, and salvation through the Means of Grace. Lutherans recognize the Means of Grace as God's Word and the Sacraments, namely, Holy Baptism and the Lord's Supper.

CHAPTER 15

A Word about God's Word

In This Chapter

- The Scriptures are the words of eternal life, the living, inspired Word of God.
- The Holy Spirit uses the Word of God in the Bible to create, feed, and sustain faith.
- It is the revelation of God's will and His plan of salvation.

The Word of God

Have you heard the story about how Jesus miraculously fed a crowd of five thousand? A boy had a few loaves of bread and a couple fish, and Jesus multiplied that small offering to feed the whole crowd. The next day the crowd came looking for Him again because they needed more food. Jesus explained, "I am the bread of life; whoever comes to Me shall not hunger, and whoever believes in Me shall never thirst" (John 6:35). This was a confusing statement for the people and the disciples to hear. Some of the disciples actually turned away and stopped following Him. He asked the remaining disciples, " 'Do you want to go away as well?' Simon Peter answered Him, 'Lord, to whom shall we go? You have the words of eternal life' " (John 6:67–68).

That is how Lutherans look at the Scriptures—the words of eternal life, the living, inspired Word of God. When everything else in life fails, the Word of the Lord endures forever and provides the bedrock for our religious life. So let us take a look at what the Bible is, where it came from, what it does, and how to use it.

Bible Basics

"Introducing . . . the Bible!"

The Bible may be the best-selling book of all time, but it is far more than a popular manuscript. It is the Word of God. It provides the basis for all of our teaching and living, so the Bible is very important and highly relevant.

When everything else in life fails, the Word of the Lord endures forever.

We know many people who believe that everything in life is relative, that it is all just a matter of opinion. For Lutherans, however, the most important "opinion" is

God's—He is the only absolute, and everything is relative to Him. In order to have more than just subjective opinions, we look to the Bible to give us something solid that we can point to as a standard outside our own sinful thinking.

Of course, there are those who will not understand this. There are those who think that the Bible is just a book of stories. So let's look at what the Bible is, how it was created, how it is organized, and how it is used.

What Is the Bible?

The Bible is a collection of sixty-six books written by many different people over thousands of years in Hebrew, Aramaic, and Greek. The type of literature varies: history, prophecy, poetry, speeches, letters, and so forth. Even from a human standpoint, the Bible has been hailed as a masterpiece of literature.

The Holy Ghost Writer

The remarkable thing about the Bible is that it was written not only by humans but also by God! He is the ghostwriter, so to speak, the author behind the authors. For the Bible to be God's Word, then God would have to be the real author, the authority behind it. This is what we mean when we say that the Bible is "inspired by God."

Now THAT'S Inspired!

> **MAKING CONNECTIONS**
>
> *Scripture Alone!*
> The reformers had three main slogans: "Scripture alone," "grace alone," and "faith alone." (See pp. 21–22.) Scripture alone reflected the reformers' belief that only the Bible could be the final determining factor in what we believe and teach in the Church. Scripture could not be joined with Church tradition, human reason or experience, or anything else. Scripture alone!
>
> More recently, some have said that Scripture is only a "conversation partner" and that the Church must decide matters based on its own judgments as well, taking into account the concerns of our modern context. However, we do not adjust God's Holy Word to fit our unholy culture.

Have you ever heard someone exclaim, "Now that was inspired"? Sometimes artists produce remarkable works that appear to be more than just the result of ordinary human effort. In fact, artists themselves sometimes feel that they could never reproduce those works because something beyond themselves had taken place. This gives us a glimpse at what inspiration is like. The writers of the Bible books had inspiration beyond themselves. The Holy Spirit of God inspired, "breathed-in," or carried along these various writers as they wrote so that they produced more than just human writings but in fact conveyed the very Word of God in the words of men.

"Now Revealing . . . "

Because the Bible is the inspired Word of God, it is also the revelation of God. It is the revelation of God's will and His plan of salvation.

It is the revelation of God's will because the Bible teaches us which actions are pleasing to God. We are given some rather clear revelation on precisely what God approves. The bigger question usually isn't whether God has spoken on a topic but whether we will listen!

Besides revealing God's will, the Bible also reveals His plan of salvation. As the story unfolds throughout the books of the Bible, we can see how God's plan takes shape. Not only do we hear the recorded history of how God created and cared for His people, but we also hear of His plan of saving us through a "chosen one," the Messiah or "Anointed One," the Christ. (More on this later.)

The Bible as Tradition—a Hand-Me-Down

The Bible as we have it now is the result of much careful work and preservation, both by God and humans. It has been handed down to us from generations of divinely inspired human writers before us. The original writings are called "autographs," and we do not have any of these originals today. Instead, what we have are copies of copies of copies.

Fortunately, our copies are quite good. Experts on such matters tell us that by comparing all the various copies, which are called the "received texts," we can see that they largely agree on the big stuff and only vary in some details here and there. That means that we can be sure that no teaching has been changed over time, which is very important.

Nothing Lost in Translation

The Bible was originally written in Hebrew, Aramaic, and Greek. Now, since most of us do not read those languages, the Bible must be translated. The Bible has been translated into only about half of all languages for the benefit of the people. While some groups will certainly create a false translation to further their own goals or false teaching, the same God who originally took such care in the writing process and the process of handing His Word down through the centuries, will also see to it that there will always be translations to truthfully convey His Word to His people today.

The Meaning and Use of God's Word

As explained above, we know that the Bible does what it does because it is what it is. Since it is God's Word, inspired by God, and the revelation of God's will and plan of salvation, the Bible is a remarkable and unique book, which means that we should expect some remarkable and unique things from it. Basically, in the Bible God speaks to us. The Bible is God's Word, so when we read the Bible, God speaks to us and works on us, creating and deepening faith through the power of His Holy Spirit.

God's Superpower

God created the entire universe simply by speaking it into being. Genesis 1 repeatedly tells us, "And God said, 'Let there be [whatever],' and it was so." God simply spoke things into being by the power of His Word. Wouldn't that be a wonderful superpower to have! In fact, isn't that everyone's fantasy? Perhaps this is why superheroes are so popular. While this is nothing but fantasy for us, it is reality for God. That is the power of God, and that is the power of His Word. God always comes with His written Word. While the authors of others books cannot travel along with their written works, God can. The Holy Spirit, who inspired the original human writers, comes to us through the words of the text as we read, and He goes to work.

TECHNICAL STUFF

God's Word Creates the Reality!

In a culture that constantly tells us we have the power to make things happen, we need to remember that the real power lies in God's Word. For example, when we partake of the Lord's Supper, what part does our faith play? The answer is this: God's Word determines the reality; our faith determines the benefit. The elements of bread and wine do actually combine with the body and blood of the Lord when the Word of God is spoken over them, regardless of what the recipients think. It is what it is because God's Word determines the reality.

However, as the Lord's Supper is received, the faith of the recipient determines the benefit. If there is proper faith in the Lord's Word, then the benefit is forgiven sins and a strengthened faith. If there isn't proper faith, then the elements are received to the person's harm, as St. Paul points out in 1 Corinthians: "Whoever, therefore, eats the bread or drinks the cup of the Lord in an unworthy manner will be guilty concerning the body and blood of the Lord. Let a person examine himself, then, and so eat of the bread and drink of the cup. For anyone who eats and drinks without discerning the body eats and drinks judgment on himself. That is why many of you are weak and ill, and some have died" (11:27–30).

The Bible—Performing Daily

Because God's Holy Spirit works through the words recorded in the Bible, we say that the Word of God not only informs but it also performs—it does things. Certainly it informs us because it is a record of God's great and merciful acts to His people in the past. However, the Holy Spirit also uses the Word of God to perform certain works and actions. We call this the "performative function" of God's Word. Whenever the Word is spoken, the Spirit is there as well to do the performative functions.

> Whenever the Word is spoken, the Spirit is there as well.

The Word of God at Work

So what performances should we expect? Well, how about this: the Holy Spirit uses the Word of God in the Bible to create, feed, and sustain faith. God created the whole universe by simply speaking it into being, and He also gives us life spiritually by speaking it into being through His Word, and through that same Word He feeds and sustains our faith.

Good Works—Result or Cause of Grace?

The good works we do are a result, not a cause of grace. In other words, good works are excluded from any consideration as the basis for salvation. God's grace alone is the basis for our salvation. Our works have no merit in that regard. However, that does not mean that they are completely excluded from the life of the Christian. To the contrary, the Christian does good works as a result of being saved. To help you remember this, always put these three things in this order:

Grace ➡ Faith ➡ Works

God's grace *results in* our faith; our faith *results in* our works.
Never do the arrows go the other way, and God gets the credit for the whole production line!

How Do We Treat the Bible?

Because the Bible is what it is and does what it does, we must treat it with great care and respect, with reverence. We revere the Bible, that is, we hold it in high esteem and treasure it. And because we know the great things that God does through it, we gladly want to read it, hear it, and learn from it. As Martin Luther says, "We should fear and love God so that we do not despise preaching and His Word, but hold it sacred and gladly hear and learn it" (SC, Third Commandment). To "hold it sacred" means to see the Bible as holy. Because it is associated with God, and God is holy, we therefore call the Bible the "Holy Bible."

How Do We Use the Bible?

With all the above in mind, let's look at how we are going to use the Bible. Because it is what it is and it does what it does, we use the Bible in faith and faithfulness.

NEED TO KNOW

God's Word = Theology

The word *theology* literally means "word of God." The more closely our theology—our teaching and living—is based on the Word of God, the better it is. When our theology differs from the Bible, that's when there are problems!

There are basically two groups of problems on how Scripture is taken: one to the right and one to the left.

1. The Sadducees were a religious group during Jesus' day. Their tendency was to the left, *accommodating* culture and *taking away* from Scripture—that is, minimizing which part of Scripture was applicable. They only held to the Pentateuch, the first five books of the Bible, and yet they did not actually believe even what was contained there; for example, they did not believe in angels, but angels do appear in the Pentateuch.
A similar tendency exists in overly liberal readings of Scripture today. These groups also tend to pick and choose which parts of Scripture are applicable. For example, they may claim: "It doesn't matter if women are pastors; it doesn't matter if people are gay; it doesn't matter if we abort our babies." However, God clearly speaks to those issues in His Word. What matters is what God says matters in Scripture.

2. The Pharisees were another religious group during Jesus' day. Their tendency was to the right, *opposing* culture and *adding* to Scripture (the Ten Commandments became 613 commandments) with the intent to "put up a fence" for extra protection. For example, to protect God's name from being misused, they simply prohibited *any* use of His name. Rather than protecting His name, what happened is that God's name was not used as it should be, in blessing the people and so forth.
A similar tendency exists in overly conservative readings of Scripture today. These groups tend to go overboard in determining what should be done. "It has to be red wine in Communion; it has to be full immersion in Baptism; it has to be organ music (or no organ music) in worship." However, what really has to be is what God says has to be in Scripture.

The Bible Is Personal but Not Private

The Bible is God's Word to all of His people, not our own private possession. Certainly God includes each of us personally, but it is not our own possession to be used as each person sees fit. Instead, we read the Bible as a community, even when we are reading alone, because we are never really alone when reading the Bible. When we read Scripture, the Holy Spirit comes with it, bonding us together with all other Christians of every time and every place. Thus, we read as a community, even if we happen to be reading on our own. We cannot read the Bible in isolation, because we need the help of this community to read it properly, to use it properly, and to live it properly.

God owns the rights, so to speak, to the Bible because it is His Word. I cannot claim to use the Bible for my own purposes, because it is not mine to use as I wish; it is God's.

How God's Word Is Organized

Let's look at two different ways in which the Bible is organized. The first way has to do with the external structure or format of the Bible; the second way has to do with the internal, thematic content of the Bible.

Structural Organization—The Container

When you open up a Bible, you can see there are two great divisions of the Bible: Old Testament and New Testament. Furthermore, each book itself is usually broken down into chapters, and each chapter has verse numbers. We will look at each of these in turn.

CHAPTERS AND VERSES

The Bible is divided up into books; each book is divided up into chapters; each chapter is divided up into verses. Only five Bible books are so short that they do not have chapter divisions: Obadiah, Philemon, 2 John, 3 John, and Jude.

This means that verses in the Bible are referred to in this standard format:

Book Chapter: Verse(s)

1 John 3:2 = 1 John (Book) 3 (Chapter): 2 (Verse)

For the five books without chapters, we simply use Book + Verse. Thus, "Obadiah 2" means the second verse in the Book of Obadiah. This system of "book, chapter, and verse" was developed so we could know which part of the Bible we are talking about at any given time. It assists us in finding sayings in the Bible, like finding a house by the street address.

THE TWO GREAT DIVISIONS—OLD AND NEW TESTAMENTS

Of the sixty-six books in the Christian Bible, thirty-nine are in the Old Testament and twenty-seven are in the New Testament. Since many of the New Testament books are shorter, the Old Testament is about four-fifths of the Bible in length.

Old and New Testaments Together

The Old Testament reveals God's mighty acts of creation, His acts of mercy on His people, and the promise of a coming Messiah (Christ). We as Christians believe and know that Jesus is indeed that Christ. Thus, in order to properly understand the New Testament, one must first understand the Old. Basically, to understand the fulfillment of God's promise of a coming Messiah, one needs to understand the promise. This means that even though Jesus is not mentioned specifically by name in the Old Testament, the basic underlying message points to Jesus and all that He is and does for us as our Messiah (Christ).

The New Testament calls Jesus the "Lamb of God." To understand the importance of this, we need to understand the sacrifices of the Old Testament. Only then can we see how God set up the sacrificial system as a way of showing mercy. God allowed His people to substitute an animal for themselves. Their sin really meant that they deserved to die, but the animal would take their place and die in their stead. Often this animal was a lamb. So in the New Testament, when John the Baptist refers to Jesus as "the Lamb of God, who takes away the sin of the world," this all makes better sense: Jesus will be our substitute. By His death our sins will be forgiven, and God Himself provides Jesus for us. Thus, the Old Testament helps us to understand the New.

NEED TO KNOW

Messiah: A Hebrew word meaning "anointed one"— that is, one chosen by God for a special purpose.

FROM THE BIBLE

"These are written so that you may believe that Jesus is the Christ, the Son of God, and that by believing you may have life in his name" (John 20:31). People commonly and mistakenly think that biblical books were written mainly to provide rules for godly living. Speaking through John, God announces the Good News that Jesus is His Son and that by faith in His name, we have life and salvation—the core message of the entire Scripture. (*TLSB*, p. 1826)

The Bible

The Bible Is Different from Any Other Book

Inspired: While other books are just collections of human thoughts, the Bible is a collection of God's thoughts transmitted to us through human prophets. It is the true and powerful Word of God.

Gospel Focus: The writings of other religions focus on how to be a good person or live a good life. The main message of the Bible is the unfolding of God's plan to save us from our sins through Jesus' death and resurrection.

True History: The stories in the Bible are not ancient myths. They really happened. Archaeologists have found numerous ancient documents and remnants of cities, which prove that the people, events, and places of the Bible all really existed.

> **FROM THE BIBLE**
>
> All Scripture is breathed out by God and profitable for teaching, for reproof, for correction, and for training in righteousness. (2 Timothy 3:16)
>
> For no prophecy was ever produced by the will of man, but men spoke from God as they were carried along by the Holy Spirit. (2 Peter 1:21)

How We Got Our English Translations

The Old Testament was originally written in Hebrew and Aramaic, and the New Testament was written in Greek. Translations are prepared by those who translate directly from the original languages.

How the Bible Is Organized

The Bible is a collection of sixty-six books, divided into two testaments. The books of the Old Testament were all written before Jesus was born. The books of the New Testament were all written after Jesus died and came back to life. Each book of the Bible is divided into chapters, and each chapter is divided into verses, except for Philemon, 2 & 3 John, and Jude, which are so short that they only have verses.

Bible Stories at a Glance

OLD TESTAMENT

Genesis: Creation, Noah's ark, the Tower of Babel, Abraham, Isaac, Jacob, and Joseph (the one with the coat of many colors)

Exodus—Deuteronomy: Exodus from Egypt, wandering in the desert for forty years, the laws God gave the Israelites

Joshua: How the Israelites entered the Promised Land

Judges: Leaders of Israel after they entered the Promised Land and before they had a king

Ruth: A widow who travelled with her Israelite mother-in-law rather than going back to her own family who did not know God

1 Samuel—2 Chronicles: Israel's kings, the fall of Jerusalem, Israelite exile in Babylon

Ezra, Nehemiah: Israelites' return to Jerusalem

Esther: Israelite woman who became queen while in exile and saved her people

Job: A man who went through terrible temptations but did not reject God

Psalms: Poetry about God's relationship with us

Proverbs, Ecclesiastes, Song of Solomon: Wise sayings

Isaiah—Malachi: Prophecies warning about exile, and stories about the Israelites' return to the Holy Land; the fiery furnace, Daniel in the lions' den, Jonah and the big fish; also many prophecies that describe the Messiah (Jesus) who was to come

NEW TESTAMENT

Matthew, Mark, Luke, John: Known as the Gospels, they tell the story of Jesus' life

Acts: Ascension of Jesus, the spread of Christianity, Pentecost, and the conversion of Paul

Romans—Jude: Letters written by Paul and other leaders of the Early Church to Christians in various cities (Rome, Corinth, Galatia, Ephesus, etc.)

Revelation: Visions of the end times and heaven

The Certainty of Faith and the Word of God

If you've lived very long, you know that human beings cannot always be trusted. No one is so perfect that you can have absolute certainty that what he or she says or does is right. Human beings must always be held accountable to a higher standard. But it is different with God. He *is* the highest standard. He is utterly good and truthful. Therefore we can have certainty and trust in Him (see Psalm 146:3). Our faith is certain not when it is based on what humans say, but only when based on what God has said. This is why we Christians think the Bible is so important. We are certain that God spoke through the prophets and apostles, and we are certain that what they wrote (the Bible) is God's Word. If we want to know what God says to us, if we want certainty of what is good and true, we should look to the Bible.

CHAPTER 16

Law and Gospel: The Two Great Doctrines of the Bible

In This Chapter

- God is the ultimate authority.
- The Law tells us that we have sinned and that our sin means a penalty must be paid.
- The Gospel tells us that Jesus paid the penalty for our sin when He died in our place on the cross.

Lutherans teach that the Word of God is divided into two doctrines, or themes, of Law and Gospel. In light of our previous discussion, it would be easy to make a correlation and say that the Old Testament equals the Law and the New Testament equals the Gospel. Unfortunately, that would be an oversimplification, because the Old Testament contains Gospel promises and the New Testament contains Law.

Defining Law and Gospel

Broadly speaking, we all know what a law is. A law sets the standard for what is expected. If the posted speed limit is 65 mph, then the legal expectation is that you will not drive faster than 65 miles per hour. If you do go faster, then you will be breaking the law and could get a ticket and face a penalty. That is how the law works.

Well, with God it is similar. God is the ultimate authority; He is the ultimate Lawgiver. He created the whole universe and us, and therefore He has the authority to set laws for our behavior. If we do not follow those laws, then we are breaking the Law and could face a penalty. God's laws tell what He expects of us, what He expects us to do.

Gospel means Good News. The Good News that Christians speak of is always centered around the message of salvation through the forgiveness of sins that comes to us because of Jesus' death on the cross in our stead. In this context of Law and Gospel, *Gospel* refers to the actions of God that are closely related to His saving plan for us in Jesus Christ.

Distinguishing Law and Gospel

As Lutherans, we believe that properly distinguishing between Law and Gospel is vitally important for properly understanding Scripture. It expresses our worldview, gives us the means to study and interpret Scripture, and protects the use, study, and application of God's Word from being hijacked by our own interests and demands.

What Is God's Purpose for the Law?

God is holy, and as such He intends to declare His holy will. This He expresses in His words of Law, with various purposes or uses. There are two uses listed below, and we will talk about a third use of the Law later.

The *first* use of the Law is that God seeks to restrain wrongdoing. The Law, with its threat of punishment, is said to have a "curbing" effect on sin. This is the basic effect of natural law on all people.

The *second* use of the Law is that it acts like a "mirror" to show us that we have sinned. Thus, through the Law, God shows us our sinfulness, and therefore we see our need for a Savior. The Holy Spirit works through this word of Law to convict us in our consciences that we have indeed transgressed or broken God's Holy Law. Then we are ready to hear the Gospel.

What Is God's Purpose for the Gospel?

Not only is God holy, but He is also love. In His love, God's purpose for the Gospel is simply that we might be saved and live as His children here and in eternity. Once we have heard His word of Law, and the Holy Spirit has done His job of convicting us of our sin, then we are ready to hear God's word of the Gospel. Because God is love, He is eager to speak that word of Gospel to us that our sins are forgiven because of our Savior Jesus Christ. More specifically, the Law tells us that we have sinned and that our sin means that a penalty must be paid. The Gospel tells us that Jesus paid the penalty for our sin when He died in our place on the cross.

Law and Gospel Working Together

The word of Law serves the purpose of getting us ready for the word of the Gospel. Without the Law, the Gospel would not make sense—who needs forgiveness if you do not know that you have sinned! And without the Gospel, the Law is mere cruelty, for what good is it to find out that you are a sinner if there is no forgiveness given! And so, throughout Scripture, these two themes run together to make sure that we actually do hear the main message of God's Word: that we are sinners who are saved because of Jesus Christ's death on the cross for us.

Many people outside of Christianity look at it as simply a religion of dos and don'ts because they do not understand the distinction between Law and Gospel.

Unfortunately, there are also many Christians who do not properly understand this, so when they read the Bible, they hear many of the demands that God makes and their consciences remain heavily burdened. However, once Christians properly understand this distinction, they are able to recognize that God is using the Law to strike their consciences and produce deserved guilt. But God does not want to stop there. He also heals their consciences and takes away their sin through the Gospel. Despite how they feel about themselves, God's word of forgiveness in the Gospel overrides any lingering feelings of guilt brought on by the Law.

Are You Smarter than a Sophomore?

In high school, the second year is called the sophomore year. The word *sophomore* means "wise-fool." After completing the first year, the second-year students walk around like they already know everything when they obviously don't. Thus, the term "wise-fool" was applied to this class.

We have a similar problem with Law and Gospel. Although the basic dynamics of grammar are simple enough to explain in a sophomore writing class, there is still a level of maturity required that goes beyond mere fundamental principles. In fact, Luther once said that someone who could properly and consistently distinguish Law and Gospel has been blessed by the Holy Spirit with a gift equal to being a "Doctor of Holy Scripture." A doctorate is considerably higher than a sophomore year in high school!

At the sophomore level, there is a simple rule of thumb for determining what is Law and what is Gospel: look at the subject of the verb. In a sentence, the verb is an action and the subject does the action. So the rule of thumb is this: In Scripture passages that tell us about winning or keeping salvation, if God is the subject of the verb, either stated or implied, then it is probably Gospel; however, if we humans are the subject of the verb, either stated or implied, then it is probably Law. By definition, Law is what God demands or requires of us—something that we are supposed to do or refrain from doing. The Law therefore focuses on *our* doing. The Gospel, on the other hand, is something that only *God* can do. He alone can send Christ to die for us. He alone can forgive us because of Christ. He alone can give us the gifts of salvation through various means of bringing us Christ. Therefore, by definition, the Gospel focuses on the action, doing, and speaking of *God*.

So . . . are you smarter than a sophomore? If the basic rule of thumb were so easy that even a sophomore could use it to distinguish Law and Gospel, then why would Luther suggest that if you do it properly and consistently then you should be considered for a doctorate? That's because what is easy to talk about in theory is more difficult to do in practice. Also, the difference between an amateur and a pro is really a degree of consistency. An amateur tennis player, for instance, will once in awhile hit an excellent shot, whereas a professional tennis player has to make excellent shots all the time. The question is always whether you can make the excellent shot at the precise time that it is needed!

Applying Law and Gospel

Applying Law and Gospel is not a matter of precision of grammar but requires wisdom. Gaining wisdom and being able to understand wise sayings takes time. In fact, some wisdom statements seem downright contradictory at face value. For example, "He who hesitates is lost" and "Only fools rush in." However, when used wisely, the parent knows when to tell a stalling child "He who hesitates is lost" and a reckless child "Only fools rush in." Each child is given the proper word of wisdom at the right time. That is also how Law and Gospel work—it takes wisdom to apply them properly.

MAKING CONNECTIONS

In his lectures on Law and Gospel, C. F. W. Walther spoke of four basic concepts.

1. All Scripture can be divided into the two fundamental yet opposing doctrines of Law and Gospel.

2. Memorizing points of doctrine does you no good unless you are able to understand and apply those statements of faith in light of Law and Gospel.

3. This kind of division and distinction is the most difficult Christian task, and the Holy Spirit is the teacher.

4. If you do not understand this distinction, Scripture will remain a closed and confusing book. If you do distinguish Law and Gospel, Scripture will become clearer to you.

Walther counted twenty-one ways in which people confuse Law and Gospel. They include making Christ into a new Moses; mixing and misapplying Law and Gospel in sermons; encouraging salvation by works; improperly understanding sorrow over sins, faith, repentance, new obedience, the sinful human condition, the Church, the Word of God, the Sacraments, and the human will; and misusing the Law and failing to let the Gospel dominate over the Law.

The distinction of Law and Gospel is a journey filled with mistakes that God will forgive and from which Christians learn by experience. It leads to heaven, where the Law no longer condemns, the Law is as easy as living, and the life-giving Gospel is eternally victorious.

Time to Afflict or Comfort?

A common saying among pastors is "Afflict the comfortable and comfort the afflicted." Now what that means is this:

For people who are *comfortable* with themselves and do not think that they are sinners, *afflict* them with the message of God's Law so that they see their sin, their sinfulness, and their need for forgiveness.

For those who are already *afflicted* (burdened) in their conscience by the weight of their sin, *comfort* them with the message of the Gospel that their sins are forgiven because of Christ.

These words are helpful for everyone, not just pastors, because you might have to use them in helping friends and family members, and you will probably need them for yourself.

For example, you could be reading the Bible and come upon some rather condemning passages. When the word of Law goes to work on your conscience, you start to feel guilty. Good! Now ask God for forgiveness. But what do you do if you still feel guilty? What if there aren't any words of Gospel in that section of Scripture? Simple, go find some. Read John 3:16 or Ephesians 2:8–10. Read some words of Gospel to make sure that you comfort that conscience. Being aware of how these two great themes work *together* helps us to get a better understanding of God's message in Scripture. (More on this later: See "Caution: The Law and Gospel Are Inseparable" on the next page.)

Law, Gospel, and Sanctification

Distinguishing Law and Gospel in the area of sanctification or the Christian life is a little tricky. Prior to conversion, there are only two effects that the Law can have. (See p. 82.) After conversion, a new creation begins. With this new creation, namely a believer, we now have a new option available for the effects and uses of the Law. Now the ***third*** use of the Law comes into play. Not only does the Law point out what actions are right or wrong (first use), or whether a person is guilty of breaking any of those laws (second use), but now the Law also points out how the person is to behave in a God-pleasing manner (third use). This third use only pertains to the believer because it is only available as an option after conversion.

Here's where it gets tricky! Now we have both God and the believer doing things at the same time. What happens to our basic rule of thumb now? Can we simply look at who is performing the action of the verbs? Well, let's not get ahead of ourselves. It is still possible to point out and isolate what is Law and what is Gospel as that which *God* is doing and that which *we* are doing.

NEED TO KNOW

Sanctification: In a wide sense, sanctification includes all effects of God's Word. In a narrow sense, sanctification is the spiritual growth that follows justification. By God's grace, a Christian cooperates in this work. Through the Holy Spirit's work, faith is increased daily, love strengthened, and the image of God renewed but not perfected in this life.

When parents wake up the children on Christmas morning and tell them that it's time to open presents, no child ever says that they are being forced to obey laws from mean and domineering parents. Although the language is in the imperative—a simple command—no one takes it as a burden because the overriding mood is one of joy and celebration. There are gifts to open! Someone went through all the time, effort, and expense to provide gifts, and now we get to open and enjoy them.

In the Christian life, we have many gifts to use and enjoy. Prayer and worship are two of the biggest gifts we have. So why do these things often seem so much like a burden instead of a gift? Why do they seem to smack of the Law's condemnation? It is because our old sinful nature still lives within each of us and still feels guilty by the implied Law that these are things we have to do. Fortunately, the Gospel also has its voice, so the new nature in the believer feels no such condemnation. As Paul says, "There is therefore now no condemnation for those who are in Christ Jesus" (Romans 8:1). This leaves things like prayer and worship as gifts to be enjoyed, and even though they do involve our action, they are taken in the overriding context of Gospel, especially as we focus on God's action for us in Christ. Yes, when we pray, *we* are praying, but the Holy Spirit is also praying, and Christ is interceding for us. And when we worship, yes, *we* are worshiping by singing and so forth, but even more important are God's actions for us in His Word and Sacraments.

Caution: The Law and the Gospel Are Inseparable

Distinguishing Law and Gospel does not mean that we distinguish them so much that they are removed from each other. Instead, we realize that they only work together and in the proper order: the Law first and then the Gospel. Also, they must be repeated throughout the life of the Christian, not as a one-time thing.

Here's where the teaching of Law and Gospel helps to keep us from going astray. There are basically two ways to stray from "the narrow path": either focusing on the Law and excluding the Gospel, or vice versa. We'll look at each in turn.

On the one hand, some people focus on the Gospel, excluding the Law. The temptation here seems to be that they let the Law bring them to the Gospel, but then they figure that they really do not need to hear the Law anymore. This happens whenever the Gospel is so separated from the Law that the Law no longer serves any function at all—everything has been reduced to Gospel only. This is called Gospel reductionism. For example: "God and I have a great relationship—I like to sin, and He likes to forgive." Obviously, the Law needs to work some true repentance here because as Christians we confess sin and flee from it; we do not accept it, like it, or embrace it.

Gospel reductionism can also be seen in how some people read Scripture. There are those, including entire Church bodies, who claim that the Gospel of Jesus Christ overrides all claims of the Law. They say that the legal requirements of God's Holy Law no longer have any bearing on how Christians should live their lives. This reduces all of God's Word down to just the word of the Gospel, and this is not a true reading of Scripture. Thus, what comes as a result is not a true form of Christianity but an aberration of Christianity.

On the other hand, some people focus on the Law, excluding the Gospel. The temptation here seems to be that they let the Law have the upper hand and the Gospel is really only needed occasionally and for extreme cases. Basically, they figure that we all can function on our own, keeping the Law and pleasing God. This is called legalism.

Legalism can be crass, where the believer thinks that his own good works earn him favor with God and thus bring about his own salvation, or legalism can be more subtle, where the believer thinks he is saved by grace but then after that his own good works serve to confirm or sustain his salvation. Here, sin simply is not taken seriously enough, and the Law is not properly understood. The Gospel is therefore eclipsed by the Law because of all the things that the believer is trying to do for himself, ignoring what only God can do for him in Christ through the Spirit and the Word.

Some people and other whole church bodies function in this way. This reduces all of God's Word down to just the word of the Law, and this is not a true reading of Scripture. Thus, what comes as a result is not a true form of Christianity, but an aberration of Christianity.

These false readings highlight the vital importance of properly distinguishing Law and Gospel. Taking the Law and the Gospel together keeps us safe between "a rock and a hard place," as it were. When we stick to God's clear Word and properly distinguish the Law and the Gospel in our teaching and in our lives, then we are certain to get it right. God's Word determines the reality, and faith determines the benefit.

Bible Study Tools

Reading and trying to understand the Bible sometimes feels overwhelming because it was written in a very different time and place than where we live. Some of the things we read about in the Bible are as unfamiliar to our culture as computers and cell phones would be to the people of the Old and New Testaments. Many people find it helpful to have some Bible study tools on hand to better understand what they are reading. There is a wide variety of these study tools on the market, so you'll be able to choose just the amount of detail that will work best for your needs.

When choosing Bible study tools, take some time to research the author and publisher of each resource. If the author or publisher is connected to a denomination or school of thought you don't agree with, you should be extra careful about using that resource. And don't forget that your pastor is a good source of Bible information. If something you read in any of these resources doesn't make sense to you, talk with him about it. As you get used to reading the Bible and using study tools, it will also be useful to see what different resources say about the same thing, but always be sure to check what the Bible says about it.

Bible Atlas: The main feature of most atlases is a selection of maps. Because the stories in the Bible are true pieces of history, seeing how the land was laid out and where each city, body of water, and mountain was located can make the Bible much easier to understand and identify with. Some atlases even include pictures and explanations of the wildlife, plants, buildings, and other features we would have seen if we had lived in Bible times.

Bible Dictionary: Bible dictionaries give detailed definitions of the words and ideas found in the Bible. They sometimes include pictures and information on where some of the words are found in the Bible.

Bible Commentary: In Bible commentaries, the authors explain the background and meaning of a piece of the Bible. Some commentaries can be very detailed, with an in-depth treatment of each verse, while others are more general in their treatment of the biblical texts.

Concordance: Concordances consist of an alphabetical list of the words found in the Bible and cite the book, chapter, and verse where you can find each word. Some concordances only list the most common words and verses that people look for. Exhaustive concordances list every word found in the Bible. Because translators can sometimes pick different English words, it is helpful to get a concordance that uses the same version of the Bible you most often use.

CHAPTER 17

Delivered in Water

In This Chapter

- In Holy Baptism, the Lord promises you the forgiveness of sins and the gift of the Holy Spirit.
- Holy Baptism is for both adults and infants, for the entire household.
- Baptism is not magic. Without faith, Baptism alone has no promise of salvation.
- Christians have the freedom to apply water in Holy Baptism in a variety of ways.

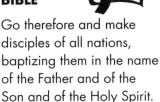

FROM THE BIBLE

Go therefore and make disciples of all nations, baptizing them in the name of the Father and of the Son and of the Holy Spirit. (Matthew 28:19)

What Is Baptism?

Simply put, Baptism is the application of water to a person in the name of the Holy Trinity—the Father and the Son and the Holy Spirit. Plain water is truly used in this Sacrament, but it is not plain water alone.

Our Lord Jesus Christ, following His death and resurrection and just before His ascension, gave the Church the gift of Holy Baptism:

MAKING CONNECTIONS

"Now when all the people were baptized, and when Jesus also had been baptized and was praying, the heavens were opened, and the Holy Spirit descended on Him in bodily form, like a dove; and a voice came from heaven, 'You are My beloved Son; with You I am well pleased.' " (Luke 3:21–22)

At Jesus' Baptism in the Jordan River, God the Holy Spirit descended on Jesus as a dove, and God the Father's voice proclaimed that Jesus is His Son. In the Church, Christians are baptized into the name of the triune God—the Father, Son, and Holy Spirit.

TECHNICAL STUFF

God gives the Sacraments to His people for their forgiveness, life, and salvation, and this happens as they call upon Him in trust and with confidence in Christ, the Savior. By the sixteenth century, the Roman Church had developed a complicated sacramental system that had transformed the Sacraments into meritorious works performed by priests. This was especially evident in the Mass, where priests "sacrificed" Christ again and again on behalf of the living and the dead. The Bible, however, reveals the key to the Sacraments: is the promises of God. God attaches His Word of promise to the element of the Sacrament—water, wine, or bread—and gives and strengthens the faith of those receiving them. (See also Ap XIII.)

So it is that the water of Holy Baptism is used according to Jesus' command and combined with the name of God and all that name stands for. This God-given reality changes everything about this particular application of water.

What Does Baptism Do?

In his Small Catechism, Martin Luther provided a concise explanation for us:

It works forgiveness of sins, rescues from death and the devil, and gives eternal salvation to all who believe this, as the words and promises of God declare. (SC, Baptism, Second Part)

Holy Baptism is a sacrament because Christ established it and invited us to do it and because it delivers the forgiveness of sins He won on the cross. Jesus suffered, died, and rose again in order to save people from the eternal death brought about by sin. Through His saving actions, Christ purchased and won salvation for all. Baptism delivers and bestows the benefits of Jesus' redemption.

How Does Baptism Work?

Again we look to Luther's explanation in the Small Catechism:

How can water do such great things?

Certainly not just water, but the word of God in and with the water does these things, along with the faith which trusts this word of God in the water. (SC, Baptism, Third Part)

How can water do such great things? It is the Word of God combined with water that makes Baptism "quite a different things from all other water . . . because something more noble is added here. God Himself stakes His honor, His power, and His might on it" (LC IV 17).

Now when you look at the Baptism font filled with water, you can replace the question "Is that all there is?" with the certain promise "There is all that!"

Baptism is not magic. Without faith, Baptism alone has no promise of salvation. Jesus said, "Whoever believes and is baptized will be saved, but whoever does not believe will be condemned" (Mark 16:16). Let's get this straight. If someone believes in Christ as Savior and is baptized, what is the promise? They will be saved. What if someone does not believe in Christ, whether they are baptized or not? This time the answer is most unpleasant: they will be condemned to hell.

TECHNICAL STUFF

Water is water . . . is Baptism?

Anabaptist: One who baptizes "again." Anabaptists rejected infant Baptism at the time of the Reformation and were termed radical for this and other views that contradicted traditional Christian and Bible teaching

John the Baptist: Also known as John the Baptizer; prepared the way of the Lord; was one like Elijah of old; baptized Jesus in the Jordan, preaching a Baptism of repentance for the forgiveness of sins. John was a relative of Jesus, son of Zechariah and Elizabeth, beheaded by Herod X at the request of his niece.

Baptist: an individual, congregation, or church body that usually teaches adult immersion Baptism as a mark of one's dedication to Christ and new life of faith. Baptism is usually called an ordinance instead of a sacrament. In addition, Baptism in a Baptist context is usually seen as the work of the Christian rather than God's work. Baptismal regeneration is usually denied.

Baptismal regeneration: In Holy Baptism, the Lord promises you the forgiveness of sins and the gift of the Holy Spirit. In theological language, this is "baptismal regeneration." Although the Bible clearly teaches it, many (Reformed) Christians still deny it. Peter had a perfect opportunity to answer the "What shall we do?" question by inviting everyone forward for an "altar call." Instead, he invited them to Baptism.

Why Be Baptized?

When one is baptized, he or she is joined to the death and resurrection of Jesus Christ. The old Adam is put to death, and a new person, who lives by faith in Christ, is raised up. This death and resurrection sets the pattern and rhythm for the daily life of the baptized, for repentance and faith. Daily, the baptized child of God of every age is to repent, that is, to turn away from sin. Daily, the baptized then turns to Christ and clings to Him in faith for the forgiveness of sins. This is the rhythm of the new life given in Holy Baptism. It is baptismal living. It is the life of the Christian.

How Should We Baptize?

The word *baptism* simply means to apply water. One could pour, sprinkle, or immerse. Some Christian groups insist that a person must be immersed in order to be truly baptized. Does Scripture insist on "dunking"? No. Christians have the freedom to apply water in Holy Baptism in a variety of ways. And as you've read before, we can't add to God's Word by insisting on something that the Lord Himself does not insist upon. That being said, most Lutheran churches will administer Baptism by pouring water over the head of the one being baptized. This became the normal practice among Lutherans during the Reformation when some insisted that Baptism was valid only by full immersion.

CHAPTER 18

Confession Is Good for the Soul

In This Chapter

- Repentance is a two-step process: first, recognizing the reality of our sin; and second, turning to God in faith for His mercy.
- Absolution is God's gift of hearing that our sins are forgiven.
- Confession is not a one-time thing, because sin is not a one-time thing.
- The Office of the Keys is the special authority Christ has given His Church to bestow or withhold the forgiveness of sins.

> **WHAT DOES THIS MEAN?**
>
> Our churches teach that there is forgiveness of sins for those who have fallen after Baptism whenever they are converted. The Church ought to impart Absolution to those who return to repentance. (AC XII 1–2)

TECHNICAL STUFF

The term *confession* is really often shorthand for two things that go together: confession *and* absolution.

- Confession. The act by which one admits or confesses sin(s) and the guilt of sin.
- Absolve. To set free from sin. By virtue of his office, in the name and stead of Christ, a pastor forgives those who repented of their sins, affirmed their faith in Christ, and want to do better (Matthew 16:19; 18:18; John 20:19–23).

Repentance and confession and absolution go hand-in-hand. They are the means by which a believer continually identifies and rejects a rebellious life, and, in faith, longs for and resolves to live in harmony with God's will.

MAKING CONNECTIONS

O almighty God, merciful Father, I, a poor, miserable sinner, confess unto You all my sins and iniquities with which I have ever offended You and justly deserved Your temporal and eternal punishment. But I am heartily sorry for them and sincerely repent of them, and I pray You of Your boundless mercy and for the sake of the holy, innocent, bitter sufferings and death of Your beloved Son, Jesus Christ, to be gracious and merciful to me, a poor, sinful being. Amen. (*LSB*, p. 184)

Lutherans are all about repentance. In fact, when Martin Luther wrote his famous Ninety-five Theses, the first four were all about repentance. This is because repentance defines the Christian life. Repentance is a two-step process: first, recognizing the reality of our sin; and second, turning to God in faith for His mercy.

Repent! No, Really!

Someone who does not believe he is a sinner cannot be repentant—what's to repent of if you are not doing anything wrong? So the first step to repentance can only happen after the Law does its accusing work. People have to hear what God's Word says so that they can recognize themselves as sinners and experience contrition, or remorse, over sin. The flesh, the world, and the devil spend all their time whispering, "What you are doing isn't that bad. In fact, it's not bad at all!" Our consciences are assaulted and dulled every day by our own sinful desires. Only the Law of God can cut us to our hearts, bring us to our knees, and show us where we are wrong (usually, that is almost everywhere). Once that message gets through and we know we are slaves to sin, the first part of repentance is accomplished.

But it is not enough just to know and believe we are sinners. If we stop there, we despair, knowing that our sin separates us from God. And trying to get out of sin by our own power will also lead us to despair, because we cannot stop sinning no matter how much we want to. So the second part of repentance is faith: believing God's promise that in Christ we are forgiven and have new life, namely a life of turning away from sin rather than into it. In particular, it means that we turn with God's help from the specific sins of which the Law convicted us. That turning goes beyond inward resolve and really wanting to do better. Repentance includes mortifying our flesh and physically, mentally, and spiritually laboring to leave the sins that plague us.

"Repent!" sounds like a harsh message, and it is harsh. Hearing what God's Word has to say about our favorite vices makes us angry, ashamed, and afraid. But it also makes us see that there is only one way out: Jesus. That is why the call to repentance is one of love. It is the call God put in the mouths of His prophets and apostles so that His people could be saved. It is the call of Jesus Himself, whose love for us was so great that He took on our flesh and lived among us. He did not come to us to give us the message we wanted to hear (you know, the one about how you are really pretty good, especially compared to that other person). He told us the truth that we needed to hear: we are perverse, we are lost, we are dead, we must be made new, and He is the one who makes all things new.

Repentance is not some theological abstraction. For Lutherans, repentance occurs in the very concrete practice of Confession and Absolution. Our pastors do not leave us hanging. The second part of repentance is also theirs to administer. They show us our sins from the Law, and they show us our Savior in the Gospel.

Our pastors convict us with God's Word and then forgive our sins in Christ's place and by Christ's command. They may do this corporately in the Divine Service, and they especially do it in private Confession and Absolution. There is no real comfort in going home and crying into our pillows about how sorry we are. Our

The call to repentance is one of love.

pastors are there to restart our crushed hearts with Jesus' words of ultimate love: I forgive you all your sins. Phew! Those words do not just comfort us, but they effectively change us, so that even in our daily lives we grow more into the likeness of Jesus.

> **MAKING CONNECTIONS**
>
> *Scripture Alone!*
>
> Hey, isn't "mortifying the flesh" a human work? I thought Lutherans didn't go for that.
>
> True, our works cannot save us. On the other hand, repentance is a lifelong work in progress. The question is, whose work is it and what does it accomplish? Well, would this work be happening if the Holy Spirit had not called you by the Gospel? Would you make changes in your life to conform it to the Word of God if God's Word meant nothing to you? So, yeah, repentance is arduous, transformative work. But it is work that would not and could not happen without the Holy Spirit.

Private Confession and Absolution

The practice of privately confessing your sins to your pastor and receiving individual Absolution is an ancient practice in the Church, but it has become less well-known among Lutherans over the last three hundred years. There are lots of historical reasons why that is so, but theologically, neglecting or rejecting confession is contrary to the intentions of the earliest Lutheran reformers. As private confession disappeared in the Lutheran churches, corporate confession became commonplace. Corporate, in this case, means something done as a group. Today, corporate

WHAT DOES THIS MEAN?

This is what true repentance means. Here a person needs to hear something like this, "You are all of no account, whether you are obvious sinners or saints <in your own opinions>. You have to become different from what you are now. You have to act differently than you are now acting, whether you are as great, wise, powerful, and holy as you can be. Here no one is godly."
But to this office of the Law, the New Testament immediately adds the consoling promise of grace through the Gospel. This must be believed. As Christ declares, "Repent and believe in the gospel" (Mark 1:15). That is, become different, act differently, and believe My promise. (SA III III 3–4)

confession is the portion of the worship service when the congregation speaks together a general confession of sin and is then absolved, or declared forgiven, by the pastor. It is usually at the beginning of a service in which Holy Communion will be given. While corporate confession is a perfectly good practice, private confession also has a strong Lutheran background.

You can fake an apology, but you cannot fake repentance. Repentance is not just devout-sounding moaning about what rotten sinners we are, but it is leaving the life of sin we love so much. It means the slanderer keeping her zingers to herself, the lecher cancelling his Internet, the glutton bypassing the buffet, the proud changing diapers all day, and the impious spending Sunday morning at church instead of the lake. It is change, and it hurts. Only the Holy Spirit could accomplish this work in us, because if there is one thing sinners do not like, it is giving up sin.

Sin dies hard, so hard that it took the Son of God with it to the grave (albeit briefly). And the sin in us kills us day after day. This is why Lutherans say the Christian life is one of repentance. Repentance is not a one-time thing, because sin is not a one-time thing. We sin daily and hourly. Everything we do is tainted by sin. So every day in a Christian's life is also characterized by repentance. In our personal prayers; in our worship together; in our private confessions and receiving of Absolution; and in our thoughts, words, and deeds, we are repenting constantly. We are always seeing our sin and throwing ourselves on God's mercy, who spared not His Son to save us. With His help, we turn away from sin again and again and again. It is hard. We fail. So we repent again, "for the kingdom of heaven is at hand" (Matthew 3:2).

Preparation for Confession

A good way of preparing for confession is to spend a few minutes thinking about the Ten Commandments and their meanings from the Small Catechism.

Ask yourself whether you have kept these Commandments perfectly in thought, word, and deed as God intended. This needs to be a fearless personal inventory, and it is never comfortable, but it should be done each time before confession, either prior to corporate confession on Sunday morning or prior to private confession at some other time.

WHAT DOES THIS MEAN?

When I urge you to go to Confession, I am doing nothing else than urging you to be a Christian. (BEC 32)

Nobody enjoys facing his or her moral and spiritual failings. As a way to make ourselves feel better, we may even be tempted to compare ourselves to other people as if to say, "I'm not so bad. Charles Manson or Adolf Hitler are really bad. I'm nowhere near that bad." But that is not how to prepare for confession, because God does not hold us to any standard but the one He has established. He holds all people to the perfect holy standard of His Law. And on that scale, every one of us falls short. So don't compare yourself to other people. Think of yourself as standing alone before God Almighty with no one there to turn to except Jesus Christ. God's verdict is "guilty" toward all who break His Law. Going to confession requires that we face up to that reality. The tendency today is to try to redefine sin so that we can feel okay about doing whatever we want to do. But denying or sugar-coating the truth about our sin is not the way to be saved. We can only be released from the punishment we deserve if we honestly acknowledge our situation.

During Confession

When you confess, it is not essential that you list every single sin. That would not even be possible. In fact, it isn't even necessary. After self-examination, talk with the pastor about those sins that particularly trouble your conscience. Be specific if you are able. But if you have trouble thinking of what to say, a general admission of guilt against God's Law is sufficient.

FROM THE BIBLE

Therefore, confess your sins to one another and pray for one another, that you may be healed. The prayer of a righteous person has great power as it is working. (James 5:16)

During the confession, your pastor might interrupt you to ask questions for clarification. But it's not the third degree. He's not on a moral fishing expedition. And he is not there to condemn you but to comfort you with God's promises.

Also, keep in mind that guilt is more than just a feeling. It is objective. A bank robber is guilty of theft whether he feels bad about his actions or not. That is why

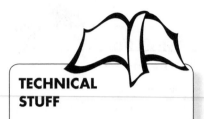

TECHNICAL STUFF

Office of the Keys is the phrase that refers to the special power that Christ has entrusted to the Church to bestow or withhold the forgiveness of sins. It's not up to the pastor or the church to decide whether to grant forgiveness. Sinners who repent are granted forgiveness. Sinners who do not repent are not forgiven. John 20:22–23 is a commonly referenced passage from the Bible as a basis for this teaching. The idea of keys locking and unlocking the gates of heaven comes from the words of Jesus: "I will give you the keys of the kingdom of heaven, and whatever you bind on earth shall be bound in heaven, and whatever you loose on earth shall be loosed in heaven" (Matthew 16:19).

we need to review the Ten Commandments and relevant passages from the Word of God. Our consciences can become hardened and calloused over time, and we need the Holy Spirit to tenderize our hearts with the Law on a regular basis. Confess your guilt, not just your guilty feelings.

After Absolution

The Lutheran pastor may speak with you during the confession and offer advice or counsel from Scripture. But the matter is closed when the Absolution is pronounced. He will not bring up the sins you confessed at a later time. Those sins are as far from you as the east is from the west. Every Lutheran pastor promises in his ordination that he will not divulge sins confessed to him. This has been called the seal of the confessional. For a pastor to break the seal would be a very grave error on his part, and he could face the sternest of consequences. You can trust your pastor to keep his mouth shut about whatever you confess.

Our assurance of God's forgiveness does not depend on the strength of our sincerity, the personal holiness of the pastor, or any action we might perform. We can be confident that the pastor's words of forgiveness are from God because Jesus promised that would be so.

Office of the Keys—God's Word on Forgiveness

Despite the historic practice of individual Confession and Absolution, there is some resistance to the practice. Some people, even some Lutherans, feel that individual confession puts too much emphasis on the pastor. Of course, the pastor does not possess any special power within himself to absolve sins. God alone has the power to forgive; the pastor acts strictly as His servant and messenger.

People will then ask why, if God forgives sins, do we need to confess to the pastor? It is not mandatory to confess your sins to the pastor. You can and should pray to God for forgiveness daily, as we do in the Lord's Prayer. However, there are times when we need to hear about God's compassion and mercy in a very personalized way. Certainly, any believer may tell the good news of forgiveness to a neighbor and be assured that real forgiveness is indeed offered there. The pastor is special only in the sense that he has been appointed by God through the Church to the official role of pronouncing Absolution. The Bible promises that when the pastor declares us forgiven for the sake of Christ, it is as if we hear it from the mouth of God Himself.

FROM THE BIBLE

The one who hears you hears Me, and the one who rejects you rejects Me, and the one who rejects Me rejects Him who sent Me. (Luke 10:16)

And when He had said this, He breathed on them and said to them, "Receive the Holy Spirit. If you forgive the sins of any, they are forgiven them; if you withhold forgiveness from any, it is withheld." (John 20:22–23)

The Certainty of Faith and the Delaying of Repentance

Your certainty comes from knowing that God will have mercy on all who repent and believe the Gospel. You can be certain of that. But you cannot be certain that you will live until tomorrow. Therefore, you cannot adopt an attitude of security, thinking, "I can sin now, and I'll repent when I'm older, before I die." The problem with this is that no one knows how long he will live. God has promised that He will always accept and forgive those who repent of their sins and believe in Jesus for forgiveness. But God has not promised that you will live until tomorrow. Therefore repent and believe now. It is like a market that is offering free groceries, but only for a limited time. If you want to have the free groceries, you will go right away. If you delay, they may be gone.

CHAPTER 19

The Lord's Supper: Given for You

In This Chapter

- Jesus is present in the Lord's Supper.
- In that bread and wine, Jesus gives us His body and blood for the forgiveness of sins.

If you hear a bell ringing in the back of your mind, there's a reason. We mentioned before that the Lord's Supper is a sacrament.

A sacrament
- is instituted by the Lord,
- contains a physical element, and
- promises forgiveness of sins.

Jesus
- instituted the Lord's Supper
- with bread and wine,
- for the forgiveness of sins.

The Lord's Supper makes the list as a sacrament.

Sacrament is Latin for "sacred rite." It has also been linked to the English word "mystery" because there are definitely things about the Lord's Supper that while we believe, we can't understand. This can be a problem for us sinners, especially in a scientific age when we want to explain everything. So here is the plan for this chapter: because it is the Lord's Supper, we are going to let the Lord have the first word. After that, we will take a look at what He says, what it means, and some of the ways that people have managed to get it wrong.

Everything You Need to Know

Jesus teaches everything you need to know about the Lord's Supper in a collection of Bible verses known as the Words of Institution. To institute something is to start or establish it. Therefore, we call these words the Words of Institution because they are the words by which Jesus started and established His Supper. These same words of Jesus are still used by the pastor today to institute the Sacrament whenever it is celebrated:

Our Lord Jesus Christ, on the night when He was betrayed, took bread, and when He had given thanks, He broke it and gave it to the disciples and said: "Take, eat; this is My body, which is given for you. This do in remembrance of Me."

In the same way also He took the cup after supper, and when He had given thanks, He gave it to them, saying: "Drink of it, all of you; this cup is the new testament in My blood, which is given for you for the forgiveness of sins. This do, as often as you drink it, in remembrance of Me." (Matthew 26:26–28; Mark 14:22–24; Luke 22:19–20; 1 Corinthians 11:23–25; *Divine Service*, The Words of Our Lord)

Let's Start Unpacking

OUR LORD JESUS CHRIST

Jesus instituted the Lord's Supper "on the night when He was betrayed"—at the Last Supper—as Jesus celebrated the Passover with His disciples one last time. Less than twenty-four hours later, He would die on the cross. The Lord's Supper is closely associated with His death for the sins of the world.

TAKE, EAT; TAKE, DRINK

Jesus used bread and wine, which He blessed with His Word. The disciples were to eat the bread and drink the wine. But this meal had a benefit that is not seen in the food of bread and wine. Jesus said the Supper was "for the forgiveness of sins."

NEED TO KNOW

Words of Institution: The words spoken by Jesus to institute, or establish, the Lord's Supper. These words are repeated over the bread and wine every time the Sacrament is celebrated.

FOR THE FORGIVENESS OF SINS

The Lord's Supper is for those who desire forgiveness. Medicine is for the sick who want to be healed. The Lord's Supper is for sinners who desire to be forgiven for their sin.

OFTEN, IN REMEMBRANCE OF ME

The purpose of the Supper is to recall and proclaim Jesus' death on the cross for the sins of the world. As St. Paul says elsewhere, "For as often as you eat this bread and drink the cup, you proclaim the Lord's death until He comes" (1 Corinthians 11:26). That proclamation is the Gospel, and the Gospel gives the forgiveness of sins, just as this Supper does. The Lord's Supper is a delivery of the Gospel.

GIVEN FOR YOU

The Lord's Supper is in fact a gift, a gift that cost Jesus much but comes to us without cost. Jesus refers to this Supper as a "testament," as in "last will and testament." By the Supper, His people receive the inheritance He leaves for them—His body and blood, forgiveness of sins, life and salvation.

We've got a lot of basics down so far. We know that Jesus instituted the Supper, telling the disciples to eat the bread and drink the cup for the forgiveness of sins. But we're still missing the central element; we're still missing the big mystery. Here is a clue: The shed blood of Jesus lies at the center of the Christian faith. It is through Christ's blood—that is, through His death on the cross—that God offers us salvation from our sins (Colossians 1:19–20). "Shed for you" (taken from the Words of Our Lord in the Divine Service) is a strange way of describing the cup. Wine isn't shed. But blood is.

The Big Mystery

Remember the warning from before: we human beings like to solve mysteries and explain everything. However, some of God's gifts to us are far too great for us to comprehend. We can't explain them. If we try, we might explain the mystery away. We may actually explain the forgiveness away. When you hear these next words of Jesus, listen to exactly what He says. Don't try to make this mystery into something you can understand:

- Of the bread, Jesus said, "This is My body."
- Of the wine, Jesus said, "This cup is the new testament in My blood."

MAKING CONNECTIONS

The Lord's Supper and the Passover
The Last Supper Jesus shared with His disciples was the Passover meal, in which they celebrated the Lord's deliverance of Israel from Egypt. At the first Passover, a lamb was sacrificed—its blood shed—then eaten for the meal.
1 Corinthians 5:7 tells us that Jesus is our Passover Lamb, sacrificed to deliver us from sin and death. The Lord's Supper, however, carries this even further: not only was Jesus sacrificed, but like the Passover lamb, He is eaten at the Supper. It is no coincidence that Jesus instituted the Lord's Supper at the Passover meal!

NEED TO KNOW

Testament: A will that establishes the disposition of one's belongings at the time of death, or a covenant established by God between God and man. The Lord's Supper fulfills both definitions: prior to the cross, Jesus leaves Christians His body and blood for the forgiveness of their sins; and this Sacrament is part of His covenant of grace for man.

TECHNICAL STUFF

Scripture and the Lutheran Confessions have several names for the Lord's Supper. Each name highlights a specific aspect:

- Lord's Supper: The meal for the forgiveness of sins was instituted by the Lord.

- Holy Communion: We are in communication with God and with one another.

- Sacrament of the Altar: Where this Sacrament is celebrated from.

- Eucharist: Greek for "giving thanks"; originates from Jesus' giving of thanks over the bread and wine at the institution of this special meal.

- Foretaste of the Feast Yet to Come: reminds us that Christ's promise of life and salvation are fulfilled in heaven where we will live forever in His nearer presence.

"Is." It's the linguistic version of an equal sign. Jesus said that in the Lord's Supper the bread is His body. The wine is His blood. This is the big mystery at the heart of the Lord's Supper: Under the bread and wine, we also receive Jesus' body and blood—the same body that was nailed to the cross and the same blood that was shed for our sin. It is also the same body and blood that Jesus showed to His disciples after He rose from the dead.

If Jesus' body and blood are there, Jesus is there. He is present under the elements of bread and wine in the Lord's Supper. We call this the real presence.

The real presence of Christ in the Lord's Supper is a mystery we can't explain. This is, however, why the Lord's Supper is also called Holy Communion. To commune is to be in intimate communication with something, and one can't be in a closer communion with the Holy Son of God than to eat His body and to drink His blood.

Beyond that, we can't explain the real presence: in that bread and wine, Jesus gives us His body and blood for the forgiveness of sins.

That hasn't stopped people from trying to explain it further though. So to help us preserve what the Lord's Supper is and what it is for, it might be helpful if we talk about what it isn't and what it isn't for.

Yikes! Are Lutherans Cannibals?

Because Lutherans teach that Jesus is really present with His body and blood, they have been accused of cannibalism. Rest easy; it isn't true. A cannibal eats physical flesh with his teeth. While we teach that Jesus is bodily present, we do not teach that He is physically present. Things are physical when they take up space; we believe that Jesus is really present with His body and blood but in a mode that doesn't take up space. Can He do that? Yes!

After rising from the dead, Jesus appeared to the disciples in a locked room and showed them His hands and His side (John 20:19–20). How did He get into the locked room? The Bible doesn't specify, but somehow He moved His body through the walls or locked door without displacing the barrier and creating a hole. As He went through, His body didn't take up space (we call this His "incomprehensible mode"). During the Lord's Supper, the bread doesn't change in size with Jesus' body present; His body is present without taking up space. One can't eat something that isn't physically present, so, no, Lutherans aren't cannibals.

The Danger of Saying More than Jesus Says

More than once in the Bible (Deuteronomy 4:2; Revelation 22:18), God warns about adding to His Word. There's a good reason for this: when we add what we mere sinful mortals think God says, we run a good chance of subtracting from what God actually meant for us to hear and to have.

TECHNICAL STUFF

One way of talking about Christ's presence in the Lord's Supper is called transubstantiation. This is the teaching of the Roman Catholic Church. This teaches that the substance of the bread changes into Christ's body so that, even though it looks like bread, no bread remains. However, Jesus didn't say, "This bread is changed into My body," but "This is My body." Elsewhere, St. Paul writes, "The bread that we break, is it not a participation in the body of Christ?" (1 Corinthians 10:16). Clearly, partakers receive both bread and Christ's body in the Supper.

Another theory is called consubstantiation, and teaches that Jesus' body is present along with the bread. Both are there, and together they form a third substance. Many think that this is what Lutherans believe, but this is not the case. Jesus didn't say, "My body is now with this bread." He said, "This is My body." Holding strictly to the words He spoke, Lutherans believe that they receive both bread and His body, because the bread is His body. It's not two different things making a third.

One more theory is that of "spiritual presence" or "symbolic presence," held by many Protestant Christians. In this theory, when Jesus said, "This is My body," He meant, "This bread symbolizes (or 'represents') My body." Many favor this over real presence because it sounds more reasonable—that Jesus can't be in the bread if He bodily sits at the right hand of God, and that the infinite Son of God can't be contained in a finite piece of bread.

One example of adding to or trying to do more than what God's Word says would be "communion in one kind." At the time of the Reformation, the Roman Catholic Church taught that only priests were to receive both bread and wine during the Distribution, while the laity received only the bread. Part of this stemmed from the concern that the cup might be spilled, as well as the rationale that the laity received Christ's blood within His body. Whatever the reason, the practice denied Christians what Jesus wanted them to have: His own blood for the forgiveness of sins. In the New Testament, however, Christians received both bread and wine: "For as often as you eat this bread and drink the cup, you proclaim the Lord's death until He comes" (1 Corinthians 11:26).

What "Is" Isn't. And Is.

Another problem arises when people try to logically explain the real presence—what the "is" means when Jesus said, "This is My body." While our example above just talks about the bread and Christ's body, the same arguments apply also to the wine and His blood.

Lutherans do not try to form theories to make the mystery make sense. They go back to Jesus' own words, and He said, "This is My body," not "This symbolizes My body." "Is" and "symbolizes" mean two very different things. To say "This symbolizes My body" is to say "This is not My body." But Jesus says, "This is." If He meant "symbolizes," He would have said so. Remember again that Paul writes, "The bread that we break, is it not a participation in the body of Christ?" (1 Corinthians 10:16). One can't participate in the body if the body isn't there.

Whoa, you might say, isn't this a little nit-picky? Well, little errors easily build into big errors over time, so we want to be as precise and faithful as we can with Jesus' words. Another good reason is that when it comes to mysteries, describing what we don't believe helps clarify what we do believe.

WHAT DOES THIS MEAN?

Martin Luther summed up all of this, saying, "[The Lord's Supper] is the true body and blood of our Lord Jesus Christ under the bread and wine, instituted by Christ Himself for us Christians to eat and drink." (SC, Sacrament of the Altar)

The Certainty of Faith and the Lord's Supper

God makes a grand and glorious promise to us in the Lord's Supper. Through His pastoral representative, Jesus takes bread and wine, speaks His words of consecration over them, and gives them to us as His body and blood for the forgiveness of our sins. Here, too, certainty is important. In the Lutheran Church, the Words of Institution (Matthew 26:26–28) are recited in the hearing of all communicants so that they know for certain that this bread and wine are the body and blood of Christ. How can they know this with certainty? Because they have heard His Word say, "This is My body; this is My blood." With certainty that the bread and wine are truly Jesus' body and blood, we Lutherans commonly honor the Sacrament with gestures, such as kneeling or standing at the altar to receive it. Our faith is directed not to Jesus in heaven but to Jesus here in the Sacrament. Without certainty, one might doubt whether he is committing idolatry—bread-worship. In order to give certainty, the Words of Institution are always recited in the hearing of those who are going to receive Communion. Certainty comes from hearing these words.

CHAPTER 20

The Lord's Supper: Dinners with Sinners

In This Chapter

- To be worthy and well prepared for the Supper is to be repentant of sin and to trust that Jesus gives you His body and blood for the forgiveness of your sins. All of this is the work of the Holy Spirit.
- Those who receive the Supper in an unworthy manner don't just receive it to no effect—they receive it to their judgment. But those who are worthy and well prepared receive the forgiveness of sins.
- Spend time in preparation before receiving the Lord's Supper.
- Both bread and wine are to be received by communicants.

"Why does He eat with tax collectors and sinners?" (Mark 2:16)

The Pharisees threw this accusation at Jesus' disciples. Jesus had just called the tax collector Matthew (also known as Levi) to be a disciple; now, He was eating at Matthew's house with many of the man's associates. Among them were other tax collectors, considered dishonest extortionists by most, and "sinners"—not just any sinful people, but outcasts of the synagogue. So if Jesus was in fact a great teacher and possibly the Messiah, why was He spending His time with the likes of these?

When Jesus heard the question, He answered, "Those who are well have no need of a physician, but those who are sick. I came not to call the righteous, but sinners" (Mark 2:17).

Jesus is making a division here. Righteous people don't need forgiveness, because they have determined that they are already righteous—it's sinners who need forgiveness. The Lord still attends meals with sinners today in the Lord's Supper. He is no longer the guest, but the host. He also continues to make distinctions between those to whom He comes and those who, because of their self-declared righteousness, do not receive His forgiveness. The question before us is this: "Who is worthy to receive the Lord's Supper?"

Who Is Worthy?

Being worthy and well prepared to receive the Lord's Supper involves believing the words "given and shed." What is given and shed? Jesus' body and blood. In other words, worthiness involves believing that you are receiving Jesus' very body and blood. In the previous chapter, we mentioned that some believe that they receive only bread and wine, not Jesus' body and blood. To believe this is to contradict what Jesus Himself says in the Words of Institution; and that makes one unprepared for the Sacrament.

Being worthy and well prepared also means believing the words "for the forgiveness of sins." It means trusting Jesus' statement that this Sacrament delivers grace. It is tempting, by design or thoughtlessness, to regard the Supper simply as an exercise that Christians do to demonstrate their love for God or one another. But Jesus gives His Supper to give us grace—it is "for the forgiveness of sins." To believe that the Supper focuses on something else is to contradict Him and say, "I am coming for some other reason, *not* for forgiveness." This is to be unworthy and ill prepared.

Finally, being worthy and well prepared also means believing the words "for you." These two words hold a lot! To believe that the Supper and its forgiveness are for you is to say, "*I* need forgiveness, because *I* am a sinner." Thus, to be worthy means to be repentant. To say "I don't need/want forgiveness" or to cling to a favored sin is to be unworthy.

> **WHAT DOES THIS MEAN?**
>
> Fasting and bodily preparation are certainly fine outward training. But that person is truly worthy and well prepared who has faith in these words: "Given and shed for you for the forgiveness of sins."
>
> But anyone who does not believe these words or doubts them is unworthy and unprepared, for the words, "for you" require all hearts to believe. (SC, Sacrament of the Altar)

For You

The words "for you" announce far better news: this forgiveness is "for *you*." The devil will sometimes tempt you to believe that Jesus forgives others but that you are unforgivable. But Jesus didn't say, "For you, unless you're really bad." He died on the cross for all. He died on the cross *for you*. The forgiveness in the Lord's Supper is "for you." To doubt that Jesus forgives you accuses Him of being unwilling or unable to forgive. To believe that is to be unworthy and ill prepared.

Therefore, to be worthy and well prepared for the Supper is to be repentant of sin and to trust that Jesus gives you His body and blood for the forgiveness of your sins. All of this is the work of the Holy Spirit. To doubt your

FROM THE BIBLE

He took bread, and when He had given thanks, He broke it and gave it to them, saying, "This is My body, which is given for you. Do this in remembrance of Me." And likewise the cup after they had eaten, saying, "This cup that is poured out for you is the new covenant in My blood." (Luke 22:19–20)

sinfulness, the Savior's presence, or His grace, is to be unprepared. This is serious! St. Paul warns in 1 Corinthians 11:27–28,

"Whoever, therefore, eats the bread or drinks the cup of the Lord in an unworthy manner will be guilty of concerning the body and blood of the Lord. Let a person examine himself, then, and so eat of the bread and drink of the cup."

Mark the words well. Those who receive the Supper in an unworthy manner do not just receive it to no effect—they receive it to their judgment. But those who are worthy and well prepared receive the forgiveness of sins, and "where there is forgiveness of sins, there is also life and salvation" (SC, Sacrament of the Altar).

Clearly, you want to be prepared.

Be Prepared

To believe in your sinfulness and Christ's presence with forgiveness in the Lord's Supper is straightforward, but the devil will tempt you at every turn to doubt these truths and come to the table unprepared. Therefore, it is good to spend time in preparation before receiving the Lord's Supper.

Bodily Preparation

In the Small Catechism, Luther favorably mentioned "fasting and bodily preparation," but he pointedly called them "fine outward training," not "ways to become worthy." Many Christians fast prior to receiving the Lord's Supper: the hunger and the weakness they feel serve as reminders that they are in need of God's gifts to live—both food for the body and grace for the soul. It can be a helpful exercise. But don't give in to the temptation that it is possible for one to earn worthiness by fasting. That is why Luther calls such exercises "fine outward training" but then goes right on to say, "But that person is truly worthy and well prepared who has faith in these words: 'Given and shed for you for the forgiveness of sins.' "

Meditation and Examination

Therefore, a good plan for preparation is to meditate upon your sinfulness, as well as Jesus' promise that He is present in the Supper to give you forgiveness. To help, there are all sorts of resources available.

One helpful resource is section 4 of the Small Catechism, "Christian Questions with Their Answers, prepared by Dr. Martin Luther for those who intend to go to the Sacrament." These are twenty questions that walk you through proper preparation for the Lord's Supper. Along with what we've already said, the final question adds another important point: "But what should you do if you are not aware of this need [for the Sacrament] and have no hunger and thirst for the Sacrament?" (SC, Christian Questions, 20). Luther doesn't say, "Wait until you feel the need," because you don't become worthy by your work of feeling needy. Instead, he provides several pertinent Scripture verses and bids you to *believe* that you need the Supper, whether or not you feel it.

There are also various prayers of preparation that are helpful for prayer and meditation. These can be found in Lutheran hymnals, prayer books, and some devotionals. Lutheran hymnals also have sections of hymns that teach about Holy Communion; singing and meditating upon them may also prove helpful for preparation.

As His pledge of love undying,
He, this precious food supplying,
Gives His body with the bread,
And with the wine the blood He shed.

Jesus here Himself is sharing;
Heed then how you are preparing,
For if you do not believe,
His judgment then you shall receive. (*LSB* 627:2–3)

Individual Confession and Absolution

Another excellent preparation is individual Confession and Absolution. This provides you with the opportunity to confess specific sins that trouble you (and which clearly demonstrate your sinfulness and need for forgiveness) and to hear from Scripture that the Lord has died for those precise sins. Following the Absolution, the pastor may also encourage you to receive Holy Communion. At the Lord's Supper, Jesus welcomes you, along with other penitent "tax collectors and sinners," to further forgive your sins and strengthen your faith.

Believing, Then Receiving

With the vital parts of the Lord's Supper, Jesus is quite specific. For instance, the elements are to be bread and wine. Both are to be received by communicants. Because Jesus specified these things, we are careful to follow them. However, Jesus didn't spell out a specific practice of Distribution; therefore, you will encounter variations in Lutheran congregations.

Traditionally, the blood of Christ has been distributed from a single chalice, the common cup. Many congregations have moved to include or solely use trays of individual cups. For many, the common cup is preferable because it most closely represents the practice of the first Lord's Supper and expresses union with Him in the Sacrament, but either may be used to deliver the blood of Christ to communicants in a reverent manner.

In some congregations, the pastor will place the host (typically wafers) into the hand of the communicants; in others, he will place it directly into their mouths. The latter method reinforces that grace is given apart from our works, as the communicant does nothing to receive it; however, both methods deliver the body of Christ to communicants.

NEED TO KNOW

Host: Latin for "sacrifice" or "victim"; the consecrated bread (and thus also Christ's body) of Holy Communion.

In many congregations, communicants come to the altar and kneel to receive Holy Communion in groups or "tables." In others, they line up in single file, receive the Lord's Supper while standing, and immediately return to their seats—this is sometimes known as continuous Communion.

Practices will vary from church to church. Regardless of the practice, the Lord's Supper should always be conducted with reverence, because God Himself is present. Most important, however, is whether or not the celebration is in accordance with Jesus' institution.

Are the Words of Institution spoken at the Sacrament faithful to the Words of Institution in Scripture?

Are the elements bread and wine?

Where this is true, you can be sure that it is the Lord's Supper.

One more variation is frequency: some congregations celebrate the Lord's Supper every Sunday, others bi-monthly, and still others less. The Lord didn't give a number; however, He did say in the Words of Institution, "Do this, as often as you drink it, in remembrance of Me" (1 Corinthians 11:25). Verse 26 reads: "For as often as you eat this bread and drink the cup, you proclaim the Lord's death until He comes." The operative word is *often*. The Church's mission is to proclaim the Lord's death for the sins of the world, and as the Lord's Supper does exactly that, "often" is far better than "occasionally."

Holy Communion is still the Supper where Jesus is present with "tax collectors and sinners" until He comes again in glory. He is present there for you, giving you His body and blood for the forgiveness of sins.

And where there is forgiveness of sins, there is also life and salvation.

On Atonement

Did Jesus die for me? How can I be sure? Can I have certainty that God forgives my sins because Jesus died for me on the cross? If peace with God depended on the sacrifice of a mere human, it would be doubtful and insufficient, because the death of a mere man, even the most perfect of human beings, would be limited in its worth. Perhaps it could only pay for one sin. "Truly no man can ransom another, or give to God the price of his life, for the ransom of their life is costly and can never suffice" (Psalm 49:7–8). But Christ is both man and God. Therefore we can be certain that His death was enough to pay the debt for the whole human race. And not only was it enough, but in fact we can be certain that Christ actually died for all. This is great news! If He died for all human beings, then I can be certain that He died for me too. No longer do I have to doubt whether I am included among God's chosen few. Christ died for all; therefore, He died for me.

CHAPTER 21

The Lord's Supper: The Lord's Care

In This Chapter

- There is no stronger personal relationship with God than when we receive the body and blood of Jesus.
- We commune with everyone who is a believer in Christ.
- God gathers His Holy Church from heaven and earth in Communion.

Life brings times of joy and times of sadness. In times of joy, we thank God for His good gifts and praise Him for our provisions. But what do we do in times of sadness? That is when we often feel God has left us. We ask where He is. How does God care for us? How can we be sure He hears our prayers, forgives our sins, and comforts our hurting hearts? As Christians, we do not avoid the difficulties of this life but face them head-on with the truth of Scripture.

How God Becomes Our Caregiver

Lutherans believe that Jesus comes to us in the Lord's Supper. (See Chapter 19.) Surely, God is everywhere. However, because we need His special attention, He comes to us in a very intimate way in the Lord's Supper. Through this Sacrament we experience God's love in the resurrected body and blood of Jesus in the bread and wine.

When we partake of the Lord's Supper, God gives us His compassionate and focused attention. There is no stronger personal relationship with God than when we receive the body and blood of Jesus. The Lord's Supper is a meal that never ends. It nourishes and gives us strength to carry on with life. But there is even more.

Who Comes to Dinner?

When you eat and drink the bread and wine in the Lord's Supper, God bestows His gift of forgiveness upon you. God's forgiveness cleans up the mess of our sinful lives. Our lives are full of moments of confusion, need, and hurt, but He makes us holy again. He does not forgive us based on the good actions we do. Instead, He gives us the perfect and holy life that Jesus lived. Our faith receives this gift. But there's more.

Those who receive the Lord's Supper are members in an exclusive family, the Church. Christ marks you as His child in Baptism. Baptism is your invitation to Communion. And like receiving an invitation to any other grand gathering, you take time to prepare. Baptism begins the time of confirming the teachings God gave you. The preparation takes place in the Church, who through her pastors and the other members instructs you in the faith through the Word and what it means as you learn it in the Confessions.

Not only does Jesus give His body, blood, and forgiveness, but He also brings everyone in heaven to be one with the believers on earth. It is a family feast with so many children that we cannot count them. At the celebration of the Lord's Supper, we rejoice in the reality that we are worshiping Christ together with "angels and archangels and with all the company of heaven," as we hear in the Proper Preface (Divine Service—Service of the Sacrament). It is heaven on earth, a foretaste of the feast to come.

The oneness of Christ's Church comes when we sing and say back to Him what He gave to us in His Word. We speak as one—the one holy body of believers. Thus, what we believe is crucial. We are sure not to say something else about God than what He has told us. This gives us the security and consistency that every child of God needs. We are sure where God comes to us, where He forgives us, and where He comforts us in His holy family.

Like our human family, God's family gathers together for the family meal. To prepare for the meal, we admit our brokenness, and He heals us; we can admit our sins, and our heavenly Father judges us as forgiven in Jesus. Our family gathering brings light to our gray lives and clarity to our confusion. The Holy Spirit gathers the family of God in forgiveness and mercy, hope and peace, life and salvation. Every Sunday is the perfect Christmas and Easter family dinner for those who believe in what He serves.

Hamburgers or Tacos?

Would we go to a hamburger place if we want tacos? Would we be surprised to receive a taco after ordering a hamburger? It isn't what was advertised. Communion is an advertisement to the whole world that says who we are and what we believe about Jesus. This is the reason why we commune in a church that teaches what we believe. It removes any doubt about God's Word when we know what a church teaches. When we commune in a particular church, we are joining our confession with theirs; we are confessing, "We say the same thing about Jesus." Some churches believe that the Lord's Supper is a symbol or does not bring forgiveness. We don't want to mislead anyone with our "advertisement" of faith, nor do we want a church to misrepresent what they advertise. This is why Lutherans commune at Lutheran churches, that is, in congregations that belong to the same Lutheran church body: so that together we tell the world what God taught us.

Heaven on Earth

The Church is a mystery from God. It is the new creation in the midst of a sinful and confused world. God gathers His Holy Church from heaven and earth in Communion. God gives you the faith to trust His Word, and the Word creates the miracle of this heavenly feast. It is why true spirituality is physical. Being spiritual is trusting in the earthly things of the bread and wine, because in them He brings His body and blood and the healing balm of salvation.

The mystery is revealed. The family feast of Holy Communion brings heaven to earth because heaven is being in the presence of God. Believing (faith) in Christ brings this. How? There is no explanation. God keeps His Word. Heaven comes to earth in God's presence because He says it happens. God's words neither lie nor change. He performs this miracle and does what He says. We can count on Him.

Family Traditions

Parents hand down wonderful traditions that bring the family together, such as holiday dinners and special anniversaries. God does the same thing. Through generations of parents and children together at church, God gathers the family for whom Jesus shed His blood. God's Word and the weekly Supper of life and salvation is handed down to their children and their children's children, so throughout history God is here for all believers, including you.

How to Receive the Lord's Supper

The Lord's Supper, often referred to as Holy Communion, is the central event of the Divine Service. This Sacrament is celebrated by those who are communicant members of (in community with) the congregation. Because in the Lord's Supper we actually receive the body and blood our Lord Jesus Christ in and with the bread and the wine, and because it is the most interactive part of the Divine Service, some may be perplexed or hesitant to receive Holy Communion.

1. Look for guidance on how to prepare. Dr. Martin Luther prepared several questions with their answers for those who intend to go to the Sacrament. These questions and answers offer a way for you to examine yourself and review what the Sacrament is. These questions can be found in the Small Catechism.

2. Look for guidance from the bulletin. The most common methods of Distribution are common cup and individual cups. Some congregations receive as small groups, often called "tables," that may be instructed to kneel at the altar railing, while others may form a continuous line going up to the altar. Very often instructions about taking Holy Communion will be in the bulletin or some announcement will be made.

3. Look for guidance from the usher. The usher takes an active part in directing the movement from the pew to the altar. Often the simplest practice is to follow the person ahead of you.

Common Cup

1. Receiving His body. Extend your hand with the palm facing up. When the server says, "The body of Christ given for you," and places the host in your hand, take the host with the fingers of the other hand and eat it.

2. Receiving His blood. The wine will be served in a large cup called a chalice. It is preferred that you assist the server by lightly grasping the foot of the chalice and guide the chalice to your lips. Drink only one sip, and remove your lips from the chalice immediately after receiving the wine. Gently release the foot of the chalice as the server moves away.

Individual Cups

1. Receiving His body. Same as above

2. Receiving His blood. Take a filled cup from the tray. When the server says, "The blood of Christ shed for you," drink it. Place the empty cup in the receptacle provided for that purpose.

PART FOUR

What you'll learn about:

- The Reformation arose out of Martin Luther's concern about how the Church thought and taught about salvation.

- How politics and theology in the 1500s influenced each other and became the seedbed of the Reformation.

- The Book of Concord contains the official confession of the Lutheran Church and is the standard by which all doctrine and practice is determined to be correct.

- Lutherans came to America during the colonial period and saw another great period of immigration between the 1850s and the 1900s.

- When Lutherans came to the New World, they brought with them a passion for education of the young, including religious instruction.

Lutherans at a Glance

Lutheranism arose out of a desire to reform the doctrine and practices of the Roman Catholic Church, but after being rejected by the Roman Church, the Lutheran Church has grown to be the fourth largest Christian tradition in the world.

CHAPTER 22

Luther: The Unlikely Reformer

In This Chapter

- For Martin Luther, the problem was not primarily the morality of the clergy, nor even its ineptitude, but rather how the Church thought and taught about salvation.

- Luther saw that at the very center there was deformation and error in the Church of his time. This error had consequences not only for the understanding of how people are saved but also in the area of how the Sacraments are understood, what the Church is, what the Church's ministry is, and what the Christian life looks like.

- The Lutheran Reformation was conservative in that it changed only what was necessary to change and did not try to start afresh and discard fifteen hundred years of Church history.

FROM THE BIBLE

For we hold that one is justified by faith apart from works of the law. (Romans 3:28)

For by grace you have been saved through faith. And this is not your own doing; it is the gift of God, not a result of works, so that no one may boast. (Ephesians 2:8–9)

Luther's Life

Martin Luther was born into an average middle-class German family. His father was a successful and pragmatic businessman who wanted his son to have a good education and career. Luther entered the University of Erfurt law school at the wishes of his father and received his master's degree in 1505, but he was unhappy with his circumstances. Then, unexpectedly, when returning to the university after a trip home, Luther encountered a severe thunderstorm and a lightning bolt struck near him. In terror of death and divine judgment, Luther cried out, "St. Anne, help me! I will become a monk!" (Okay, so maybe this story can't be completely substantiated, but it has been included in most major Luther biographies.)

After this turn of events, Luther entered the Augustinian monastery in Erfurt in 1505. Although Luther dedicated his life to the disciplines of the monastery, he still felt uncertainty and doubt about his salvation. He regularly engaged in fasting, flagellation, and confession, but still he experienced continual deep spiritual despair. To distract him from his depression, Luther's supervisor, Johann von Staupitz, ordered that Luther pursue a degree in theology. So, after being ordained as a priest, he started theological studies at the University of Erfurt in 1507.

At the University of Erfurt, Luther was exposed to the current humanist ideology. His studies were influenced by the dominant philosophy of returning "Back to the source!" that is, the original texts in each area of study. For theologians like Luther, that meant the Hebrew and Greek texts of the Bible. After receiving his doctorate in theology in 1512, he became professor at Wittenberg University. For Luther, this became a period of intense study. He prepared and gave lectures on Psalms (1514–15), Romans (1515–16), Galatians (1516–17), and Hebrews (1517–18). It was in his study that Luther encountered the words of Romans 1:17: "The righteous shall live by faith." According to Luther himself, "Here I felt that I was altogether born again and had entered paradise itself through open gates." This marked the turning point for Luther.

> **WHAT DOES THIS MEAN?**
>
> There I began to understand that the righteousness of God is that by which the righteous lives by a gift of God, namely by faith. And this is the meaning: the righteousness of God is revealed by the gospel, namely, the passive righteousness with which merciful God justified us by faith, as it is written, "He who through faith is righteous shall live." Here I felt that I was altogether born again and had entered paradise itself through open gates. There a totally other face of the entire Scripture showed itself to me. (AE 34:337)

While professor at the University of Erfurt, Luther also was priest at Wittenberg's City Church. During this time, the popes were often more concerned with political questions than with the duties of their office as supreme governors of the Roman Catholic Church. They led wars and were more interested in their position as princes of the territory of the church state and the enlargement of their political powers. Wars and huge building projects like St. Peter's Basilica in Rome were costly, and so the raising of money became an issue. It was a common practice in the Roman Catholic Church to raise money by selling indulgences, a piece of paper stating their sins were forgiven. Unfortunately, there were some in the church who took advantage of the poor in the selling of these indulgences. John Tetzel, a Dominican monk, was notorious for this practice. On October 31, 1517, when Tetzel came to a town near Wittenberg to peddle these indulgences, Luther posted his Ninety-five Theses, or propositions, condemning this practice and other abuses within the Roman Catholic Church. (This event might be familiar to you if you have seen images of Luther nailing a piece of paper to a wooden door.)

Luther's intent by posting his theses was not to break away from the Roman Church, but to stimulate academic debate and draw attention to the practices of the Church. For Martin Luther, the problem was deeper. It was not primarily the morality of the clergy, nor even its ineptitude, but rather how the Church thought and taught about salvation that got him interested in the reform of the Church. He ultimately wanted to convince the Church of its errors, thus reforming its doctrine. The Ninety-five Theses were quickly printed through the availability of the printing press (see p. 174) and spread all over Germany.

WHAT DOES THIS MEAN?

Though there may be many people who look upon this whole movement as a diabolical affair, who so call it and condemn it . . . who think it fitting that Wittenberg and all that has been begun there be allowed to go to destruction, this does not excuse me; for God will not judge me by the faith of others, whether they be many or few, but by my own conscience. And I know that my message and what I have begun to do are not of myself but of God, nor will death or persecution teach me other wise. (*What Luther Says*, 3795)

Here I Stand

Luther saw that there was error in what the church of his time was proclaiming. This error had consequences not only for the understanding of how people are saved, but also in the area of how the Sacraments are understood, what the Church is, what the Church's ministry is, and what the Christian life looks like. Luther engaged in much dialogue and writing during this period in an effort to persuade the Roman Catholic Church to reform its views.

The Church's response was to declare Luther a heretic and insist that he retract his positions. In 1520, Luther was excommunicated from the Roman Catholic Church and in 1521 was summoned to defend his doctrinal positions at the Diet of Worms. During his defense he replied,

Unless I am convinced by the testimony of the Scriptures or by clear reason (for I do not trust either in the pope or in councils alone, since it is well known that they have often erred and contradicted themselves), I am bound by the Scriptures I have quoted and my conscience is captive to the Word of God. I cannot and I will not retract anything, since it is neither safe nor right to go against conscience. I cannot do otherwise, here I stand, may God help me, Amen. (AE 32:112–13)

Luther was summarily declared an outlaw. Upon his return home, he was "kidnapped" by his benefactor, Frederick of Saxony, and hidden for a time for protection. During this time Luther translated the Greek New Testament into German. For the first time Scripture was available in the language of the common people for all to read. Later, he also translated the Hebrew Old Testament into German.

Luther continued to press for reform and defend the centrality of the Gospel through preaching, writing, and teaching. He was distraught at the lack of spiritual knowledge among the common people about faith and the Bible. In response, Luther wrote the catechism to aid in instruction of families and children at home. (See p. 180.) He also wrote many hymns to aid and instruct the common people during worship. (See p. 225.)

Are Lutherans Evangelical?

Lutherans are the original Evangelicals. The word *evangelical* comes from the Greek word *euangelion*, meaning "good message." Luther and those who followed his teachings began to call their churches "evangelical" (Gospel proclaimers) because of the focus on the Gospel's good news centered on the death and resurrection of Jesus Christ as a sole means of salvation. This is different than "Evangelicalism," which is a later term that describes a Protestant movement that originated in Great Britain in 1730. This movement focused on the need for personal conversion, being "born again," and biblical fundamentalism. These same needs inform much of American Evangelicalism yet today. Because modern-day Evangelicals teach about the faith much differently than the Lutherans, few Lutheran churches in America today use the name *Evangelical*.

NEED TO KNOW

What Does This Mean?

Catholic: universal, including all.

Concord: agreement between people or groups.

Diet: a formal meeting of princes and emperors.

Edict: an announcement of a new law.

Papal Bull: a letter sent by the pope. *Papal* tells us it has something to do with the pope, and *bull* comes from the same root word as *bulletin*.

Theses: A thesis is a statement that is being presented for discussion or explanation. *Theses* is the plural of *thesis*.

Are Lutherans Protestant?

By definition, Lutherans are the only "Protestants." In 1529 at the Diet (Imperial Assembly) of Speyer, legal restrictions were placed upon the Evangelicals that restricted their ability to spread Evangelical teaching, and the right to assembly, among others. The Evangelical delegation filed a formal protest. When the protest was rejected, the delegation at Speyer filed an appeal with the emperor. Historically, then, to refer to the "Protestants" comes from this specific protest, one lodged only by the Lutherans.

Later reformers tried to strengthen their cause by joining themselves with this historic protest. Because so many people taught differently from the Evangelicals, the "Lutherans" ended up largely rejecting the title for themselves.

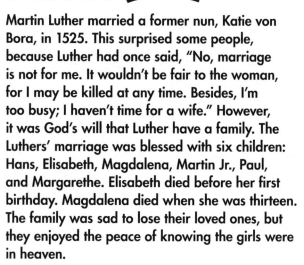

MAKING CONNECTIONS

Martin Luther married a former nun, Katie von Bora, in 1525. This surprised some people, because Luther had once said, "No, marriage is not for me. It wouldn't be fair to the woman, for I may be killed at any time. Besides, I'm too busy; I haven't time for a wife." However, it was God's will that Luther have a family. The Luthers' marriage was blessed with six children: Hans, Elisabeth, Magdalena, Martin Jr., Paul, and Margarethe. Elisabeth died before her first birthday. Magdalena died when she was thirteen. The family was sad to lose their loved ones, but they enjoyed the peace of knowing the girls were in heaven.

Reformation Events

1517 Luther nailed his Ninety-five Theses to the door of the Castle Church in Wittenberg on October 31. His goal was to start discussions about indulgences and other questionable practices of the Catholic Church in order to reform (fix) it.

1520 Pope Leo X issued a "papal bull" giving Luther sixty days to recant (take back what he had said against the Roman Catholic Church). Luther later burned the bull publicly.

1521 Luther was excommunicated (kicked out of the Catholic Church) by Pope Leo X.

1525 The Anabaptist movement began when a group of people who had been baptized as infants gathered to be rebaptized as adults. Mennonite, Amish, Hutterite, and Brethren groups of today are Anabaptists.

1526 At the Diet of Speyer, German princes were given the right to choose whether their territories would be Roman Catholic or Protestant.

1529 Luther published his Large and Small Catechisms. He wrote the catechisms after he visited Saxony and realized how little most Christians and even most pastors knew about God and the Bible. The Small Catechism became an instant best seller.

1530 The Augsburg Confession was prepared by Philip Melanchthon to explain what Lutherans believe. It was presented to Emperor Charles V by a group of Lutheran princes at the Diet of Augsburg in June. The emperor did not like what was said in the Augsburg Confession and prepared his own statement, the Pontifical Confutation of the Augsburg Confession, to explain what he thought was wrong with the Augsburg Confession.

TECHNICAL STUFF

Apology: Were they sorry?

The word *apology* means "defense" in Greek. People who are apologists or study apologetics use the Bible and logic to prove truths about God.

MAKING CONNECTIONS

The Book of Concord, also known as The Lutheran Confessions, is made up of several documents:

- **Three creeds: Apostles', Nicene, Athanasian**
- **The Augsburg Confession**
- **The Apology of the Augsburg Confession**
- **The Smalcald Articles**
- **The Power and Primacy of the Pope**
- **The Small Catechism**
- **The Large Catechism**
- **The Formula of Concord: Epitome and Solid Declaration**

Philip Melanchthon spent about half a year preparing the Apology of the Augsburg Confession in which he worked through each of the points of the emperor's confutation and explained the errors in the confutation and the truth in the Augsburg Confession.

1531 The Augsburg Confession and the Apology of the Augsburg Confession were published.

1534 Henry VIII created the Church of England (origin of Anglicans). Society of Jesus (Jesuits) founded by Ignatius of Loyola.

1538 Martin Luther's Smalcald Articles were published. Luther had been asked to prepare a statement of faith that would clearly explain the difference between Lutheran and Roman Catholic beliefs.

Pope Paul III decided to call a council to discuss how to reform the Catholic Church. The Council of Trent met between 1545 and 1563.

1540 Philip Melanchthon's Treatise on the Power and Primacy of the Pope was published. In it, Melanchthon pointed out three main false teachings about the pope.

1546 Soon after Martin Luther died (February 18, 1546), Pope Paul III and Emperor Charles V made an agreement to stop the Protestant Reformation and force the Lutherans to become a part of the Catholic Church again. The Smalcaldic War broke out. By the middle of 1547, the emperor had defeated all the Lutheran princes. Philip Melanchthon decided to compromise some of his beliefs in an effort to get along with the pope and the emperor. Lutherans became split between those compromising like Melanchthon and those who held tightly to what they believed.

1552 The Elector of Saxony drove the emperor and his troops out of Saxony. Two treaties, in 1552 and 1555, gave religious freedom back to the princes.

1560 The Church of Scotland broke from the Roman Catholic Church (origin of Presbyterians).

1563 The Council of Trent met for the last time after making many decisions about official beliefs and practices of the Roman Catholic Church.

1576 The Epitome of the Formula of Concord was completed at the Torgau Conference. Six Lutheran theologians, including Martin Chemnitz, met to create a document they hoped would end the theological disagreements between Lutherans who were compromising with the pope on some articles of the Augsburg Confession and other Lutherans who were trying to hold to everything Luther taught based on the Bible.

1577 The Solid Declaration of the Formula of Concord was completed. The Solid Declaration is a longer, more detailed version of the Epitome.

1580 The Book of Concord was published exactly fifty years after the Augsburg Confession was presented at the Diet of Augsburg. Over eight thousand signed it to show that they agreed with everything in it.

CHAPTER 23

The World of the Reformation

In This Chapter

- The spread of information was rapidly growing in Europe.
- The Northern Renaissance emphasized learning the ancient languages and going back to the original source texts.
- Throughout the Middle Ages, there had been a growing problem of corruption within the Roman Catholic Church and a number of attempts at reform.

The Expanding World

In the 1500s, Europeans were encountering rapid change. During this time period, their world grew larger—figuratively and literally. Figuratively, education and literacy for the common people was swiftly spreading. Literally, the world was revealed as bigger than they had realized.

"Land, Ho!"

The start of the Reformation is generally dated from Martin Luther's posting of his Ninety-five Theses in 1517. Yet just twenty-five years earlier, in 1492, Christopher Columbus made his famous voyage that led to the discovery of the New World, reforming the intellectual thought of the time. Now the people of Europe were wrestling with the reality that the world had two more continents than anyone had imagined.

Different Beliefs

Europeans were also well aware of those groups that held different beliefs. For most of the medieval period, Muslims controlled much of the area that is now Spain and Portugal. In fact, it was in 1492, the same year of Columbus's famous voyage, that the last of the Muslim states in Spain were defeated. This did not mean an end to European dealings with Muslims, just a shift of directions, since at this time there was a great invasion of Europe from the southeast by the Ottoman Turks. They even got as far as laying siege on Vienna in 1529, the year before the Diet of Augsburg.

Printing for the People

Intellectually, the spread of information was rapidly growing in Europe. Around 1439, Johannes Gutenberg invented the moveable type printing press. It is hard to understand the impact of this invention. The printing press created a means of quickly disseminating information that was previously unheard of. Books were often hand-copied and expensive to own. Think of how the world of information for us changed because of the Internet. All of a sudden it was possible for ideas to travel faster than previously imagined. On top of this, the cost of printed materials went way down, which meant that the common people could purchase and read tracts and join in the ideas that were rippling through their world—and what ideas there were!

The Renaissance and the Reformation

Renaissance Men

The era of the Reformation was in fact the same era as the Renaissance. Most likely you think of the great Renaissance men of Italy, such as Leonardo da Vinci and Michelangelo, who were early contemporaries of the reformers (da Vinci died just two years after Luther posted his Ninety-five Theses, and Michelangelo was a mere eight years older than Luther). Martin Luther, Philip Melanchthon, and the other reformers were really figures of the *Northern* Renaissance, not the Italian Renaissance.

MAKING CONNECTIONS

An example of the many ways politics and theology influence each other is that one of the main reasons for the Diet of Augsburg and the subsequent writing of the Augsburg Confession was that Emperor Charles V wanted the people of the Holy Roman Empire united in order to fight the invading Turks. (See pp. 179–83.)

The Northern Renaissance emphasized learning the ancient languages and going back to the original source texts rather than trusting in later summaries and translations. This is what led Melanchthon to become one of the best biblical Greek scholars of the age and Luther to cling to the Bible as the source of our faith. Further, Luther learned both Greek and Hebrew to first study the Bible in its original language and then later to translate them into German. Luther learned that in religion, even more than in other things, he must ultimately hold to the original text of God's Word and not to other people's biased translations. The idea of studying the Bible in its original languages was not unique to the reformers, as Luther used a

Greek New Testament that was compiled by great Renaissance humanist Erasmus of Rotterdam.

Education

A key aspect of Renaissance thought was the movement of humanism. This movement led to a revival in the study of the humanities with a great emphasis on ancient languages and texts. This led to a debate within the greater European culture as to how education should be formed. Throughout the medieval era, education relied heavily on Aristotle, largely as he was interpreted by Thomas Aquinas. However, during the Renaissance there was a growing swell of support for making education less dependent on Aristotle and more on learning languages and other ancient authors.

As a result, men such as Luther were formally trained in the old way of Aristotle, but in the informal discussions around the universities, the new way of humanism was taking root. During the era of the Renaissance, this emphasis on the ancient languages led to many of the thinkers embracing Latin and taking on alternate forms for their names, including Luther and his friend and supporter Philip Melanchthon. Luther often signed his name in the Latinized form of "Martinus Lutherus." Melanchthon went a step further, as he was actually born Philip Schwartzerd, but then translated his name (which simply means "black earth") into Greek and become Philip Melanchthon. When Luther was called as a professor of theology at the University of Wittenberg, he started working not only to study the Bible but also to adjust the teaching format at the university. This movement led to Melanchthon joining the faculty. As a result, the great Reformation of the Church was first seen by many as a reformation of education!

TECHNICAL STUFF

Northern Renaissance: a movement within the greater Renaissance that took place in Northern Europe, including the German lands, the Netherlands, France, England, and Poland. This movement was less influential in the arts, but placed greater stress on education and was closely linked to the Reformation.

TECHNICAL STUFF

Renaissance humanism, not to be confused with today's secular humanism, was a school of thought that emphasized grammar, rhetoric, moral philosophy, history, and poetry—especially through the study of Greek and Latin classical writers.

MAKING CONNECTIONS

During this time, Copernicus challenged the ancient idea that the earth was at the center of the universe. He claimed that the sun is at the center and the earth revolves around the sun. Copernicus wrote this idea first in 1530, the same year as the Augsburg Confession, though he held off publishing it for a few years.

Early Attempts at Reformation

Reformation Men

The Reformation was not the product of a few smart men (and these guys were definitely smart!) who impulsively decided to shake things up in the Roman Catholic Church. Throughout the Middle Ages there had been a growing problem of corruption within the Church and a number of attempts at reform. Many of the attempts had simply been movements to curtail abuses of power and promote better piety. However, there had been several men who saw that the real problem came from the Church straying from reliance on the Bible.

There was John Wycliffe (d. December 31, 1384) in England, who argued that the Bible belonged to the Church and therefore should be available to all believers, including a translation for the laity. Many of Wycliffe's early efforts at limiting the power of the Church hierarchy were supported by the English royalty. However, as some of his supporters become more radical and demanded changes to the laws, support for the reform movement died down. After his death, the Council of Constance condemned him as a heretic, and in a symbolic (and to us seemingly silly) measure, they ordered that his bones be dug up and burned.

Jan Hus (d. July 6, 1415) of Bohemia took up many of Wycliffe's ideas. Hus challenged the Roman Catholic Church, particularly on the celibacy of priests and the idea that the laity should only receive Communion in one kind. This was the practice that only the priests could partake of Christ's blood in the wine, and the rest only got His body in the bread. Hus was summoned to the Council of Constance in 1415 (the same one that condemned Wycliffe). He was guaranteed safe conduct to and from the council by the Holy Roman Emperor; however, at the council he was condemned and burned at the stake.

The Holy Roman Empire

Why didn't Luther and his supporters suffer the same fate as Wycliffe and Hus? To understand, we need to take into account the political situation at the time of the Reformation. First, when we speak of the Reformation happening in Germany, this is only partly right. The area was known as Germany because the people spoke

German, but there was no official country of Germany until the nineteenth century. Rather, the official country was the Holy Roman Empire, which was a loosely connected set of mostly independent princedoms with a few free cities thrown in. The Holy Roman Emperor was not a hereditary position like a king; there were seven electors who would vote for the next emperor when the previous one died. This meant that the emperor had a very limited power base, but the electors were especially powerful. In order for the emperor to move much forward in the empire, he had to call a Diet, a meeting of the princes.

King Charles: Holy Roman Emperor

The emperor at the time of the Reformation was Charles V, a man of tremendous power. He was also known as Charles I, king of Spain, and held the throne of Austria as well. If you count the official control of the Americas by Spain, Charles was technically ruler over more of the earth than anyone in history! As king of Austria and Spain, he was not only a devout Catholic, but he also was ruler of these strongly Catholic lands. Therefore, Charles tried to stamp out the movement of the Reformation in order to consolidate his power. In fact, declared by the electors to be king of the Romans and later by the pope to be the Holy Roman Emperor, Charles was the official protector of the Catholic faith, which is why when Luther was declared a heretic, Charles declared him an outlaw and free to be killed by anyone.

However, as much as Charles wanted to stop Luther and the Reformation, his power in many parts of the Empire was greatly limited, and this was especially true in Saxony. Luther lived and worked in Saxony as a subject of Duke Frederick the Wise. Besides being a duke, Frederick was one of those powerful electors. (Ironically, Frederick cast the deciding vote to place Charles on the throne of the empire.) While Frederick did not dare openly defy the rule of Charles, he was willing and able to subvert the attempts to squash the Reformation. This included a move that probably saved Luther's life when Luther was called to stand trial before a council of the Church. Frederick, remembering what happened to Hus, insisted that as a citizen of the Holy Roman Empire, Luther

NEED TO KNOW

Holy Roman Empire: This was the name of the loose confederation of Germanic states during the Middle Ages and Reformation. It drew its name from the false idea that this was the continuation of the empire of Charlemagne, which was wrongly considered a continuation of the Roman Empire. It was simply a standard nation, with nothing particularly holy about it, and it was far from an empire in scope. So it was not really holy or Roman or an empire. Other than that, the name fit perfectly!

should stand trial in the empire, and so when Luther was condemned, he was still allowed safe conduct to leave the Diet of Worms. Also, it is important to remember that Charles was ruler of two other countries, and as such was often distracted from dealing with the reformers by little things like ruling Austria and Spain, trying to limit papal reaches for power in his lands, a Turkish invasion, and possible war with France.

Does It Still Matter?

After nearly five hundred years, does the Reformation still matter? The Roman Catholic Church is not the same as it was at the time of Luther. Lutheran churches do not agree among themselves what it means to be Lutheran.

Well, are the questions debated during the Reformation still important?
• Are we saved by grace from God or by what we do?
• Is the Bible held up as the authority?
• What do the Sacraments mean?

Yes, the Reformation still matters.

Confession of Faith

What Is a Lutheran?

While there is a variety of ways one could answer this question, one very important answer is simply this: "A Lutheran is a person who believes, teaches, and confesses the truths of God's Word as they are summarized and confessed in the Book of Concord." The Book of Concord contains the Lutheran Confessions of faith.

When a pastor is ordained, he promises that he will perform the duties of his office in accord with the Lutheran Confessions. When people are confirmed, they are asked if they confess the doctrine of the Evangelical Lutheran Church as they have learned to know it from the Small Catechism to be faithful and true.

These solemn promises indicate to us just how important the Lutheran Confessions are for our church. Let's take a look at the various items contained in the Book of Concord, and then we will talk about why the Lutheran Confessions are so important for being a Lutheran.

What Are the Ecumenical Creeds?

The three Ecumenical Creeds in the Book of Concord are the Apostles' Creed, the Nicene Creed, and the Athanasian Creed. They are described as "ecumenical" [universal] because Christians worldwide accept them as correct expressions of what God's Word teaches.

What Is the Augsburg Confession and Apology of the Augsburg Confession?

In the year 1530, the Lutherans were required to present their confession of faith before the emperor in Augsburg, Germany. Philip Melanchthon wrote the Augsburg Confession, and it was read before the imperial court on June 30, 1530. One year later, the Lutherans presented their defense of the Augsburg Confession, which is what "apology" here means. It, too, was written by Philip Melanchthon. The largest document in the Book of Concord, its longest chapter is devoted to the most important truth of the Christian faith: the doctrine of justification by grace alone, through faith alone, in Christ alone.

What Are the Small and Large Catechisms?

Martin Luther realized early on how desperately ignorant the laity and clergy of his day were when it came to even the most basic truths of the Christian faith. Around 1530, he produced two small handbooks to help pastors and the heads of families teach the faith.

The Small Catechism and the Large Catechism are organized around six topics: the Ten Commandments, the Apostles' Creed, the Lord's Prayer, Holy Baptism, Confession, and the Sacrament of the Altar. So universally accepted were these magnificent doctrinal summaries by Luther that they were included as part of the Book of Concord.

What Are the Smalcald Articles and the Treatise on the Power and Primacy of the Pope?

In 1537, Martin Luther was asked to prepare a statement of Lutheran belief for use at a Church council, if it was called. Luther's bold and vigorous confession of faith was later incorporated into the Book of Concord. It was presented to a group of Lutheran rulers meeting in the town of Smalcald. Philip Melanchthon was asked to expand on the subject of the Roman pope and did so in his treatise, which also was included in the Book of Concord.

What Is the Formula of Concord?

After Luther's death in 1546, significant controversies broke out in the Lutheran Church. After much debate and struggle, the Formula of Concord in 1577 put an end to these doctrinal controversies, and the Lutheran Church was able to move ahead united in what it believed, taught, and confessed. In 1580, all the confessional writings mentioned here were gathered into a single volume, the Book of Concord. *Concord* is a word that means "harmony."

What Is the Connection between the Bible and the Confessions?

Lutherans confess that the Word of God is and should remain the sole rule and norm of all doctrine. What the Bible asserts, God asserts. What the Bible commands, God commands. The authority of the Scriptures is complete, certain, and final. The Scriptures are accepted by the Lutheran Confessions as the actual Word of God. The Lutheran Confessions urge us to believe the Scriptures, for they will not lie to you and cannot be false and deceitful. The Bible is God's pure, infallible, and unalterable Word.

The Lutheran Confessions are the basis, rule, and norm indicating how all doctrines should be judged in conformity with the Word of God. Because the Confessions are in complete doctrinal agreement with the written Word of God, they serve as the standard in the Lutheran Church to determine what is faithful biblical teaching, insofar as that teaching is addressed in the Confessions.

What Is the Main Point of the Lutheran Confessions?

The Lutheran Reformation was not a revolt but rather began as a sincere expression of concern with the false and misleading teachings, which, unfortunately, even to this very day, obscure the glory and merit of Jesus Christ. What motivated Luther was a zealous concern about the Gospel of Jesus Christ. Here is how the Lutheran Confessions explain what the Gospel is all about:

A person has not kept God's Law, but has transgressed it when his corrupt nature, thoughts, words, and works fight against it. Therefore, he is under God's wrath, death, all temporal calamities, and the punishment of hellfire. The Gospel is properly a doctrine that teaches what a person should believe, so that he receives forgiveness of sins with God. In other words, it teaches that God's Son, our Lord Christ, has taken upon Himself and borne the Law's curse and has atoned and paid for all our sins. Through Him alone we again enter into favor with God, receive forgiveness of sins through faith and are delivered from death and all the punishments of sins, and are eternally saved. . . . It is a good and joyful message that God will not punish sins, but will forgive them for Christ's sake. (FC SD V 20, 21)

What Is a "Confessional" Lutheran?

The word *confession* is used in a variety of ways, but when we speak of a confessional Lutheran, we mean a Lutheran who declares to the world his or her faith and most deeply held belief and conviction in harmony with the documents contained in the Book of Concord. You will catch the spirit of confessional Lutheranism in these, the last words written in the Book of Concord:

> In the sight of God and of all Christendom <the entire Church of Christ>, we want to testify to those now living and those who will come after us. This declaration presented here about all the controverted articles mentioned and explained above—and no other—is our faith, doctrine, and confession. By God's grace, with intrepid hearts, we are willing to appear before the judgment seat of Christ with this Confession and give an account of it [1 Peter 4:5]. We will not speak or write anything contrary to this Confession, either publicly or privately. By the strength of God's grace we intend to abide by it. (FC SD XII 40)

What Is an Unconditional Subscription to the Confessions?

Confessional Lutheran pastors are required to subscribe unconditionally to the Lutheran Confessions because they are a pure exposition of the Word of God. This is the way our pastors and every layman who confesses his belief in the Small Catechism is able with great joy and without reservation or qualification to say what it is that he believes to be the truth of God's Word.

> An unconditional subscription is the solemn declaration which the individual who wants to serve the church makes under oath that he accepts the doctrinal content of our Lutheran Confessions, because he recognizes the fact that they are in full agreement with Scripture and do not militate against Scripture in any point, whether the point be of major or minor importance; and that he therefore heartily believes in this divine truth and is determined to preach this doctrine. (C. F. W. Walther)

So What Is It to Be a Lutheran?

Being a Lutheran is being a person who believes the truths of God's Word, the Holy Bible, as they are correctly explained and taught in the Book of Concord. To do so is to confess the Gospel of Jesus Christ. Genuine Lutherans, confessional Lutherans, dare to insist, "What is contrary to these confessions is to be rejected and condemned, as opposed to the unanimous declaration of our faith" (FC Ep 6).

Such a statement may strike some as boastful. But it is not; rather, it is an expression of the Spirit-led confidence that moves us to speak of our faith before the world.

To be a confessional Lutheran is to be one who honors the Word of God. That Word makes it clear that it is God's desire for His Church to be in agreement about doctrine and to be of one mind, living at peace with one another. It is for that reason that we so treasure the precious confession of Christian truth that we have in the Book of Concord. For confessional Lutherans, there is no other collection of documents or statements or books that so clearly, accurately, and comfortingly presents the teachings of God's Word and reveals the biblical Gospel as does our Book of Concord.

Hand in hand with our commitment to pure teaching and confession of the faith is, and always must be, our equally strong commitment to reaching out boldly with the Gospel and speaking God's truth to the world. That is what "confession" of the faith is all about. Indeed, "Since we have the same spirit of faith according to what has been written, 'I believed, and so I spoke,' we also believe, and so we also speak" (2 Corinthians 4:13). This is what it means to be a Lutheran.

CHAPTER 24

Lutheranism after Luther

In This Chapter

- Luther's death brought in a time of challenges to the rapidly growing Reformation in the Church.
- Following the devastation of the Thirty Years' War, many in Europe lost their zeal for things religious.
- After the American Revolution, a growing influx of Lutherans came to America.

TECHNICAL STUFF

Council of Trent: A council of the Roman Catholic Church that met in Trent in Northern Italy from 1545 to 1563. This council solidified Roman Catholic doctrine and rallied the Roman Catholic Church in what has been called both the Counter-Reformation and the Catholic Reformation. Many of the official Roman Catholic teachings to this day were actually set formally at the Council of Trent.

Divisions and Concord

In some ways, it is unfortunate that this whole theological movement became known by the name of one man: Martin Luther. Luther himself didn't want it that way and preferred that the church be called "Evangelical" or Gospel-centered. However, the name "Lutheran" stuck. All too often, because this movement is called Lutheranism, people think that it is all about Luther. Nothing could be further from the truth! Yes, Luther started the movement, but it has long survived and grown since his time. In fact, Lutheranism, in its many forms, is actually the fourth largest Christian tradition in the world!

This doesn't mean that there were not struggles in Lutheranism as it grew and expanded after Luther. By the time of his death on February 18, 1546, the Reformation had ballooned in many ways. In Switzerland, under Ulrich Zwingli, what became known as the Reformed movement had started. This was the movement that John Calvin later led. Also, the "Radical Reformation," which led to the Anabaptist movement, had also arisen. In 1533, Henry VIII of England had instituted the English Reformation, which allowed him his desired divorce, but soon was influenced first by Lutherans and later by Reformed thinkers. Further, the Lutheran Reformation had expanded into Denmark and Norway and would soon move into Sweden, Finland, Russia, and other parts of Europe.

The great outside challenge that arose at this time was that the Roman Catholic Church finally called a council to address the Reformation. It met in Trent from 1545–1563. (Obviously, it happened on and off during this time—people were not literally there for nineteen years straight.) This council responded to the Protestant Reformation by solidifying Roman Catholic doctrine and unifying the Roman Catholic Church against the Protestants.

Luther's death also brought in a time of challenges to the rapidly growing Reformation. The burning question, especially in the German lands of the Lutheran Reformation, was who would be the one to rise up and take the helm (unofficially) of the movement. The natural choice for this was Luther's close friend and supporter Philip Melanchthon. Melanchthon appeared to have a perfect résumé for this: a brilliant mind (academically even smarter than Luther); a close friend of Luther's; the author of the Augsburg Confession, the Apology to the Augsburg Confession, and the Treatise on the Power and Primacy of the Pope; and a highly respected professor at the University of Wittenberg. The problem was that for all of his academic brilliance, Melanchthon was not the strong leader the times demanded. In particular, when the leadership of the Roman Church rejected Luther and his insistence that the Gospel be central to the Church, this led to divisions within the Church, first between the Lutherans and the Roman Church, but then also between the Reformed and the Anabaptists. These divisions weighed heavily on Melanchthon's conscience.

To try to bring about more unity, Melanchthon proceeded to make changes to the Augsburg Confession. In particular, he tried to downplay the sections on the Lord's Supper, so that those who didn't take Jesus' words "this is My body" and "this is My blood" literally could now agree to the Confession. This, along with a few other controversies, led to splits within Lutheranism.

Just when it looked like the whole Lutheran Reformation would implode, a group of theologians led by Martin Chemnitz produced the Formula of Concord in order to bring resolution to the issues and theological unity back to Lutheranism. This was formally released in 1577, and then included with the rest of

TECHNICAL STUFF

Anabaptism: This is a term that literally means "rebaptism." This was a series of groups that arose during the Reformation that rejected the traditions of the Church, including infant Baptism, insisting on rebaptizing adults. The Mennonites of today are the direct descendants of this movement.

Unaltered Augsburg Confession: Look at the cornerstone or sign on many Lutheran churches and you will see the letters *U. A. C.* This is not some odd Latin phrase, but simply stands for "Unaltered Augsburg Confession," which is a simple way of stating that this church holds to the Augsburg Confession— the original one that was presented in Augsburg and not one of Melanchthon's later editions.

the Lutheran Confessions (including the Unaltered Augsburg Confession) in 1580 to form the Book of Concord.

The publishing of the Book of Concord in 1580 brought in a period of relative theological stability for Lutheranism in what has become known as the Age of Orthodoxy. This age stretched into the eighteenth century, though there is debate over the exact dating. During this period, the Lutheran theologians focused on systematizing Lutheran doctrine and establishing the proper theological understandings of various questions.

Unrest and Splintering

This does not mean that all was peaceful and quiet in the lands of Luther! Rather, from 1618–1648 the Thirty Years' War ravaged much of central Europe, especially the German lands of the Reformation. Some historians look on this as a war of religion, but this is only partly true. In fact, the Thirty Years' War was really a series of wars for power within Europe. While the start of the war(s) revolved around struggles between Protestant powers and Catholic ones, it devolved into simply fighting for political control of Europe. This was shown especially when heavily Roman Catholic France, whose Prime Minister was a Catholic cardinal, Cardinal Richelieu, joined the "Protestant" side of the war in 1635.

Following the devastation of the Thirty Years' War, many in Europe lost their zeal for things religious. This included a splintering in Lutheran theology. While the Age of Orthodoxy continued, the end of the Thirty Years' War was also the time of the rise of pietism under Philip Jacob Spener and others. The erosion of Christian morals in and after the war concerned Spener, and he emphasized pious living.

During this same time, another direction that Lutheran theology took was that of Rationalism. This was a movement related to the Enlightenment in philosophy, which emphasized the ability of the human mind to understand all things and an insistence that all should be in accord with human reason. This movement led to what has become known as theological liberalism, where miracles, divine inspiration of Scripture, and others things that we do not see and experience in our daily lives were rejected out of hand.

Coming to America

You might remember from history that this same time period (the eighteenth century) is also the time of the Industrial Revolution and the expansion of colonial America. While far from the majority, there were Lutherans who emigrated from Europe to America at this time. These Lutherans were in no way organized and tended to end up in various places around the English colonies. These people were generally without pastors, let alone any sort of church body to support them. Finally, the first Lutheran organization in America came about by the work of Henry Melchior Muhlenburg in Pennsylvania when he formed the Pennsylvania Ministerium in 1748. In fact, this was the closest thing to a Lutheran church body in all of colonial America.

NEED TO KNOW

Synod: Literally, in Greek, means "to come together" or to "walk together." This is one of the preferred terms by Lutherans to describe a church body or a portion of a church body that is formed of fellow Lutherans who have chosen to "walk together" or work together for their common mission.

Following the American Revolution, a growing influx of Lutherans came to America; however, they were far from organized or unified. Many of these immigrants slowly started to band together in bodies named for the state in which they lived. These included the New York Ministerium (1786), the North Carolina Synod (1803), the Evangelical Lutheran Synod of Maryland and Virginia (1820), the Tennessee Synod (1821), and, well, you get the picture.

Many of these ended up joining together in the cooperative General Synod that first formed in 1820. In the General Synod, the various local synods kept their autonomy, but they also worked together on a more national scale.

Back in the German lands, there still was no united Germany but a series of independent German kingdoms. Here pietism and rationalism took root and caused many Lutherans to downplay the differences between Lutheran teachings and other Protestant churches' teachings. This led the king of Prussia, Frederick Wilhelm III, a Calvinist married to a Lutheran, to declare that on the three hundredth anniversary of Luther's posting of the Ninety-five Theses (1817), the Calvinist and Lutheran churches in Prussia would be united to form what became known as the "Prussian Union."

While this technically only affected the kingdom of Prussia, orthodox Lutherans in the other German nations, such as Bavaria and Saxony, were concerned that similar orders would be given in their country as well. After all, Prussia was the largest and most influential of the German states. This fear, along with the desire for opportunities in the new world, led a number of conservative Lutherans to leave their various German lands for America.

NEED TO KNOW

Pietism: The movement within Lutheranism that started in the seventeenth century; emphasized personal piety over doctrinal correctness. This movement expected members to refrain from frivolous entertainment and focus purely on personal spiritual improvement. It saw biblical doctrine as less important than "a religion of the heart."

Rationalism: A philosophical movement that is often hostile to Christianity, especially the Bible's teachings about miracles and faith. Rationalists decide what is true on the basis of human reason rather than Holy Scripture.

One of these migrations, which was to have a large impact on much of American Lutheranism, took place when a group of Saxons set sail for America in November 1838 under the leadership of Martin Stephan. This group intended to create a Lutheran settlement in Missouri. While still on their ships after having crossed the Atlantic, they named Stephan bishop. This group of over five hundred landed in America and first settled briefly in St. Louis in early 1839. As settlement in this area was rejected by Stephan, plans were made for the whole group to move to Perry County, Missouri. When some, under Stephan's leadership, went down to Perry County, some women from the group still in St. Louis confessed to having illicit relations with Stephan. Shortly thereafter, the group deposed Stephan for sexual and fiscal misconduct, and false doctrine.

For over a year and a half, the Missouri Saxons in Perry County suffered doubt about their emigration and debated the question of whether they were even a church. During this time, they faced hunger, sickness, and death. Ultimately, at a debate at Altenburg, Missouri, in April 1841, C. F. W. Walther emerged as the new theological leader among the Missouri Saxon pastors and congregations.

Under Walther's leadership, the group began to reach out to other Lutherans in America. These efforts led to the creation of the *Die Deutsche Evangelisch-Lutherische Synode von Missouri, Ohio und anderen Staaten* (German Evangelical Lutheran Synod of Missouri, Ohio, and Other States).

Confessional Revival

During this same period, many of the Lutherans of the General Synod, who had been in America for a couple of generations, were reconsidering their connection to their confessional roots. There was a renewal of confessional interest but in a couple of different directions. On the one extreme was Samuel Simon Schmucker, who in 1855 put forth the idea of rewriting the Augsburg Confession to make it more palatable for those Americans who were closely tied to the Puritan tradition. Others responded against this and argued that the Lutheran Confessions were an important portion of their theological heritage. On the opposite extreme of Schmucker was Walther, who argued that the Lutheran Confessions are a right exposition of the Bible and should be held to because of this.

As the nineteenth century drew to a close, the Lutheran churches in America experienced a time of incredible growth. A large number of immigrants from Germany poured into America and were in need of churches. In particular, the Lutheran bodies that had been formed by recent immigrants grew quickly at this time, as they spoke the same language as these new arrivals and shared closer ties with their culture.

CHAPTER 25

Changes and Challenges to Lutheranism

In This Chapter

- As late as the 1930s, Lutherans in America were printing periodicals for their members in not only German, but also Slovak, Danish, Norwegian, and Finnish.
- In the twentieth century, a new movement toward unity in the American Lutheran churches developed.
- The biggest theological issue that plagued and divided many American Lutherans throughout the twentieth century was the issue of theological liberalism and biblical inerrancy.

Continued Growth from the Outside

The twentieth century carried its share of upheavals, struggles, and great changes. This is also true of American Lutheranism in the last century. However, in the nineteenth century, Lutheranism in America initially saw relatively little change. The era of tremendous growth due to immigration continued apace. The one change was a small shift in where the immigrants hailed from, as there was a slight drop-off in the number of immigrants from Germany; however, this was offset by a growing number of immigrants from other largely Lutheran lands. These included many from Scandinavia as well as an influx of Lutherans from Russia. Therefore, the Lutheran churches in America continued to grow in both numbers and optimism with this constant influx of Lutheran immigrants from Europe.

This is not to say that all was equal amongst the various Lutheran bodies in America. Rather, these growth trends illustrated some of the historic differences between the Lutheran synods in America. The Missouri Synod, a church built on recent immigration, continued to lead the growth as they reached out to their fellow immigrants. On the other end of the spectrum was the General Synod, with its long history in America and predominance of English, which showed the smallest growth with new immigrants.

Americanization and the Use of English

At the start of the twentieth century, a full 80 percent of Lutherans in America were speaking one of almost thirty different non-English native languages! For some of the churches, this came not only from immigrants but also from the education of the next generation. The Missouri Synod led the way, as it had many German schools that preserved this language in the children and grand-children of immigrants. In many ways these Lutherans had simply transplanted their home culture to their new life in America, rather than becoming mainstream Americans.

However, the first decade of the twentieth century also saw the start of great change in the form of a new movement toward the use of English in many American Lutheran church bodies. Even the Missouri Synod, which was so heavily invested in its German heritage, voted in 1911 to allow the "English Evangelical Lutheran Synod of Missouri and Other States" to join the Missouri Synod as a nongeographical, English-language district. As Lutherans are typically reluctant to change, it should be noted that the transition to English for these immigrant churches tended to be slow, and as late as the 1930s, Lutherans in America were still printing periodicals for their members in not only German, but also in Slovak, Danish, Norwegian, and Finnish.

The main factor that eventually forced the dropping of the German language was World War I. Suddenly, it became very unpopular to sound too German, and many German-Americans downplayed their German heritage, including many Lutherans. It went so far that several states attempted to outlaw German-language schools, a movement that ended with the Missouri Synod suing the State of Nebraska and winning the right at the U.S. Supreme Court to have German-language schools. However, by then the move to English was very well underway in American Lutheranism.

Another change that came over Lutheranism in America in the twentieth century was a sudden growth in foreign mission efforts. Prior to this, most of the missionary efforts of American Lutherans were focused on immigrants to America, with a few missions to Native Americans and freed slaves after the Civil War. In the twentieth century, American Lutherans awoke to needs elsewhere and became more focused on the mission fields in areas such as India, Africa, and South America.

The Movement toward Unity

One of the great shifts in American Lutheranism in the twentieth century was a new movement toward unity in the American Lutheran churches. As the nineteenth century saw the development of countless Lutheran synods, in the twentieth century there was much more done to unite these groups.

The Missouri Synod, with its characteristic theological conservatism, continued to emphasize full unity only in complete doctrinal agreement. As a result, it worked slowly through the Synodical Conference, along with the Wisconsin Synod and some smaller bodies, to try to find doctrinal agreement with other Lutherans. This was a process that included more talking than anything else, but whenever unity was reached, it was a very strong, organic unity.

The first group to overcome great differences to reach unity was the Norwegians. In 1917, the Hague Synod, the Norwegian Synod, and the United Norwegian Lutheran Church of America all united to form the Norwegian Lutheran Church of America, which was later called the Evangelical Lutheran Church. Following this, the more Americanized and more Eastern Lutherans in the General Synod and the General Council united to form the United Lutheran Church in America. A little later, in 1930, the Buffalo Synod, the Iowa Synod, and the Ohio Synod united to form the American Lutheran Church.

World War II and Renewed Growth and Unity

The rising specter of Nazism and the subsequent Second World War led to some challenges to Lutherans in America, but far less than the First World War had done. There is a common misconception that the German Lutherans in America were largely Nazis. This is simply not true. There were a few Nazi supporters within American Lutheranism, but they were a tiny minority. Some of the German Lutherans early on hoped that Hitler would help their fatherland out of its terrible depression, but soon this hope was lost. Rather, the overwhelming sentiment was that something had gone terribly wrong, and there was also a great dismay at the destruction that was brought to the birthplace of Lutheranism.

Following the Second World War, in general, American churches grew at a tremendous pace in the 1950s. Lutheranism was no exception in this area. This can best be illustrated with the Missouri Synod, which at its peak growth was opening on average a new congregation every fifty-four hours! This was a time of great optimism throughout the country and all of Christendom, but it was not to last.

When we think of the changes and challenges that arose in twentieth-century America, one of the most prominent periods was the 1960s, along with all of the social turbulence. This time also brought about changes within American Lutheranism, albeit of a different stripe. While much of the country was facing disunity over Vietnam and social issues, the Lutherans experienced a new surge of unity. Starting in 1960, the American Lutheran Church, the Evangelical Lutheran Church, and the United Evangelical Lutheran Church merged to form The American Lutheran Church (notice that the new body has "The" capitalized to differentiate it from the previous American Lutheran Church). This was followed in 1962 by the formation of the Lutheran Church in America, bringing together the American Evangelical Lutheran Church, the Augustana Lutheran Church, the Suomi Synod, and the United Lutheran Church in America. This trend toward unity was completed in 1987 when these two bodies, along with a couple of smaller ones, merged to form the Evangelical Lutheran Church in America (ELCA). To give you an idea about just how many Lutheran bodies merged in the twentieth century, what started out as forty-eight independent church bodies in 1900 now constituted one—the ELCA.

The Theological Divide

However, in a different way, the twentieth century was also a time of disunity. The biggest theological issue that plagued and divided many American Lutherans throughout the twentieth century was the issue of theological liberalism and biblical inerrancy. The mainline churches generally view the Bible as inspired by God but historically conditioned and imperfect. On the other side of the debate are those, like confessional Lutherans, who regard the Bible to be incapable of error (infallible) and free from error (inerrant), because the very words and phrases of Scripture were inspired by God the Holy Spirit. Consequently, the Word of God does not lie or deceive. American Lutherans were divided over this issue, due to differences between liberal Lutheran churches and the more conservative Lutheran churches.

On one hand, many of the more conservative Lutherans, such as the Missouri and Wisconsin synods, remained committed to the historic position of Lutheranism about the Bible's reliability and truthfulness. Others, such as the United Lutheran Church in America, were more open to new interpretive methods such as historical criticism, while trying to maintain a Lutheran emphasis on the Gospel.

NEED TO KNOW

The Bible is the "Holy Scripture" because God the Holy Spirit gave to His chosen writers the thoughts that they expressed and the words that they wrote (verbal inspiration). Because God's Spirit worked through the writers of Scripture, it is God's infallible Word and is completely reliable. Therefore, the Bible is God's own Word and truth, without error (inerrancy).

NEED TO KNOW

Historical criticism: An approach to studying the Bible in which the Bible is treated as any other historical document. This includes the assumptions that the Bible is historically conditioned, that it has been adapted over time, and that miracles and other extreme supernatural portions are suspect.

Following the Second World War, there was even within the Missouri Synod a growing fascination with German theological insights, including historical criticism. This led a number of the new faculty members of the Missouri Synod's largest seminary, Concordia Seminary in St. Louis, to adopt historical criticism. This led to a grassroots and political backlash in the early 1970s. Ultimately, the majority of the faculty walked out in 1974 in protest of what they saw as a lack of trust and limits to their intellectual freedom. Much to the surprise of the protesting faculty, the leadership of the Missouri Synod did not ask them to come back, and many of this side, both in the seminary and in the greater church membership, left the Missouri Synod and eventually joined the ELCA.

As the twenty-first century began, the ELCA continued on its path of seeking unity with other Christians through a number of means. It is very active with the ecumenical movement and the Lutheran World Federation. The ELCA also reached out to other Christians through agreements of fellowship with the United Church of Christ, the United Methodist Church, the Presbyterian Church (U.S.A.), the Protestant Episcopal Church, and other church bodies. Meanwhile, the smaller Lutheran bodies in America, including the Missouri Synod, the Wisconsin Synod, and the Evangelical Lutheran Synod have continued to stress full theological agreement as necessary for unity.

Lutheran Church Bodies in the United States

EVANGELICAL LUTHERAN CHURCH IN AMERICA (ELCA)

Congregations: 10,396
Member of Lutheran World Federation
Headquarters: 8765 W. Higgins Road, Chicago, IL 60631
www.elca.org
Publishing Company: Augsburg Fortress
www.augsburgfortress.org
Seminaries and Extension Centers:

Luther Seminary (St. Paul, MN)
www.luthersem.edu

Lutheran School of Theology at Chicago (Chicago, IL)
www.lstc.edu

Lutheran Seminary Program in the Southwest (Austin, TX)
www.lsps.edu

Lutheran Theological Center in Atlanta (Atlanta, GA)
www.itc.edu

Lutheran Theological Seminary at Gettysburg (Gettysburg, PA)
www.ltsg.edu

Lutheran Theological Seminary at Philadelphia (Philadelphia, PA)
www.ltsp.edu

Lutheran Theological Southern Seminary (Columbia, SC)
www.ltss.edu

Pacific Lutheran Theological Seminary (Berkeley, CA)
www.plts.edu

Trinity Lutheran Seminary (Columbus, OH)
www.trinitylutheranseminary.edu

Wartburg Theological Seminary (Dubuque, IA)
www.wartburgseminary.edu

THE LUTHERAN CHURCH— MISSOURI SYNOD (LCMS)

Congregations: 6,123
Member of International Lutheran Council
Headquarters: 1333 S. Kirkwood Rd., St Louis, MO 63122
www.lcms.org
Publishing Company: Concordia Publishing House
www.cph.org
Seminaries:

Concordia Seminary (St. Louis, MO)
www.csl.edu

Concordia Theological Seminary (Fort Wayne, IN)
www.ctsfw.edu

WISCONSIN EVANGELICAL LUTHERAN SYNOD (WELS)

Congregations: 1,290

Member of Confessional Evangelical Lutheran Conference

Headquarters: 2929 N Mayfair Road, Milwaukee, WI 53222

www.wels.net

Publishing Company: Northwestern Publishing House

www.nph.net

Seminary: Wisconsin Lutheran Seminary (Mequon, WI)

www.wls.wels.net

ASSOCIATION OF FREE LUTHERAN CHURCHES

Congregations: 270

Headquarters: 3110 E Medicine Lake Blvd., Plymouth, MN 55441

www.aflc.org

Seminary: Association Free Lutheran Theological Seminary (Plymouth, MN)

www.aflts.org

EVANGELICAL LUTHERAN SYNOD

Congregations: 140

Member of Confessional Evangelical Lutheran Conference

Headquarters: 6 Browns Court, Mankato, MN 56001

www.evangelicallutheransynod.org

Publishing Company: Ambassador Publications

www.aflc.org/publications/

Seminary: Bethany Lutheran Theological Seminary (Mankato, MN)

www.blts.edu

CHURCH OF THE LUTHERAN CONFESSION

Congregations: 92

Headquarters: 501 Grover Road, Eau Claire, WI 54701

www.clclutheran.org

Publishing Company: CLC Bookhouse

www.clcbookhouse.org

Seminary: Immanuel Lutheran High School, College, and Seminary (Eau Claire, WI)

www.ilc.edu

AMERICAN ASSOCIATION OF LUTHERAN CHURCHES (AALC)

Congregations: 78

Member of International Lutheran Council

Headquarters: 6600 N. Clinton Street, Augustine Hall, #13, Fort Wayne, Indiana 46825

Mail Address: The AALC, 921 East Dupont Rd., #920, Fort Wayne, IN 46825-1551

www.taalc.org

Seminary: American Lutheran Theological Seminary in Fort Wayne, IN

alts.edu

There are also several smaller Lutheran groups and independent Lutheran congregations in the United States.

CHAPTER 26

No Lazy Bellies Allowed!

In This Chapter

- It was education that started the revolution in Christianity that is now referred to as the Reformation.
- To make teaching God's Word easier, Martin Luther wrote the Small Catechism.
- When Lutherans came to the New World, they brought with them a passion for education of the young, including religious instruction.

Education of the masses is something quite modern. During medieval times, education was reserved for those who could afford it, usually the nobility and those in the Church—priests, monks and nuns. During the Renaissance (fourteenth to seventeenth centuries), education again became something that was valued and promoted. Universities began to be established across Europe. And it was the invention of the mechanical printing press by German goldsmith Johannes Gutenberg that made it possible for new ideas to be shared and studied not only in schools but, eventually, even by the average person.

The printing press also brought new scholarship and ideas in the Church. Before the 1500s, hand-copied Bibles were rare, expensive, and generally unavailable to most people; many priests had never read from one. Without access to the Scriptures, folks simply believed what they had been taught. The Church taught that how you lived mattered the most because it was your good works that earned your entry into heaven. As a result, following the rules set by the Church became very important. Now with Bibles being printed and more available in languages other than Latin, people were able to study, teach, and preach from the Scriptures themselves.

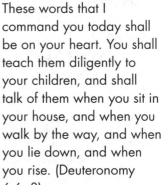

FROM THE BIBLE

These words that I command you today shall be on your heart. You shall teach them diligently to your children, and shall talk of them when you sit in your house, and when you walk by the way, and when you lie down, and when you rise. (Deuteronomy 6:6–8)

NEED TO KNOW

Grace is the unearned and undeserved gift of forgiveness and eternal life received by faith and given to all who believe. Ephesians 2:8–9 shows us that this gift is free to those who receive it but was purchased at great cost by Jesus' life, death on the cross, and resurrection.

By 1517, after many years of teaching classes in biblical studies, Dr. Martin Luther noticed that Scripture did not exactly support the teaching of good works earning salvation. He became convinced that God's love and forgiveness is a free gift received through faith, not something earned by works (Ephesians 2:8–10). Scripture calls this gift "grace."

Luther's education convinced him that the Church's teachings were not always following Scripture's teachings. It was education that started the revolution in Christianity that is now referred to as the Reformation. Luther's scholarly objection to some of the Church's teachings began what is now known as Lutheranism.

"Lazy Bellies"

In Luther's day, schooling was expensive and not available to most people. For them, teaching happened in the church and in the home. Luther turned to the family as the place where basic religious education should take place. To make teaching God's Word easier, Luther wrote the Small Catechism as a summary of the basic teachings of Scripture and as a tool for the head of the household to "teach it in the simplest way to his household," saying, "Catechism study is a most effective help against the devil, the world, the flesh, and all evil thoughts. It helps to be occupied with God's Word, to speak it, and meditate on it" (LC Preface 10).

Luther also wrote a catechism for pastors so that they could faithfully preach and teach these basic teachings from God's Word. And when some pastors would not even teach the catechism to their people, he called them out as a bunch of "lazy bellies" or "arrogant saints."

Establishing Schools

When Lutherans came to the New World, they brought with them a passion for education of the young, including religious instruction. Henry Muhlenberg, a Lutheran pastor from Germany, helped to establish a "charity school" in

Pennsylvania and St. Matthew Lutheran School in New York City in 1752.

In the 1830s, a new wave of Lutheran immigration began. Lutherans coming to the Midwest from Saxony in Germany placed an even greater emphasis on education than had been seen among the Lutheran congregations in the East. In fact, when the Saxon Lutherans began founding congregations, one of the fundamental goals was that each congregation would establish and support a parochial school.

Today

Lutherans continue to value and promote education. The family is still seen as the first and primary place where faith is taught and nurtured. Each day Lutheran schools support families in the task of teaching and nurturing faith in their children, as the school becomes a workshop of Christian love. In this schools, children experience God's love and forgiveness, even as they learn math, history, language, arts, and science.

The largest Protestant single denomination school system in the United States is run by the The Lutheran Church—Missouri Synod. The congregations of the LCMS operate 1,406 elementary schools, 976 early childhood centers, and 103 high schools, enrolling more than 270,000 children. The two

WHAT DOES THIS MEAN?

This sermon is designed and undertaken to be an instruction for children and the simple folk. Therefore, in ancient times it was called in Greek *catechism* (i.e., instruction for children). It teaches what every Christian must know. So a person who does not know this catechism could not be counted as a Christian or be admitted to any Sacrament, just as a mechanic who does not understand the rules and customs of his trade is expelled and considered incapable. (LC Short Preface 1–2)

WHAT DOES THIS MEAN?

Martin Luther used the term "lazy bellies" to refer to those who regarded "the catechism as a poor, common teaching, which they can read through once and immediately understand" (LC Preface 5). He added: "Therefore, for God's sake I beg such lazy bellies or arrogant saints to be persuaded and believe that they are truly, truly not so learned or such great doctors as they imagine!" He noted: "Even if they know and understand the catechism perfectly (which, however, is impossible in this life), there are still many benefits and fruits to be gained, if it is daily read and practiced in thought and speech" (LC Preface 9).

WHAT DOES THIS MEAN?

Whenever God's Word is taught, preached, heard, read, or meditated upon, then the person, day, and work are sanctified. This is not because of the outward work, but because of the Word, which makes saints of us all. Therefore, I constantly say that all our life and work must be guided by God's Word, if it is to be God-pleasing or holy. (LC 1 92)

seminaries and ten schools of the Concordia University system offer training and degrees across all of the arts and sciences, as well as preparing qualified educators and pastors for its schools and churches.

Top Ten List of Luther's Writings

10. **On the Councils and the Church** (1539) Did Luther start a "new" church? This work first explains the great ancient councils of the Christian Church and then shows ways in which we can recognize where the true Church of Christ can be found today.

9. **Genesis** (1535–45) Luther spent his last years lecturing to students on Genesis. This work shows God the Holy Trinity at work in the Old Testament to teach and save His people.

8. **Confession concerning Christ's Supper** (1528) Luther's disagreement with Ulrich Zwingli on the Lord's Supper was crucially important. Luther holds to the literal understanding of Jesus' words in the Supper and concludes with his own statement of faith.

7. **Galatians** (1535) "The Epistle to the Galatians," Luther said, "is my epistle, to which I am betrothed." Here is Luther's teaching of salvation in all its clarity and beauty.

6. **Bondage of the Will** (1525) Sinful human beings are not free to choose between God or the devil, good or evil, salvation or damnation. Luther shows that, instead, God chose us Christians.

5. **Freedom of a Christian** (1520) This early work helped clarify Luther's theology: a Christian is totally free from sin through faith in Christ but must also serve his or her neighbor in love.

4. **Church Postil** and **House Postil**. After Luther's catechisms, his sermons have been his most popular writings through the centuries. These sermons follow the life of Christ through the Church Year and provide a wealth of Christian teaching.

3. **Smalcald Articles** (1537) Luther prepared this statement of faith for a council announced by Pope Paul III in 1536, a council that did not actually take place until after Luther's death. With the two catechisms, this writing was included in the Book of Concord (see p. 186) and is a standard for Lutheran teaching and practice.

2. **Large Catechism** (1529) Based on sermons in 1529, this book explains the Ten Commandments, Creed, Lord's Prayer, Baptism, and the Sacrament of the Altar in a conversational style.

1. **Small Catechism** (1529) After visiting the churches in Saxony, Luther was convinced that people needed a short manual on the basics of Christianity. The Small Catechism has been Luther's most popular and important work ever since.

PART FIVE

What you'll learn about:

- The Divine Service is the chief worship service among Lutherans.

- The Christian Church Year is used to not only mark time but also to set the story of Jesus in an orderly pattern for teaching.

- The sign of the cross is given to each of us in our Baptism and is used by Lutherans as a token of our salvation.

Worship: The Blessings of God

People often think that worship is about what we do for or toward God. The reality is quite different. In the Divine Service, God comes to us and provides His service for us. The work we do in worship is to receive the gift of God's grace and respond.

CHAPTER 27

Finding Meaning in the Words

In This Chapter

- The words and ways of Lutheran worship stretch back to the very beginning of the Old Testament and its prophecies.
- Nothing in the worship service—not the candles, not the flowers, not the music, not the prayers, not the praise—makes us worthy of anything before God.
- God initiates a holy conversation: He speaks first. Only then do His people respond.

You walk into the examination room of an orthopedic surgeon. A quick knock on the door, and in walks the doctor. "What seems to be the problem?" he asks as he pulls up the round stool-on-wheels.

As you point to the aching spot, you begin, "Well, you see, I have this pain in my"—

"Ulna," he says.

"Um, yeah, my arm, and the pain seems to be reaching down into my wr"—

"Articulatio radiocarpea?"

"Sure, Doc, whatever. Say, can we just use simple words?"

When attending a Lutheran worship service, you may have a similar feeling of confusion. As you look at a page in the hymnal, puzzling words and headings appear. There are simple words used in the Divine Service, and there are technical words. Most words used are of Latin origin, but there are a couple of Greek and Hebrew words. These words themselves reflect the history of Lutheran worship, which is primarily from the Western Christian Church, that is, historically, the Latin-speaking church of Europe and North Africa, but not exclusively so. The Greek and Hebrew words tie us to the ancient Mediterranean and Middle Eastern Christians. Don't let these words scare you. Short definitions will be given along the way.

These unusual words help us realize that in the Divine Service we are standing in the steady stream of history that has come to us now. The words and ways of Lutheran worship stretch back to the very beginning of the Old Testament and its prophecies. That same worship finds its full meaning and expression in the death and resurrection of Christ Jesus as handed down to us in the New Testament.

The Christ-centered focus of the Divine Service used by Lutherans is the result of the reforming work of Martin Luther, who removed the unbiblical barnacles that had attached themselves through the centuries and that hid the grace and forgiveness of Jesus. At the very heart of the Divine Service is the Lord Jesus, the Son of God, the Savior of the world. Jesus has fulfilled His promises to free us from sin and to forgive us. In response we sing to Him, petition Him, and give eternal thanks to Him. As Jesus says of Himself, "The Son of Man came not to be served but to serve, and to give His life as a ransom for many" (Matthew 20:28).

What Is Worship and the Divine Service?

The Athanasian Creed teaches us that true Christian worship can be recognized in two ways. First, we worship the triune God, that is, the Father, the Son, and the Holy Spirit. The second way we recognize Christian worship is that it is centered on Jesus Christ, the only-begotten Son of God. Our worship is "divine" because it is Christ centered.

The Lutheran Confessions teach us about the "service" of Divine Service: "The worship and divine service of the Gospel is to receive gifts from God" (Ap V 189). In the Divine Service, God, who calls, gathers, and enlightens the whole Christian Church on earth, comes with His gracious gifts to serve us.

Though the Divine Service may simply be called a "worship" service, these words *Divine Service* say much about the focus of the worship service and what happens. This most important worship service for Lutherans is "divine" in that it finds its source and origin in the triune God Himself: Father, Son, and Holy Spirit.

> **FROM THE BIBLE**
>
> Therefore let us be grateful for receiving a kingdom that cannot be shaken, and thus let us offer to God acceptable worship, with reverence and awe, for our God is a consuming fire. (Hebrews 12:28–29)

This worship service is also "service" in that Christ Jesus serves us His Word and His Supper. Only then through the working of the Holy Spirit do we serve Him in prayer and praise and serve our neighbor through offerings and acts of love.

Worship can be a troublesome word. Who begins the act of worship? What or whom is being worshiped? It is at this point where we can become confused and begin to think that God has come to be entertained by us, that somehow what we say and do in the worship service makes us more worthy of God's free gift of love. Nothing in the worship service—not the candles, not the flowers, not the music, not the prayers, not the praise—makes us worthy of anything before God. We do not appease God's wrath, nor do we earn His forgiveness by anything we do. Rather, it is "Jesus who delivers us from the wrath to come" (1 Thessalonians 1:10).

In the Divine Service, God provides His service for us. In the reading, the preaching, and the proclamation of His Word, in His Sacraments of Holy Baptism and Holy Communion, God comes to us. The work we do in worship is to receive the gift of God's grace and respond.

> Our Lord speaks and we listen. His Word bestows what it says. Faith that is born from what is heard acknowledges the gifts received with eager thankfulness and praise. Music is drawn into this thankfulness and praise, enlarging and elevating the adoration of our gracious giver God. Saying back to him what he has said to us, we repeat what is most true and sure. (LW, p. 6)

The key to understanding the way Lutherans worship is realizing that God initiates a holy conversation: He speaks first. Only then do His people respond, not the other way around. Such is the way God has worked from the very beginning of creation (Genesis 1:3). God speaks into nothingness, emptiness—and then there is something to talk about!

Because of our sin, we cannot come to God; God must come to us. This is what takes place in the Divine Service. Through the Word and Sacraments, God speaks to His people. He reminds us of our sinfulness and failure to love completely, and He then forgives us and assures us of the grace we have in Jesus Christ.

If worship begins with you or me, honestly it is going to be terrible worship: self-centered, egotistical, one huge "me-fest." That may sound appealing, but in the long haul of life, such worship is boring, gasps for air, and is ultimately a dead end. We need something outside of us, and God supplies that very need in the Divine Service.

The Divine Service Tells the Story of Salvation

The structure of the Divine Service is the story of God's work of salvation—the essence of the Bible itself. In the Divine Service, God invites us to take part in that story, to be immersed in it and find our place at the table. As we take part regularly, this story becomes our story. The **Gloria** begins at the beginning—the Christmas announcement of the angels—but in the process makes of us messengers bringing the news of peace on earth, reminds us that the God we worship has come in the flesh, and points forward to the Lord's Supper that will come later. The **Kyrie** joins us to those lepers, the blind, the deaf, the sick, and all those who call upon the Lord for mercy and gives us the hope that as they graciously received it, so will we as we meet Christ in this service. The **Readings** place us within the biblical narrative at a specific time and place to hear the Word alongside its original hearers, both believers and doubters, the obedient and the disobedient. The **Agnus Dei** puts us alongside John the Baptizer and once again enables us to ask for mercy. The **Sanctus** reminds us that the Christ who is acclaimed with the Palm Sunday crowd is none other than the Messiah whom Isaiah saw high and lifted up, the one we will meet in the flesh momentarily. The **Words of Institution** are the purest narrative, explaining, interpreting, and offering what we have asked for all along—Kyrie eleison, Lord have mercy. The **Nunc Dimittis** brings the worshiper full circle to where it all began and makes of us Simeons who have held the Lord in our hands and have thus seen the promise fulfilled. We are ready to go in peace.

MAKING CONNECTIONS

Our Lord is the Lord who serves. Jesus Christ came into the flesh not to be served, but to serve and to give His life as a ransom for many. On the cross He offered Himself as a spotless sacrifice for the sin of the whole world. . . .

Our Lord serves us today through His holy Word and Sacraments. Through these means, He comes among us to deliver His forgiveness and salvation, freeing us from our sins and strengthening us for service to one another and to the world. . .

Having been called, gathered, enlightened, and sanctified by the Holy Spirit, we receive His gifts with thankfulness and praise. With psalms, hymns, and spiritual songs, we joyfully confess all that God has done for us, declaring the praises of Him who called us out of darkness into His marvelous light. (*LSB*, p. viii)

Sacraments and Rites

TECHNICAL STUFF

Rubric: Rubrics are the directions for leading worship—such things as determining who sings or says what at a specific point of the service, when the congregation stands or kneels, or what kind of procession may be conducted. The word *rubric* means "red." Traditionally rubrics are printed in red ink.

WHAT DOES THIS MEAN?

It seems proper that those rites be called Sacrament which contain promises with signs attached to them. The remainder, not connected to signs, are only promises. Hence it follows that there are, strictly speaking, only two Sacraments in the Church of God: Baptism and the Bread; for in these alone we note both the divinely instituted sign and the promise of the forgiveness of sins. For the sacrament of repentance, which I added to these two, lacks a visible and divinely instituted sign, and I have said that it is really nothing else than a return to Baptism. (*What Luther Says*, 3933)

Rite: a prepared order to aid the leader in conducting the ceremony for solemn or religious acts.

Sacrament: a sacred act
- instituted by God
- in which God Himself has joined His Word of promise to a visible element (water, bread, wine)
- and by which He offers and gives the forgiveness of sins earned by Christ.

One of the main differences among denominations is their beliefs about sacraments and rites. These disagreements about which rites are also sacraments hinges on whether a person believes a certain rite is also a "Means of Grace." Lutherans believe that Holy Baptism and the Lord's Supper meet the requirements to be called Sacraments. (See also Part 3.)

Sacraments in the Lutheran Church

Holy Baptism: Lutherans baptize infants because we recognize that God chooses us before we ever even think about choosing Him. Those who have not been baptized as young children go through classes to learn the basics of Christianity before being baptized. While most Lutheran Baptisms involve water being sprinkled or poured on the person's head, any amount of water, including full immersion, is considered acceptable.

Lord's Supper: Also known as Holy Communion, Eucharist, the Sacrament of the Altar. Jesus instituted this Supper the night before He was crucified (Luke 22:19–20). When we receive the Lord's Supper, Jesus is present "in, with and under" the visible elements of the bread and wine. He is right there personally with each person.

Common Rites among Lutherans

Confession and Absolution: Lutheran services include a time of Confession, when we admit to God that we have sinned, and Absolution, when the pastor announces God's forgiveness of our sins.

Confirmation: For people who were baptized as young children, confirmation provides an opportunity to study what we believe, publicly declare our faith in Jesus, and to promise lifelong faith in Him. Because it is important for people to have instruction before they receive Holy Communion for the first time, most congregations find it convenient for people to receive Holy Communion after they are confirmed.

Holy Matrimony: Holy Matrimony provides a context of praise, Scripture, and prayers within which the Church, through her pastors, gives the heavenly Father's blessing to the willing consent and solemn promises of a man and a woman. Lutherans do not categorize it as a sacrament because it does not include a Means of Grace.

Ordination/Commissioning: When a man has completed his training to become a pastor, and has been called by a congregation to serve in the Office of the Holy Ministry, he goes through a rite called ordination to officially become a pastor. Lay professional church workers, such as deaconesses, directors of Christian education, and Lutheran school teachers go through a rite called commissioning.

Funeral: The several rites associated in Lutheran burial of the dead provide a time to remember that "all who believe and are baptized will be saved."

MAKING CONNECTIONS

One way to remember the meaning of the word *grace* is

G od's
R iches
A t
C hrist's
E xpense

Grace is the forgiveness God gives us even though we are all sinful. Jesus took the fair punishment for our sins so that we could be forgiven by God.

"For by grace you have been saved through faith. And this is not your own doing; it is the gift of God, not a result of works, so that no one may boast." (Ephesians 2:8–9)

Prayers for Worship

On entering a church

Lord, I love the habitation of Your house and the place where Your glory dwells. In the multitude of Your tender mercies prepare my heart that I may enter Your house to worship and confess Your holy name; through Jesus Christ, my God and Lord. Amen.

Before worship

O Lord, my creator, redeemer, and comforter, as I come to worship You in spirit and in truth, I humbly pray that You would open my heart to the preaching of Your Word so that I may repent of my sins, believe in Jesus Christ as my only Savior, and grow in grace and holiness. Hear me for the sake of His name. Amen.

After worship

Almighty and merciful God, I have again worshiped in Your presence and received both forgiveness for my many sins and the assurance of Your love in Jesus Christ. I thank You for this undeserved grace and ask You to keep me in faith until, with all Your saints, I inherit eternal salvation; through Jesus Christ, my Lord. Amen.

Before communing

Dear Savior, at Your gracious invitation I come to Your table to eat and drink Your holy body and blood. Let me find favor in Your eyes to receive this holy Sacrament in faith for the salvation of my soul and to the glory of Your holy name; for You live and reign with the Father and the Holy Spirit, one God, now and forever. Amen.

Thanksgiving after receiving the Sacrament

Almighty and everlasting God, I thank and praise You for feeding me the life-giving body and blood of Your beloved Son, Jesus Christ. Send Your Holy Spirit that, having with my mouth received the holy Sacrament, I may by faith obtain and eternally enjoy Your divine grace, the forgiveness of sins, unity with Christ, and life eternal; through Jesus Christ, my Lord. Amen.

For blessing on the Word

Lord God, bless Your Word wherever it is proclaimed. Make it a word of power and peace to convert those not yet Your own and to confirm those who have come to saving faith. May Your Word pass from the ear to the heart, from the heart to the lip, and from the lip to the life that, as You have promised, Your Word may achieve the purpose for which You send it; through Jesus Christ, my Lord. Amen.

CHAPTER 28

Order in the *Order*

In This Chapter

- The order of worship is based exclusively on Scripture and is focused completely on Jesus Christ.
- Through the Word and Sacraments, God speaks to His people.
- We choose hymns that are doctrinally sound and theologically significant.

The Divine Service is the chief worship service in the Lutheran Church. The order of worship is basically the same in all orthodox Lutheran hymnals. This order of service is not unique to Lutherans. We did not invent it. It is the ancient form of worship that has been developed among Christians the world over from the very beginning of the New Testament era. It is based exclusively on Scripture and is focused completely on Jesus Christ and His saving grace on the cross of Calvary.

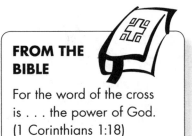

FROM THE BIBLE

For the word of the cross is . . . the power of God. (1 Corinthians 1:18)

Because of our sin, we cannot come to God, but God must come to us. This is what takes place in the Divine Service. Through the Word and Sacraments, God speaks to His people. He reminds us of our sinfulness and failure to love completely and He then forgives us and assures us of the grace we have in Jesus Christ.

This grace is central to our lives as Christians, and we must treat it with all reverence and respect. It was not of our doing, and it is not ours to tamper with. Therefore, worship is not a matter of novelty or entertainment, much less a matter of attempting to please the masses. For this reason we choose hymns that are doctrinally sound and theologically significant to round out our worship. Hymns, like the Divine Service, must reflect this Christocentric "God coming to man" theology or else they are unfit for the service. May our worship always be pure and always emphasize this biblical Christocentric attitude. The rest of this chapter explains the different parts of the Divine Service so you can feel a little more comfortable during worship by understanding what is happening.

The Preparation

INVOCATION

Since Lutherans are trinitarian, we call upon the triune God to bless our time together in worship. The trinitarian Invocation also recalls our Baptism. We call on the Father, Son, and Holy Spirit, in whose name we were baptized. "For through Him we both have access in one Spirit to the Father" (Ephesians 2:18).

We do not come before God on our merits or by our deeds. We come because He has called us by His Holy Spirit, who calls, gathers, enlightens, and sanctifies the Church. Divine Service is first and foremost an activity of a Christian congregation, members of which have been joined to the Lord by the work of the Holy Spirit in Baptism.

The Invocation is addressed to God, so the pastor will face the altar. Facing the altar, the sign of the cross connected to the Invocation is a personal signature, and it is appropriate that all may join in this act as a remembrance of their Baptism.

CONFESSION AND ABSOLUTION

As Christians, our lives are to be ones of continual repentance as God promises eternal forgiveness. "If we confess our sins, He is faithful and just to forgive us our sins and to cleanse us from all unrighteousness" (1 John 1:9).

The expression, "we are by nature sinful and unclean," comes from the Augsburg Confession (II 1) and is unique to Lutheranism in its structuring of the preparatory rites. The statements made in this prayer of confession are a summary of Romans 7:14–8:14.

NEED TO KNOW

Invocation: From the Latin for "call upon"; the words "In the name of the Father and of the Son and of the Holy Spirit" spoken at the beginning of the service; serves as a reminder of Holy Baptism.

NEED TO KNOW

Confession: The act by which one admits or confesses sin(s) and the guilt of sin.

Absolution: The act of setting free from sin.

FROM THE BIBLE

I acknowledged my sin to You, and I did not cover my iniquity; I said, "I will confess my transgressions to the Lord," and You forgave the iniquity of my sin. (Psalm 32:5)

Service of the Word

The Service of the Word is the second part of our Divine Service. The purpose of the Service of the Word is to present Christ to the assembled congregation as they prepare to meet Him in His Supper.

The changeable texts, known as the Propers, bring variety into the worship, as they follow the seasons of the Church Year and the readings.

With the Introit, the service proper begins. The Preparation can be omitted altogether, as it is when we celebrate Holy Baptism immediately after the Opening Hymn.

INTROIT

The Introit is a collection of passages from Scripture that set the tone for the service. The verses chosen are different each Sunday and reflect the theme of the Holy Gospel to come. It is itself Scripture.

KYRIE

As we draw toward the reading of God's Word, we join with all the faithful through the ages and ask the Lord for mercy. The Kyrie is a litany, the first prayer of the gathered congregation. It is encountered frequently in Scripture—for example, the Canaanite woman (Matthew 15:22) and the ten lepers (Luke 17:13). It is a cry for mercy that our Lord and King will hear us and help us in our necessities and troubles. "His mercy is for those who fear Him from generation to generation" (Luke 1:50).

GLORIA IN EXCELSIS OR HYMN OF PRAISE

Confident that the Lord is merciful, we join the whole Church and all the angels in singing glory to God. The pastor begins with the angelic hymn in Luke 2:14: "Glory to God in the highest, and on earth peace among those with whom He is pleased!" The congregation follows with the earthly confirmation of the praise.

SALUTATION AND COLLECT

The phrase "Let us pray" is an invitation and admonition.

The Collect is the pastor's first prayer in the name of the people; he speaks for the congregation. The Collect "collects" in a concise and beautiful manner the

NEED TO KNOW

Introit: (inn-TRO-it) From the Latin for "enter."

Kyrie: (KIH-ree-ay) From the Greek *Kyrie eleison*, which means "Lord, have mercy."

Gloria in Excelsis: (GLOW-ree-uh in ex-SHELL-sis) Latin meaning "glory in the highest."

Salutation: Special greeting between pastor and people: "The Lord be with you," followed by the response "And also with you" or "And with your spirit."

Collect of the Day: (KAH-lekt). A brief, structured prayer.

theme for the day. Most of the Collects have been in continuous use in the Church for over fifteen hundred years. In these historic prayers we join with the great body of believers, the communion of the saints, and the generations yet to come.

The Collect is preceded by the Salutation. The Salutation is indicative of the special relationship between the congregation and its representative before God—the called pastor. This is found in Ruth 2:4; Luke 1:28; 2 Thessalonians 3:16; and elsewhere. The response parallels biblical usage in passages like Philemon 25 and Galatians 6:18.

OLD TESTAMENT READING AND EPISTLE

The actual bestowal of the grace of God, which was announced in the Introit and prayed for in the Collect, is now about to take place in the reading and preaching of the divine Word. This is the climax of the Service of the Word. Selected portions of the Word are appointed to be read according to the arrangement of the Church Year. It has been traditional for the congregation to be seated for the Old Testament Readings and Epistle, because these are seen as instruction in contrast to the Gospel, which is an account of the life and words of Jesus, the Lord of the Church.

VERSE

In response to the Epistle, we sing the appropriate verse. Except during Lent we sing the Alleluia or the words of St. Peter in John 6:68: "Lord, to whom shall we go? You have the words of eternal life."

HOLY GOSPEL

From earliest times the Gospel has been given pride of place in the readings of the Divine Service. It is always read last. The congregation stands for the reading. The Gospel is properly announced and read by the pastor or an ordained assistant as part of his work in the holy ministry of Word and Sacrament to proclaim the person and work of Christ to all.

CREED

Placed here, the Creed is a solemn confession and response of faith to the Word, which has just been proclaimed and heard. We confess the faith that the Christian Church has confessed from the beginning. We take our stand among those who have held the same Gospel from time immemorial.

The Nicene Creed is the proper creed for Sunday and festival celebrations of Holy Communion because of its expanded confession of the person and work of Jesus, the Christ.

HYMN OF THE DAY

Sometimes known as the Sermon Hymn, this is the principal hymn of the Divine Service. Efficiently used, it highlights the theme of the day and/or the theme of the Sermon that follows.

SERMON

The preacher "says what the Word says" to those whom the Word has gathered here and now to hear it with open hearts and receive it in faithful hearts

Martin Luther designated the omission and abuse of preaching as two of the three serious abuses that had crept into the Church of his day. He expressed his concern in his typical blunt fashion in 1523, saying, "When God's Word is not preached, one had better neither sing nor read, or even come together" (AE 53:11).

> **NEED TO KNOW** /!\
>
> **Votum:** short prayer based upon a promise from God.

VOTUM

The Sermon begins with a blessing upon the hearers, or an Invocation. A Votum concludes the Sermon. The ancient Votum is Paul's words to the Philippians: "The peace of God, which surpasses all understanding, will guard your hearts and your minds in Christ Jesus" (4:7).

OFFERING

While the Offering symbolizes the "spiritual worship" (Romans 12:1) of Christian lives offered in response to God, it also unites the faithful in an act of fellowship (Acts 2:42). The gifts that are shared represent the gifts of creation and are offered as a sacrifice of thanksgiving to the Lord so that by means of them He might accomplish His purpose to bless His people.

PRAYERS

Here we pray that what we have heard from God may be taken to heart. We also ask God to take care of our needs. We give Him thanks, praise, and honor as well.

OFFERTORY

The Offertory allows us to accompany our gifts to the Lord with praise for His many benefits in our lives, the very benefits from which our gifts were taken. These texts extol the extremely Lutheran idea of giving back to the Lord from the riches He has given to us (see Psalm 51:10–12).

Service of the Sacrament

In the Service of the Sacrament of the Altar, God joins His act and deed to His Word; He gives us the body offered and the blood shed for the forgiveness of our sins and for strength for Christian living.

NEED TO KNOW

Preface: Proclamation of praise and thanksgiving that begins the Service of the Sacrament.

Proper Preface: A special prayer said before the Lord's Supper that emphasizes the key themes of the feast, occasion, or season of the Church Year.

Sanctus: (SAHNK-toose) Latin for "holy."

PREFACE

There is little in the liturgy of the evangelical church that is older than the versicles and responses, the dialogue between the pastor and the people, known as the Preface.

P: The Lord be with you.
C: And with your spirit.

Similar to the beginning of Divine Service itself, the first word spoken to begin the Lord's Supper is the name of the Lord. The Lord is Host, the Head of the family of God. The Lord is serving (Luke 22:27), giving out His gifts—gifts given with the words that carry and bestow what they say.

During the Preface, the pastor and the people encourage one another in the way St. Paul encouraged the Thessalonians: "That He may establish your hearts blameless in holiness before our God and Father, at the coming of our Lord Jesus with all His saints" (1 Thessalonians 3:13).

PROPER PREFACE

During each of the major festival seasons of the Church Year, the Proper Preface gives glory to God, recalling the specific mercy emphasized during that season and leads into a united praise of the Church on earth, the saints above, and all the heavenly hosts, worshiping the Holy Trinity in the Sanctus.

SANCTUS

The people's response to the Proper Preface is the Sanctus (Latin, meaning "holy")—"Holy, holy, holy is the Lord Almighty; the whole earth is full of His glory." The text is built on the opening verses of Isaiah 6 and John 12:41. The Sanctus has two other distinct parts, the Hosanna and the Benedictus.

HOSANNA

An expression of joy for what Christ has done; it has been sung since Jesus triumphantly entered Jerusalem to give Himself for our sins. It can also be found in the Psalms. "Hosanna to the Son of David! Blessed is He who comes in the name of the Lord! Hosanna in the highest!" (Matthew 21:9).

BENEDICTUS

The words come from Psalm 118:26 and are quoted by Zechariah at the birth of his son, John the Baptist, in Luke 1:68–79, in a prayer of thanksgiving. "Hosanna"—"Praise the Lord" (see Psalm 117). We join with the angels, archangels, and all the company of heaven in singing.

PRAYER OF THANKSGIVING

Before the altar, the presiding pastor offers the Prayer of Thanksgiving on behalf of the assembled congregation. Its text affirms the Sacrament of the Altar as an ordinance graciously instituted by God, thanking Him for sending Jesus and for His Son's body and blood about to be given in the Sacrament for the forgiveness of our sins. This sets the proper framework for our "remembering": participation in the worship that God has established and blessed through Word and Sacrament.

LORD'S PRAYER

The Lord's Prayer (Matthew 6:9–13; Luke 11:2–4) is the "Prayer of the Faithful" children of the heavenly Father, who tenderly invites them to call upon Him as His beloved children. This is the family prayer of Christ's Church. It has been associated with the Words of Institution in all Lutheran Communion rites. The conclusion is found in Galatians 1:5; Hebrews 13:21; and Revelation 1:6.

As we pray the prayer that Jesus Himself taught us, we are preparing for the second great moment of the Divine Service—the Lord's Supper.

WORDS OF INSTITUTION

The pastor recites the words of Jesus Himself recorded in the Gospels of Matthew, Mark, and Luke, and in St. Paul's First Letter to the Corinthians. Yet these words are not merely the recitation of a historical narrative concerning the original institution of the Supper in the Upper Room. They are the words of consecration. Christ speaks them again by and through the pastor to do and to give now what He did and gave then. In these words Christ Himself assures us that He is indeed bodily present in the Sacrament of the Lord's Supper and that through it our sins are forgiven.

> **NEED TO KNOW**
>
> **Benedictus:** Latin for the first words: "Blessed is he."
>
> **Lord's Prayer:** The model prayer Jesus taught to the disciples (Matthew 6:9–13). Sometimes it is called the Our Father, after the first words of the prayer.
>
> **The Words of Institution:** The words spoken by Christ when He instituted the Sacrament of the Altar (Matthew 26:26–28; Mark 14:22–24; Luke 22:19–20; 1 Corinthians 11:23–25).

PAX DOMINI

In anticipation of the blessings to be received through the body and blood of our Lord in, with, and under the bread and wine, the pastor and the people announce the peace of God to one another, as Christ Himself did on that first Easter. Jesus came and stood among them and said, "Peace be with you" (John 20:19).

AGNUS DEI

The wording in the text is taken from the words of John the Baptist in John 1:29. It serves as a hymn of adoration to the Savior who is present in the body and blood. For this reason it has not been seen in the liturgies of the Reformed churches.

NEED TO KNOW

Agnus Dei: (AHG-noose DAY-ee) Latin for "Lamb of God" (John 1:29).

Canticle: Latin for "little song"; Scripture texts sung as part of the liturgy.

Amen. Hebrew word meaning "it is true; reliable."

Benediction: From the Latin for "[The Lord] bless [you]"; the Aaronic Blessing (Numbers 6:24–26) is commonly used in connection with Holy Communion, while the Apostolic Blessing (2 Corinthians 13:14) is used at other times.

THE DISTRIBUTION

In the Lord's Supper, we receive the body and blood of Jesus Christ. Through it our sins are forgiven because we have been given faith in the words "Given and shed for you" in our Baptism. At this, the climax of the second half of the Divine Service, we are reminded of the way in which we began, recalling our Baptism.

POST-COMMUNION CANTICLE

Following reception of our Lord's forgiving body and blood, we join in singing a hymn of thanks. Usually this hymn is called the Nunc Dimittis ("Depart in peace") or "Simeon's Song" and is recorded in Luke 2:29–32. The use of the Nunc Dimittis is unique to the Lutheran liturgy.

PRAYER OF THANKSGIVING

"Amen." We add our own and the Church's undying gratitude in this Collect of Thanksgiving—a prayer that the gifts now received from the Lord may accomplish His purpose in His people.

BENEDICTION

Also known as the Aaronic Blessing or the Priestly Blessing, the Benediction is the blessing the Lord directed Moses to use when he blessed the people in the Lord's name. See Numbers 6:24–26.

The Certainty of Faith and How Lutherans Worship

Certainty is also important for how we worship God together. What God says in the divine Scriptures is decisive. We don't use worship practices if we have doubts about whether they are true or pleasing to God. For example, we know with certainty that God wants us to pray to Him, to sing, to read the Scriptures, to confess our faith, to listen to the pastor's preaching, to celebrate the Lord's Supper, to baptize new believers, to confess our sins, and to believe the pastor's proclamation of forgiveness. We have certainty that these things are pleasing to God, and therefore our worship is centered on these things, while we avoid other things.

Symbols of God's Presence
What You Might See in Church

Altar. A stone or wooden structure at the center of the chancel from which the Lord's Supper is celebrated; the sacramental focus from which God gives His gifts; the sacrificial focus of the congregation's worship.

Baptismal font. The baptismal font is often made of stone or wood with a metal bowl to hold the water used for Baptism and a lid to cover the metal bowl when a Baptism is not taking place. The baptismal font may be located in the chancel area, in the narthex, or in a room of its own called a baptistery.

Chancel. The chancel is the area at the front of a worship space where the altar, pulpit, lectern, and often the baptismal font are located.

Narthex. The narthex is the room or area where people gather just outside the nave. This is where ushers usually hand out bulletins and where the pastor might greet people after a service.

Nave. Latin for "ship"; the main portion of a church building where people gather to worship and pray.

Pew. Long benches in a church are called pews. Some churches now use rows of individual chairs instead of pews.

Pulpit. The pulpit is an enclosed and often raised piece of furniture where a pastor commonly stands when delivering the sermon. Preaching from the pulpit reminds everyone that the pastor is God's representative, speaking God's Word to the congregation. Some pastors prefer to stand between the chancel and the nave while they preach their sermons in order to remind everyone that Jesus' death and resurrection have taken away the separation sin once caused between God and His people.

Lectern. A piece of furniture similar to, but often smaller than, the pulpit. The lectern is the appropriate place for a pastor or member of the congregation to read the Bible readings of the day or make announcements. Not all churches have lecterns. If there is no lectern, readings take place at the pulpit.

Sanctuary. Officially, the sanctuary is the area around the altar in the chancel. It is sometimes separated from the rest of the chancel and the nave by a Communion rail. People often use the term *sanctuary* to refer to the whole worship area, including both the nave and the chancel.

Sacristy. A room, usually near the chancel, where paraments, linens, sacramental vessels (Communionware), and other altar supplies are kept. In churches that do not have a vestry, vestments are also kept in the sacristy. Sometimes there is a sink and counter area in the sacristy for the altar guild to prepare items for Holy Communion and to clean up the Communionware items after Holy Communion.

Vestry. A small room where the pastor and his assistants keep their vestments and prepare for worship services. Some churches have one room that serves as both sacristy and vestry.

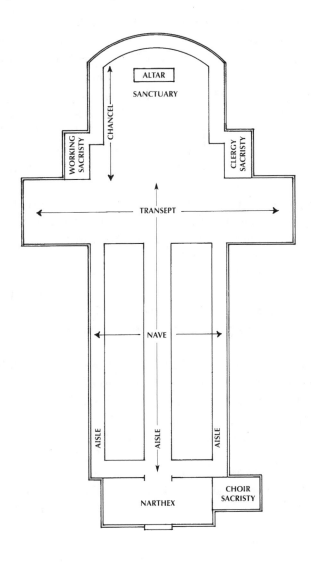

Nothing Else Than Faith

BY REV. LARRY M. VOGEL

Wherever you find Christians, you will find worship, for one simple reason: we worship because of Jesus. The words He spoke to a Samaritan woman are unforgettable (see John 4:5–30). She asked Him where to worship. He answered by telling her that God had brought salvation to the world through His people Israel, who gathered for worship festivals in Jerusalem. But contrary to expectation, Jesus didn't send the woman to Jerusalem, as if worship were primarily a geographical question. Instead, He said: "The hour is coming, and is now here, when the true worshipers will worship the Father in spirit and truth, for the Father is seeking such people to worship Him" (John 4:23).

Every religion worships somehow, giving honor or homage to a single deity (Muslims), to many deities (Hindus), to ancestors (folk religions), or perhaps simply to spiritual ideas (Buddhists). Yet Christians cannot consider such worship to be worship done "in truth," because the object of such worship is not the triune God.

In addition, just because people go to worship in a church that teaches the truth about God does not mean they have worshiped "in spirit." If they merely warm a seat without any genuine response or attention to God, they didn't truly worship either.

So what is Christian worship? As he studied Genesis (4:26), Martin Luther discovered what he considered to be a "most excellent definition" for worship, namely, "to call upon the name of the Lord" (AE 1:327). He connected that definition with Romans 10:13–14, which says, "For 'everyone who calls on the name of the Lord will be saved.' How then will they call on Him in whom they have not believed? And how are they to believe in Him of whom they have never heard? And how are they to hear without someone preaching?"

Luther also commented on Jesus' words to the Samaritan woman: "For from this you see that true worship can be nothing else than faith; it is faith's sublimest activity with respect to God. For no one is capable of such heartfelt confession, adoration, bending, and bowing (or whatever you want to call it) before God in his heart, unless he unwaveringly holds God to be his Lord and Father, from whom he receives and will receive all good things, and through whom, without any merit on his part, he is redeemed and preserved from all sins and evil" (AE 36:293).

In other words, faith in Christ is true worship. Where there is true faith in Christ, there is true worship. When Lutherans talk about worship, it must be Christ focused and faith focused. "God wants to be worshiped through faith so that we receive from Him those things He promises and offers" (Ap IV 49). Imagine: no matter what you do in a "worship" setting—sing, give an offering, pray, or anything else—if it isn't done with genuine faith, it isn't really worship! Moreover, genuine faith is astoundingly simple: believing acceptance of God's gracious "promises and offers" in Jesus Christ.

If worship is Christ focused and faith focused, then the location for worship isn't the important thing (the reason Christians, unlike Jews and Muslims, have no "holy cities"). Moreover, the faith focus also means that external aspects of worship, such as musical instruments, specific songs, architectural customs, postures, clothing styles, languages, and so on are also not decisive for genuine worship. Times of controversy compelled Lutherans to point out that such external worship matters "are neither commanded nor forbidden in God's Word, but have been introduced only for the sake of fitting and good order" (FC Ep X 3).

The Bible gives only general instruction on worship. There is no point-by-point "order of service" in the New Testament. What is clear is that whenever Christians assembled, there were opportunities for faith to be created and nurtured, and there were opportunities for faith to be expressed. So Jesus commanded that His followers baptize in the triune name and teach His Word (Matthew 28:19–20). When He first gave His body and blood with bread and wine, He told His disciples to "do this" as well, originating the Lord's Supper (see Luke 22:19–20). These emphatic concerns of our Lord Jesus were the very means by which He had personally gathered His first disciples: He spoke to them and He ate with them (see Luke 5:15; 15:2, for example).

It should be no surprise then, that after His resurrection and ascension, Jesus provided the means by which people would continue to become His disciples, being baptized into Him (Acts 2:38), hearing Him (Acts 2:22), and eating and drinking His very body and blood (Acts 2:42; 1 Corinthians 11:23–25). Just as Israel "called on the name of the Lord" in faith, so Jesus' disciples call on His name as Lord, in faith (Romans 10:9). Notice how Paul addressed the Corinthians as a called and calling people: "To the church of God that is in Corinth . . . called to be saints together with all those who in every place call upon the name of our Lord Jesus Christ, both their Lord and ours" (1 Corinthians 1:2). Since faith comes by hearing, and faith believes the promises of forgiveness, life, and salvation conveyed by means of Baptism and Communion, how could it be otherwise?

By such language, the New Testament makes clear that the Christian Church is nothing more than the people who have been called by Jesus to leave their routines and gather around Him, hearing Him (Word), receiving His gifts (Sacraments), and calling on Him in prayer and praise. That, simply, is the Lutheran understanding of Christian worship.

This understanding has persisted in historical worship practices and, from Luther's time, in Lutheran churches. Christian worship is rightly built on the twin pillars of (1) the Word of God and (2) the Sacraments (Baptism and Communion). The Word and Sacraments, not other customs, are the core of Christian worship because they are the means by which the Holy Spirit creates and nurtures faith.

This view is built on the Lutheran understanding of the Church as the people God has called together in faith. The Church, properly speaking, is not like some outward club or institution. "Rather, the Church is people scattered throughout the whole world. They agree about the Gospel and have the same Christ, the same Holy Spirit, and the same Sacraments, whether they have the same or different human traditions" (Ap VII and VIII 10).

Lutheran congregations today are far from uniform about how they conduct worship services. Throughout most of its history, the Lutheran Church has tended to be liturgical in worship, largely maintaining the worship practices they inherited from the time of the Reformation. The desire to respect tradition and the desire to respect contemporary culture have found themselves at odds in the Lutheran Church. Every church that calls itself Lutheran is careful neither to scorn traditional practices of Christian worship nor to neglect the concern to express itself in language and customs its community can understand and appreciate.

Hymns of Martin Luther

A Mighty Fortress Is Our God
Ein feste Burg ist unser Gott
LSB 656/7

All Glory Be to God Alone
All Ehr und Lob soll Gottes sein
LSB 948

Although the Fools Say with Their Mouth
Es spricht der Unweisen Mund
AE 53:229

Christ Jesus Lay in Death's Strong Bands
Christ lag in Todesbanden
LSB 458

Come, Holy Ghost, God and Lord
Komm, Heiliger Geist, Herre Gott
LSB 497

Dear Christians, One and All, Rejoice
Nun freut euch, lieben Christen
LSB 556

Flung to the Heedless Winds
Ein neues Lied wir heben an
TLH 259

From Depths of Woe I Cry to Thee
Aus tiefer Not schrei ich zu dir
LSB 607

From Heaven Above to Earth I Come
Vom Himmel hoch, da komm ich her
LSB 358

Grant Peace, We Pray, in Mercy, Lord
Verleih uns Frieden gnädiglich
LSB 777/8

Happy Who in God's Fear Doth Stay
Wohl dem, der in Gottes Furcht steht
AE 53:242

Herod, Why Dreadest Thou a Foe
Was fürchst du, Feind Herodes, sehr
AE 53:302

If God Had Not Been on Our Side
Wär Gott nicht mit uns diese Zeit
TLH 267

In Peace and Joy I Now Depart
Mit Fried und Freud ich fahr dahin
LSB 938

In the Very Midst of Life
Mitten wir im Leben sind
LSB 755

Isaiah, Mighty Seer in Days of Old
Jesaja, dem Propheten, das geschah
LSB 960

Jesus Christ, Our Blessed Savior
Jesus Christus unser Heiland, der von uns
LSB 627

Jesus Christ, Our Savior True
Jesus Christus unser Heiland, der den Tod
AE 53:258

Lord, Keep Us Steadfast in Your Word
Erhalt uns, Herr, bei deinem Wort
LSB 655

Man, Wouldst Thou Live All Blissfully
Mensch, willst du leben seliglich
AE 53:280

May God Bestow on Us His Grace
Es wollt uns Gott gnädig sein
LSB 823/4

Now Praise We Christ, the Holy One
Christum wir sollen loben schon
TLH 104

O Lord, Look Down from Heaven, Behold
Ach Gott vom Himmel, sieh darein
TLH 260

O Lord, We Praise Thee
Gott sei gelobet und gebenedeiet
LSB 617

Our Father, Who from Heaven Above
Vater unser im Himmelreich
LSB 766

Savior of the Nations, Come
Nun komm, der Heiden Heiland
LSB 332

These Are the Holy Ten Commands
Dies sind die heilgen zehn Gebot
LSB 581

Thou Who Art Three in Unity
Der du bist drei in Einigkeit
AE 53:308

To God the Holy Spirit Let Us Pray
Nun bitten wir den Heiligen Geist
LSB 768

To Jordan Came the Christ, Our Lord
Christ, unser Herr, zum Jordan kam
LSB 406/7

To Me She's Dear, the Worthy Maid
Sie ist mir lieb, die werte Magd
AE 53:292

To Shepherds as They Watched by Night
Vom Himmel kam der Engel Schar
TLH 103

Triune God, Be Thou Our Stay
Gott der Vater wohn uns bei
LSB 505

We All Believe in One True God
Wir glauben all an einen Gott
LSB 954

We Praise You, Jesus, at Your Birth
Gelobet seist du, Jesu Christ
LSB 382

We Sing Thy Praise, O God
Herr Gott, dich loben wir
ELH 45

AE   *Luther's Works, American Edition, vol. 53, 1965*
ELH *Evangelical Lutheran Hymnary, 1996*
LSB *Lutheran Service Book, 2006*
TLH *The Lutheran Hymnal, 1941*

CHAPTER 29

A Time for Everything

In This Chapter

- The Church Year is divided into three parts: the Time of Christmas, the Time of Easter, and the Time of the Church.
- The Time of Christmas deals with who Jesus is: God in the flesh.
- The Time of Easter deals with what Jesus came to do.

No story is complete without understanding the order of things. You cannot have a story without order and time. If the prince kisses Sleeping Beauty in chapter 1, but the evil spell that put her to sleep does not come until chapter 5, well, that story just does not make sense.

The Church has a story to tell as well. Indeed, Martin Luther said that the Church is a "mouth house" (AE 68)—a place where the true story of Jesus is the main event. This is one story we do not want to get wrong, and that is why the Church uses the rhythms of the festivals and seasons of her year to teach the story of Christ.

Jesus Time

Everybody loves Christmas—even cultures with no historic ties to Christianity have adopted silver bells, carols, and gift-giving in late December. But Christmas is just the tip of the iceberg when it comes to the Church's year—just one part of the story the Church has to tell.

The Church Year is divided into three parts: the Time of Christmas, the Time of Easter, and the Time of the Church. Each has its own piece of the story of Jesus to tell.

Time of Christmas

The time of Christmas begins with Advent, which is Latin for "He's coming." These four Sundays before Christmas are dedicated to preparing our

BELIEVE, TEACH, CONFESS

Lutherans keep the church year that has been used for hundreds and hundreds of years—tying us together in our way of worship with countless Christians of past and present. "We do not abolish the Mass, but religiously keep and defend it." (Ap XXIV 1)

hearts for the coming of Christ, teaching us to hope for the right things. At this time of year, the television commercials and newspaper advertisements are trying to convince us to hope for all the wrong things: more toys (for kids and grown-ups alike), more debt, more worry, more stuff, more discontent with what we already have.

But if you wander into a Lutheran church during Advent, you will get a very different feel. Even the colors in the church (blue or violet) say it is just not Christmas yet: we are taking our time and still getting ready. Ready for what? Listen to the readings in Advent—we are waiting in hope for a King who will come and save us from our need to justify our lives with stuff. While the world is running haphazardly, the Church is at peace, waiting in anticipation for the King of peace.

That is why the Church still has plenty of energy for a celebration of Christmas that keeps going through Epiphany (the coming of the Wise Men) to the celebration of the Baptism of Jesus, His first miracles, and His glorious transfiguration.

Time of Easter

The Time of Christmas deals with who Jesus is: God in the flesh. Now the Church considers what Jesus came to do. This is the Time of Easter, which begins with the solemn rites of repentance on the first day of Lent, Ash Wednesday.

This focus on repentance becomes ever sharper as the forty days of Lent close in on Holy Week and the events remembered on Maundy Thursday (the day Jesus was arrested), Good Friday (the day of His sacrifice on the cross), Holy Saturday (His rest in the tomb), and Easter Sunday—the day of Resurrection.

While the world uses Easter as a convenient excuse for a day of springtime fun, for the Church it is the center of the year and the pivot of history. Christ is risen from the dead! Death no longer has mastery over Him or His faithful! Death has been defeated, and we, too, shall rise with Christ on the Last Day!

That is an event that is worth more than just one day's celebration. So the Church celebrates Easter for fifty days, until the day of the Spirit's coming to enliven the Church on Pentecost (Acts 2), which ushers in the Time of the Church.

Time of the Church

All that Jesus did for our salvation would do us no good if that salvation were not delivered to us. That delivery of Jesus' work is what happens in the Church. It began on Pentecost with Peter's first sermon and the gathering of the people around the Word and Sacraments (Acts 2:36–42), and it continues today. The readings and worship on the Sundays after Pentecost focus on our life in Christ, a life of continual growth in the fear and instruction of the Lord.

And then . . . back to the beginning, to Advent and another year of God's grace. And so the Church goes on proclaiming Christ year after year in a story that is new with each telling.

Seasons and Colors of the Church Year

Season of Advent

Advent starts four Sundays before Christmas and ends on December 24. The color for the season of Advent is blue to emphasize hope and preparation for Jesus' coming. You may also see violet used during Advent as a symbol of repentance to remind us to feel sorry for our sins.

Christmas and the Christmas Season

Nobody knows the exact date of Jesus' birth. About three hundred years after Jesus was born, Christians chose December 25 as the day we celebrate the nativity, or birth, of Jesus. After four weeks of Advent anticipation, Christmas has more good news than a single day can hold. The Christmas season begins on Christmas Eve and ends on January 5, the day before Epiphany. The season of Christmas is also known as the twelve days of Christmas. The color for the season of Christmas is white.

Epiphany and the Epiphany Season

Epiphany is on January 6. Epiphany means "to show" or "to make known" and is often called the Gentile Christmas because this is the celebration of when the Magi, who were Gentiles, came to worship Jesus. The Epiphany season continues until the day before Ash Wednesday. The color for most of the season of Epiphany is green. White is used on the Day of Epiphany, on the first Sunday after January 6 when we celebrate the Baptism of Our Lord, and on the last Sunday before Ash Wednesday when we celebrate the Festival of the Transfiguration.

Season of Lent

Lent is a season set apart to prepare for the Resurrection of Our Lord on Easter. During Lent we focus on our need to repent of our sin and our need of a Savior from sin. The season begins on Ash Wednesday. Many churches have Ash Wednesday worship services during which the pastor will take ashes from the previous year's palm branches and draw a cross on each person's forehead. We remember that "the wages of sin is death" and that our bodies came from ashes/dust and will become ashes/dust again after we die. The color for Ash Wednesday is black.

Lent is forty days long; we do not count the Sundays *in* Lent as part of the season of Lent. Even during Lent, Sundays are to remember and celebrate Jesus' resurrection. The color for the Lenten season is violet.

Holy Week

As we get closer to Good Friday and Easter, the Lenten preparation and repentance deepens. This final week of Lent is called Holy Week. Apart from the special days, the color of Holy Week is scarlet or the violet of Lent.

Palm Sunday: Holy Week begins with Palm Sunday. On Palm Sunday we remember when Jesus entered Jerusalem riding on a donkey and was welcomed by people waving palm branches and shouting "Hosanna!"

Holy (Maundy) Thursday: On the last Thursday before Easter, we celebrate Jesus' institution of the Sacrament of the Altar during His Last Supper. The color for the Divine Service on Holy Thursday is white.

Good Friday: On the last Friday before Easter, we remember Jesus' crucifixion. We call it "Good" because it is the day when Jesus paid for our sins by dying in our place. Many churches take everything off the altar and drape it with black cloth on Good Friday. The color for Good Friday is black or no color at all.

The Christian Year

Easter Vigil: The last celebration of Holy Week is actually the first celebration of the Resurrection of Our Lord. Easter Vigil is a nighttime celebration on Saturday when the whole congregation is invited to remember their Baptism into Christ's death and resurrection.

The Resurrection of Our Lord and the Season of Easter

Easter Sunday is celebrated on the first Sunday after the first full moon falling on or after March 21 (the first day of spring). This means Easter's date is not fixed and changes each year. Easter is the celebration of Jesus' resurrection. The season of Easter extends the Easter celebration for fifty days. The color for Easter and its season is white.

Pentecost and the Season after Pentecost

Pentecost is celebrated fifty days after Easter and celebrates the fulfillment of Jesus' promise to send the Holy Spirit to the Church. Red, the color of fire and blood, is the color for Pentecost. The Sundays after Pentecost make up the longest portion of the Church Year. During the season after Pentecost, we focus on growing together in the life God has given us through the Means of Grace. The color for most of the season of Pentecost is green, but other colors are used for some special days. Red is used when celebrating Reformation and special days that commemorate those who died for the faith. White is used when celebrating special feast days that mark celebrations in the life of Christ or His Church.

CHAPTER 30

The Sign of the Cross

In This Chapter

- Luther suggested the sign of the cross as a daily practice.
- The sign of the cross is a way of declaring your salvation.
- Making the sign of the cross or not making the sign of the cross is part of our Christian liberty.

Making the sign of the cross is a physical action that draws the whole self into the act of worship. You don't have to be in any Lutheran congregation very long to see that there is no uniformity about this practice of signing the cross. Some Lutherans may consider this a Catholic practice, and in the past this connotation caused many Lutherans to abandon its use. Yet in the hymnal, at several points in the worship service, a red cross ☩ appears. Luther suggested the sign of the cross as a daily practice, directing in his Small Catechism that the head of the household should teach the family the Morning and Evening Prayers in this way:

In the morning when you get up, make the sign of the holy cross and say:

In the name of the Father and of the Son and of the Holy Spirit. Amen.

Luther teaches the believer to begin prayer in the morning and prayer in the evening by making the sign of the cross. The sign of the cross is made by placing the thumb and the first two fingers of the right hand together as a reminder of the Trinity. Touch your head at the naming of the Father; then bring your hand to the middle of your chest (over your heart) at the naming of the Son. At the naming of the Holy Spirit, touch your right shoulder and then your left shoulder.

But let us be clear, making the sign of the cross or not making the sign of the cross is part of our Christian liberty. It should never be made a criterion for being viewed as more or less confessional, more or less liturgical, or more or less Lutheran. While the sign of the holy cross is the property of each and every baptized child of God, it is up to the individual to determine when and how he or she will use it.

In the church's worship, it is a laudable custom to cross ourselves at the beginning and end of all services and at the following places in the Divine Service or in the Order of the Holy Communion Service: during the opening words, "In the name," etc.; at the end of the Absolution; at the beginning of the Introit; at the end of the Gloria in Excelsis; when the Gospel is announced (at this point the sign is made with the hand closed using the tip of the thumb upon the forehead, lips, and breast); at the end of the Creed; during the Sanctus at the words "Blessed is He"; after the consecration at "The peace of the Lord"; when we receive the holy body and precious blood of Christ; when the minister says "Depart in peace"; and at the end of the Benediction. Throughout the liturgy and these notes, a ✠ indicates some of the appropriate places to make the sign of the cross as token of our salvation.

The Possession of the Christian

We were signed with the cross when we were baptized. The sign of the cross is a way of declaring your salvation. In Holy Baptism Jesus has made His cross to be yours so that you do not have to suffer for your sin.

> Receive the sign of the holy cross both upon your ✠ forehead and upon your ✠ heart to mark you as one redeemed by Christ the crucified. (*Holy Baptism*, LSB, page 268)

The signing of the cross is the way the Church blesses people and things, setting them apart as belonging to God and service in the Church.

By it we become part of the wonderful history of our faith and companions in the company of the saints. It is right that we should make the sign of the cross frequently and glory in it.

The Christian also finds comfort in making the sign of the cross in a time of tragedy, in the face of danger, or in the presence of heresy and evil. Within the liturgy itself, this use of

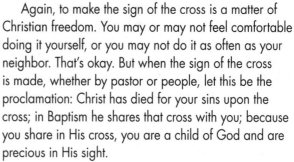

making the sign of the cross is why it is included in the Lord's Prayer at the speaking of the words "And lead us not into temptation, but ✠ deliver us from evil."

Again, to make the sign of the cross is a matter of Christian freedom. You may or may not feel comfortable doing it yourself, or you may not do it as often as your neighbor. That's okay. But when the sign of the cross is made, whether by pastor or people, let this be the proclamation: Christ has died for your sins upon the cross; in Baptism he shares that cross with you; because you share in His cross, you are a child of God and are precious in His sight.

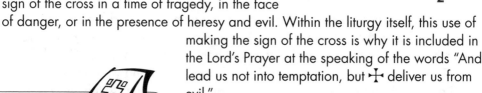

FROM THE BIBLE

But far be it from me to boast except in the cross of our Lord Jesus Christ, by which the world has been crucified to me, and I to the world. (Galatians 6:14)

Top Twenty-five Hymns Lutherans Love to Sing

Hymn	LSB
A Mighty Fortress Is Our God	656/657
Amazing Grace	744
Beautiful Savior	537
Children of the Heavenly Father	725
Crown Him with Many Crowns	525
Dear Christians, One and All, Rejoice	556
Go, My Children, with My Blessing	922
God's Own Child, I Gladly Say It	594
I Know That My Redeemer Lives	461
Jesus Has Come and Brings Pleasure	533
Let Us Ever Walk with Jesus	685
Lift High the Cross	837
Lord, Keep Us Steadfast in Your Word	655
Now All the Vault of Heaven Resounds	465
O Lord, We Praise Thee	617
O Morning Star, How Fair and Bright	395
O Sacred Head, Now Wounded	449/450
Praise God, from Whom All Blessings Flow	805
Praise to the Lord, the Almighty	790
Savior of the Nations, Come	332
Silent Night, Holy Night	363
Soul, Adorn Yourself with Gladness	636
The Church's One Foundation	644
The Tree of Life	561
Thy Strong Word	578

PART SIX

What you'll learn about:

- The Church has formulated clear confessions of faith in response to both the lack of faith and attacks on faith.

- The good works we do are a great benefit to our family, friends, neighbors, and all the people with whom we share God's good earth.

- This desire to go tell others about Jesus is the result of the Holy Spirit's work in each believer, and it is at the heart of the Church's mission.

- What we do with our time, talents, and treasures flow from our relationship with God.

Living as Lutherans

Having received from God all good things for our body and for our soul, as Christians we live in relationship with not only God but also our neighbors. The love we have received becomes active in our faith. In this way the believer becomes the mouth confessing the Good News of Jesus Christ and the hands of God working for the good of the neighbor.

CHAPTER 31

We Confess

In This Chapter

- The person, word, and work of Jesus cannot be shaken.
- Leaders of the Early Church felt a need to formulate concise, memorable statements of the sure and foundational truths of Christianity.
- Historically, the Christian Church has recognized three Ecumenical Creeds: the Apostles' Creed, the Nicene Creed, and the Athanasian Creed.

"I find your lack of faith *disturbing*," says Darth Vader after Admiral Motti criticizes him for his devotion to the mysterious Star Wars "Force." Darth Vader is right—not about the "Force," but about a lack of faith. A lack of faith is disturbing. For instance, when a student's faith is attacked by a cynical college professor, she is inevitably disturbed. Or when a child's faith in a friend's loyalty is betrayed, he is inexorably troubled. A shaken or shattered faith is a very disturbing thing.

We all encounter moments that fracture our faith and shake up our souls. It is in these moments that we often find ourselves groping for something sure—something solid that will not shudder. Scripture tells us that we have something sure, or rather someone sure, and that someone is Jesus Christ.

The person, word, and work of Jesus cannot be shaken. Therefore, we gladly build our faith upon the rock, who is Christ, with full confidence that He will never betray or break our faith.

FROM THE BIBLE

"Everyone then who hears these words of Mine and does them will be like a wise man who built his house on the rock. And the rain fell, and the floods came, and the winds blew and beat on that house, but it did not fall, because it had been founded on the rock." (Matthew 7:24–25)

The Need for Creeds

Shortly after the Church was birthed, opponents arose who ruthlessly and relentlessly attacked the Christian faith. At first, folks like the Roman emperors, some of whom demanded that all Romans worship the emperor as god, persecuted Christians. The Gnostics, who taught that access to secret knowledge rather than faith in the Son of God was the key to salvation, also sought to suppress Christianity during this period. Later, attacks came from those within the Church itself. For instance, a fourth-century priest from Egypt named Arius taught that though Jesus was *a* god, He was not *the* God. This is in direct contradiction to John 1:1, 14, which teaches that "the Word," Jesus, "was God" and "dwelt among us."

The leaders of the Christian Church found both the lack of faith and the attack on faith disturbing! They felt a need to formulate concise, memorable statements of the sure and foundational truths of Christianity. Such is the origin of creeds.

The earliest Christian creeds are actually found within the very pages of Scripture. For example, when the apostle Paul writes in Romans 10:9, "If you confess with your mouth that Jesus is Lord and believe in your heart that God raised Him from the dead, you will be saved," the phrase "Jesus is Lord" is an early Christian creed. Thus, creeds are as old as Christianity.

The Big Three

Historically, the Christian Church has recognized three Ecumenical Creeds: the Apostles' Creed, the Nicene Creed, and the Athanasian Creed. A brief word about each of these creeds is helpful. See also pp. 18–19.

Apostles' Creed

The Apostles' Creed is the shortest and simplest of the "big three" creeds, and finds its origins in the writings of the first- and second- century Church Fathers. For

TECHNICAL STUFF

The word *faith* is regularly used in two ways. On the one hand, it describes a person's trust in God. On the other hand, it describes the content of what we believe as Christians. The creeds invoke both uses of the word *faith*, for they describe what we believe as well as inviting us to believe.

BELIEVE, TEACH, CONFESS

"New Arians teach that Christ is not true, essential, natural God, of one eternal divine essence with God the Father. They say He is only adorned with divine majesty inferior to, and beside, God the Father. Some Anti-Trinitarians reject and condemn the ancient, approved Nicene and Athanasian Creeds. They condemn both their sense and words. These people teach that there is not just one eternal divine essence of the Father, Son, and Holy Spirit." (FC SD XII 36–37)

NEED TO KNOW

Creed: From the Latin word *credo*, "I believe"; a summary of what the Church believes; refers to any of the three Ecumenical Creeds used in worship: the Apostles' Creed, often used at Baptisms, funerals, and non-Communion services; the Nicene Creed, often used at services with Holy Communion; and the Athanasian Creed, often spoken on Trinity Sunday.

TECHNICAL STUFF

An ecumenical creed is a creed that is accepted by the Christian Church *as a whole*. In other words, it doesn't matter if you are Lutheran, Roman Catholic, Methodist, or Presbyterian. If you are a Christian, you can joyfully confess the Ecumenical Creeds!

instance, Ignatius of Antioch writes this around AD 107:

"Be deaf, therefore, whenever anyone speaks to you apart from Jesus Christ, who is of the stock of David, who is of Mary, who was truly born, ate and drank, was truly persecuted under Pontius Pilate, was truly crucified and died in the sight of beings of heaven, of earth and the underworld, who was also truly raised from the dead." (John Leith, *Creeds of the Churches*, 3rd ed. [Louisville: John Knox Press, 1982], 16–17.)

These words are an almost verbatim repetition of what Christians around the world confess even today in the Second Article of the Apostles' Creed. Thus, the Apostles' Creed is nearly as ancient as the Church itself.

Nicene Creed

The origins of the Nicene Creed go back to AD 325 during the Church's Council of Nicaea. It was during this period that Arius attacked the teaching that the Father and Son were both coeternally and coequally God. Hence, the Nicene Creed confesses that Christ is "God of God, Light of Light, very God of very God . . . being of one substance with the Father" (*LSB*, p. 158). This creed, then, is largely devoted to defending Christ's divinity.

Athanasian Creed

The longest of the "big three" creeds is the Athanasian Creed, containing some 656 words. Although its composition is traditionally attributed to Athanasius, who lived in Alexandria in the fourth century, its author is technically anonymous. Nevertheless, this creed carefully addresses and defends the doctrine of the Trinity in a highly technical and in-depth way.

Back to the Basics

In the sixteenth century, as Martin Luther led a reformation of the Christian Church, he took painstaking precautions to assure others that he had no aspirations of starting a new religion or sect. Rather, he maintained, he was simply seeking to return the Church to its orthodox roots. This is why the Augsburg Confession, a statement of what Lutherans believe, opens: "Our churches teach with common consent that the decree of the Council of Nicaea about the unity of the divine essence and the three persons is true. . . . God is one divine essence" (AC I 1, 2). In order to make its case that Lutherans are part of the universal Christian Church, the Augsburg Confession appeals to the universal Christian creeds. The reformers are thus arguing that they are only teaching what has always been taught in the creeds. They are simply going "back to the basics" of creedal Christianity.

Martin Luther himself used the Apostles' Creed as a "back to the basics" teaching tool when he wrote his Small Catechism. He begins his comments on this creed by explaining, "[This is how] the head of the family should teach it in a simple way to his household" (SC, The Creed). Luther believed that every Christian should know the creeds because they contain elementary and vital teachings of the Christian faith.

Say What?

Although the creeds contain elementary and vital teachings of the Christian faith, you may have wondered what certain phrases meant. So here are two of the most common questions concerning the Apostles' Creed.

Why do some versions of the Apostles' Creed say, "I believe in the holy catholic Church," while we say, "I believe in the holy Christian Church"?

TECHNICAL STUFF

An article is a given section of a creed. Both the Apostles' Creed and Nicene Creed have three articles: one devoted to God the Father, a second devoted to God the Son, and a third devoted to God the Holy Spirit.

TECHNICAL STUFF

To be "orthodox" means to believe and teach correctly about the Christian faith. Martin Luther, as well as other reformers in the Church, maintained that orthodox theology is to be based in and guided by Scripture alone. The creeds provide helpful touch-points to orthodox, scriptural, Christian teaching. This is why Luther found them so helpful.

These statements are different ways of confessing the same thing. The word *catholic* comes from the Greek word *katholikos*, meaning "according to the whole." Thus, to say "I believe in the holy catholic Church" is to say "I believe according to the whole, or universal, Church," which is none other than "the Holy Christian Church!"

Why do we say that Jesus "descended into hell"? Is that in the Bible?

The Apostles' Creed derives its confession of Jesus' descent into hell from 1 Peter 3:18–19: "For Christ also suffered once for sins, the righteous for the unrighteous, that He might bring us to God, being put to death in the flesh but made alive in the spirit, in which He went and proclaimed to the spirits in prison." Lutheran theologians take the reference to "the spirits in prison" as a declaration that Jesus descended into hell to proclaim His victory over hell through His death and resurrection.

Credo!

Credo is a Latin word meaning "I believe." The ultimate goal of the creeds is to give us a form by which to confess what Christians both corporately and as individuals believe about God: This is what I believe. And this is in whom I believe. I believe in God. And even if I have to suffer death, this I will still believe.

In basic training, a Marine quickly learns to salute the flag every time the Marine passes it. This is both to show respect to the flag as a symbol of our country and to express a willingness to defend our nation at any cost—even if that cost be life itself. Hence, a Marine will proudly declare, "Semper Fi! I will be always faithful to the Marine Corps and to my country, even it costs me my very life."

Whenever young people are confirmed in their Christian faith, immediately after they confess the Apostles' Creed, they are asked, "Do you intend to continue steadfast in this confession and Church and to suffer all, even death, rather than fall away from it?" The young people respond, "I do so intend with the help of God." Like Marines, they declare in front of all those assembled, "*Semper Fi!* I will be always faithful—not just to my flag, but to the faith, even if it costs me my very life."

BELIEVE, TEACH, CONFESS

"Therefore, we have declared to one another with heart and mouth that we will not make or receive a separate or new confession of our faith. Instead, we will confess the public common writings, which always and everywhere were held and used as such symbols or common confessions in all the churches of the Augsburg Confession." (FC SD Summary 2)

This is the power of the creeds in a Christian's life. The creeds are so powerful that they would move a child of God to shout "Credo!" The creeds are so powerful that they would move a confirmand to promise to die for the faith expressed by them. The creeds are so powerful because they point us to our Savior who died for the forgiveness of our sins. The creeds are so powerful because for over two thousand years, the Christian Church has proclaimed, "Credo! I believe! I believe in God: the Father, Son, and Holy Spirit. And even if I have to suffer death, I will still believe." So, we join in the refrain of the creeds. The creeds are not only expressions of the Church's faith, they are expressions of our faith—a faith that is always sure, for it is a faith that clings to Christ.

Scripture Passages Containing Early Creedal Formulas

Creeds express what we believe and who we believe in. The three Ecumenical Creeds were not the first time that Christians had used creedal statements. Here are some examples from Scripture:

Now when Jesus came into the district of Caesarea Philippi, He asked His disciples, "Who do people say that the Son of Man is?" And they said, "Some say John the Baptist, others say Elijah, and others Jeremiah or one of the prophets." He said to them, "But who do you say that I am?" Simon Peter replied, "You are the Christ, the Son of the living God." (Matthew 16:13–16)

Thomas answered [Jesus], "My Lord and my God!" (John 20:28)

Have this mind among yourselves, which is yours in Christ Jesus, who, though He was in the form of God, did not count equality with God a thing to be grasped, but made Himself nothing, taking the form of a servant, being born in the likeness of men. And being found in human form, He humbled Himself by becoming obedient to the point of death, even death on a cross. Therefore God has highly exalted Him and bestowed on Him the name that is above every name, so that at the name of Jesus every knee should bow, in heaven and on earth and under the earth, and every tongue confess that Jesus Christ is Lord, to the glory of God the Father. (Philippians 2:5–11)

[Christ] is the image of the invisible God, the firstborn of all creation. For by Him all things were created, in heaven and on earth, visible and invisible, whether thrones or dominions or rulers or authorities—all things were created through Him and for Him. And He is before all things, and in Him all things hold together. And He is the head of the body, the church. He is the beginning, the firstborn from the dead, that in everything He might be preeminent. For in Him all the fullness of God was pleased to dwell, and through Him to reconcile to Himself all things, whether on earth or in heaven, making peace by the blood of His cross. (Colossians 1:15–20)

The saying is trustworthy, for: If we have died with Him, we will also live with Him; if we endure, we will also reign with Him; if we deny Him, He also will deny us; if we are faithless, He remains faithful—for He cannot deny Himself. (2 Timothy 2:11–13)

CHAPTER 32

We Love God and Our Neighbors

In This Chapter

- God does not match the contributions of our works with His grace.
- Good works are the fruit of faith.
- The good works we do give evidence of a living faith.

The good works we do are a great benefit to our family, friends, neighbors, and all the people with whom we share God's good earth. The key question this: do we do good works for God, for us, or for our neighbor? The most appropriate answer is that our works serve our neighbor.

Yet we humans are bound to think that good works are for God so that we can get on God's good side. But God does not need your good works. They can do nothing to make Him love you or love you more. In fact, thinking about good works in this way leads you away from the heart of His love: grace. God's love for you is pure grace. Grace is God's desire from the depths of His heart for you to be His. At the center of His heart of grace is His Son. And there is nothing anyone's works could do to make the Father's heart fill with more grace for him or her.

BELIEVE, TEACH, CONFESS

"Our churches teach that this faith is bound to bring forth good fruit [Galatians 5:22–23]. It is necessary to do good works commanded by God [Ephesians 2:10], because of God's will. We should not rely on those works to merit justification before God. The forgiveness of sins and justification is received through faith." (AC VI 1–2)

It Begins with Christ

Since the Father chooses freely to love His despicable creatures, human works cannot be part of any conversation with God. Thus, Lutherans prohibit talk of works when discussing God's desire that people be restored to a relationship with Him. God the Father's Son, Jesus Christ, stands at the center of that restored relationship. His mercy is God's mercy. His grace is God's grace. In Christ's death and resurrection, He is merciful to a rebellious humanity alienated from His Father. Here is a gift beyond all measure: that God loves us by means of our very act of crucifying His Son. If this is how God loves His creatures, even to the point of dying at their hands, then what could He want with our parade of good works? He is gracious to you because He wants to love you in His Son. He freely gives you His heart, His very self. Bargaining with Him with our works mocks His grace.

The point being made here is that God is the cause of your salvation. You have absolutely nothing to do with it. Lutherans have said that justification is by grace through faith for Christ's sake alone. You are made righteous by grace through faith alone apart from works. We are all familiar with retirement accounts in which employers provide matching funds to the contributions the employees make. But this is not how justification works. God does not match the contributions of our works with His grace. That is works-righteousness. God's righteousness is the free gift of God in Christ. If God were a banker, He would be out of business because He would have given all the bank's assets away! And He acts without any investment of works on your part.

Faith Bearing Fruit

This doesn't mean Lutherans just throw up their hands and say, "Who needs good works!" Instead, Lutherans believe good works have their right place in human life. Good works are the fruit of faith.

While you may not be a fruit grower, imagine a yard with two apple trees and a peach tree. One of the apple trees always produces a solid crop of apples. The peach tree is much more fickle. In some years an early frost can kill its fruitfulness. The other apple tree is more often than not a failure, with many of the apples simply bad. It is an apple tree in name only.

We expect fruit trees to produce the fruit that they were created and cultivated to produce. So Christians are expected to be like the first apple tree: consistently filled with fruit. Likewise, Christians bear fruit appropriate to the tree into which they have been implanted: Jesus Christ, the faithful Son of God. The heavenly Father wants to renew and re-create His creatures so that they become what He intended them to be: children that trust Him and are faithful to His desires and will. In a word, fruitful. By uniting you to Christ and His resurrection through the gift of His life-creating Spirit, God makes you fruitful apple trees like God's Great Apple Tree, Jesus Christ (there is a classic American hymn by that name, "Jesus Christ the Apple Tree" by Elizabeth Poston). This is what Lutherans mean when they say that good works follow from true, living faith as certainly and without doubt as fruit from a good tree. Good works are the fruit of faith and of justification through Christ alone.

What Are Good Works?

If good works are the fruit of faith, this begs the question: what kinds of works are good? Since they are the fruit of faith, works that are good are works related to faith in God. Good works are related to faith because God has freed those who believe to truly do good works. If people trust that God loves them graciously in Christ, then they have been freed from worrying about their eternal future. They have certainty about who they are and where life and death are ultimately leading. They can freely love God and spontaneously love their neighbors, all those around them, by attending to their needs.

People love God by trusting in Him, receiving good gifts from Him, praying to Him, and thanking, praising, and worshiping Him. People love and serve their neighbors by supporting their neighbors' lives, honoring authority and the rule

BELIEVE, TEACH, CONFESS

"Good works certainly and without doubt follow true faith—if it is not a dead, but a living faith—just as fruit grows on a good tree [Matthew 7:17]." (FC Ep IV 6)

WHAT DOES THIS MEAN?

Luther wrote that good works are God's work in us: "For if it is a good work, God has done it through me and in me. But if God has done it and it is God's work, what is the whole world in comparison with God and His work? Now although I do indeed not become pious through such works (for this must have taken place previously, through Christ's blood and grace without works), yet I do them for the praise and honor of God and for the benefit and welfare of my fellow man." (*What Luther Says*, § 4881)

of law, honoring their spouses, parenting well, and defending the possessions and reputations of their neighbors. It may appear that this brief list of good works echoes the Ten Commandments. It does. They are works that are according to God's will. And if we trust God, then we know that following His will is what is best for us and for those around us. Thus, good works are the fruit of faith in God.

Good Works Are Necessary

Because good works are God's will for your life in Christ, they are necessary. They are not necessary as a way of assuring that God loves you and is gracious to you. But they are necessary for the sake of your neighbor's life and as a sign that faith is living in you. It's much like making waffles. Many waffle recipes call for baking powder. If an inexperienced chef thinks that substituting baking soda will work just as well, the end result will be something that looks like a waffle but tastes extremely bitter.

Good works are essential for enabling those around you to live healthy, productive, full, and faith-centered lives. In addition, good works are necessary as markers that assure us that faith is alive in us. The good works we do give evidence of a living faith. We know the tree is living if it is producing good fruit.

FROM THE BIBLE

"So also faith by itself, if it does not have works, is dead. But someone will say, 'You have faith and I have works.' Show me your faith apart from your works, and I will show you my faith by my works." (James 2:17–18)

Furthermore, our good works serve us as a fence around the garden of our faith. The more good works cover the fences of our lives, the less likely the diseases and destructive insects of sin can penetrate faith's garden.

Abound in good works! God doesn't need them for Him to love you. But your neighbor needs them to live. And you will have proof that you are a living branch in the Great Apple Tree: Jesus Christ.

Living in Two Kingdoms

By Rev. John T. Pless

Created and redeemed by God, Christians are sanctified to serve Him in the ordinary places of life. Martin Luther called these ordinary places of life the "three estates" of Church, civil government, and family. It is within these earthly places where God is served through the loving service rendered to the neighbor. We have become accustomed to think of vocation only in terms of an occupation or a job. A vocational counselor is one who helps you determine what line of work you should pursue. A vocational school provides you with training to perform a particular job. If you are asked, "What is your vocation?" you are likely to answer, "I am an accountant, a farmer, or a pastor." Now such an answer would be partially correct. The work you do with your head and hands to provide others with needed services and earn a wage for yourself is indeed part of your vocation. But it is only part. Vocation means "calling," and this calling embraces the whole of your life.

God Himself Does the Calling

The apostle Peter says that God has "called you out of darkness into His marvelous light" (1 Peter 2:9), thus giving you a high and holy status as a member of a chosen generation, a priest in His royal priesthood, a citizen in that holy nation of the elect. This calling is the calling to faith itself. Therefore, Paul writes to the Thessalonians, "But we ought always to give thanks to God for you, brothers beloved by the Lord, because God chose you as the firstfruits to be saved, through sanctification by the Spirit and belief in the truth. To this He called you through our gospel, so that you may obtain the glory of our Lord Jesus Christ" (2 Thessalonians 2:13–14). On the basis of God's redeeming work in Christ, the apostle implores the Ephesians "to walk in a manner worthy of the calling to which you have been called" (4:1). Luther reflects the language and thought of Paul when he has us confess in the explanation of the Third Article of the Creed that "the Holy Spirit has called me by the Gospel." This is the calling to faith in Christ, and this calling gives us a new identity and status before God not determined by achievements or capacities.

The Scriptures also speaking of "calling" in connection with our place in creation. For example, in his first letter to the congregation at Corinth, the apostle Paul reminds these Christians that they were bought with the price of the Lord's own blood. Then, he continues "So, brothers, in whatever condition each was called, there let him remain with God" (1 Corinthians 7:24). Those who are married may not use their faith as an excuse for divorce. The slave may not use his or her freedom in Christ as the grounds for running away from an earthly master.

The Christian Calling Is Twofold

- First, it is a calling faith (Third Article).
- Second, and at the same time, it is a calling to a life of love that flows from faith (Ten Commandments).

In this calling, the heavenly and the earthly are joined together. While both Christians and non-Christians are parents, children, governors, citizens, employers, and employees, only believers can be said to have a calling. In other words, the Christian who occupies a particular station in life fulfills his or her spiritual calling in that sphere.

On the other hand, the unbeliever may perform works that are outwardly good in his or her particular station as a parent, worker, or citizen, but as this work is done apart from faith, it may not be said to be

WHAT DOES THIS MEAN?

Luther's doctrine of vocation is about "being" before it is about "doing." In one of his essential treatises, "The Freedom of a Christian" (1520), Luther writes: "Good works do not make a good man, but a good man does good works; evil works do not make a wicked man, but a wicked man does evil works." Consequently it is always necessary that the substance or person himself must be good before there can be any good works, and that good works follow and proceed from the good person, as Christ also says 'A good tree cannot bear evil fruit, nor can a bad tree bear good fruit' [Matt. 7:18]. It is clear that the fruits do not bear the tree and that the tree does not grow on the fruits, also that, on the contrary, the trees bear the fruits and the fruits grow on the trees. (AE 31:361)

a calling. Such work indeed falls under the realm of "civic righteousness." It has great value before man and is used by God for the good of His creation. The pagan farmer who provides us with food is a mask or covering of God, through which God gives us daily bread. But in the presence of God such work is without holiness; indeed this work is altogether sinful because the person who does it is a sinner without faith in Christ.

The dual calling of a Christian to faith and love means that we are not evacuated from the world, sucked up by a celestial vacuum cleaner into the safety of heaven. Like salt, believers are sprinkled through creation. Like light they are left in the world to penetrate its darkness. Faith receives God's gifts, and as these gifts have their way with us, they move us to give as the Lord has given all things to us. Luther crafted a prayer for use in the liturgy after the congregation had received the body and blood of Christ in the Sacrament of the Altar. Luther's prayer, called the Post-Communion Collect, reads in part, "We give thanks to You, almighty God, that You have refreshed us through this salutary gift, and we implore You that of Your mercy You would strengthen us through the same in faith toward You and in fervent love toward one another" (LSB, p. 166). The Sacrament strengthens us in faith toward God and in love toward the neighbor. God's service to us cannot but lead to our service of the neighbor. That is the movement of the Lutheran understanding of vocation.

WHAT DOES THIS MEAN?

The dual calling of the Christian is well expressed by Luther: "We conclude, therefore, that a Christian lives not in himself, but in Christ and in his neighbor. Otherwise he is not a Christian. He lives in Christ through faith, and in his neighbor through love."

The existence of the old Adam is focused on self. The old Adam is curved in on himself to use the imagery of Luther. This existence stands in bold contrast to the life of the new man in Christ. The new man lives outside of himself for his calling is to faith in Christ and love for the neighbor. Again, listen to Luther: "By faith he is caught up beyond himself into God. By love he descends beneath himself into his neighbor." (AE 31:371)

CHAPTER 33

We Tell Others

In This Chapter

- Those who know the Good News will want to share it with others.
- God carries out His mission through the men and women who make up the Church.
- Lutheran churches all around world send their emissaries to locations near and far to announce the Good News of God's love to a world that is in need of hope and life.

When we believe that Jesus Christ is the only answer to humankind's dilemma and the only means by which anyone can have a right relationship with God, then those who know the Good News will want to share it with others.

When we believe that without faith in Jesus Christ there can only be eternal separation from God here and in eternity (called hell), then those who have been saved will want to tell others about the true life that can be found only in Jesus.

FROM THE BIBLE

"For the love of Christ controls us, because we have concluded this: that one has died for all, therefore all have died; and He died for all, that those who live might no longer live for themselves but for Him who for their sake died and was raised." (2 Corinthians 5:14–15)

The Heart of Mission Work

This desire to go tell others about Jesus is the result of the Holy Spirit's work in each believer, and it is at the heart of the Church's mission.

The **basis** for Christian mission to the world, then, is the universal dimension of the Gospel. By that we mean the reality that the work of Christ was effective for all people, everywhere. This is seen most explicitly in the "Gospel in a nutshell," John 3:16: "For God so loved the world, that He gave His only Son. . . ." The Lutheran believes that he or she can tell anyone, no matter how serious his or her fault or errors, "Christ died for you."

The **goal** of mission from a Lutheran perspective is expressed in the Lord's Prayer (Matthew 6:9–13), taught by Jesus Himself, who said one should pray,

"Thy kingdom come." When we pray that petition of the Lord's Prayer, we are asking that God's kingdom would come not only to us, but that the Gospel would be preached to all the world so that others who do not know of the depth of God's love for them may hear that news and trust in Christ.

The **source** of Christian mission, however, is to be found in God Himself; therefore, when we speak of missions, we often use the term *Missio Dei* because it points to the primary source of Christian mission: it is the mission of God. But God carries out His mission through the men and women who make up the Church. For example, God sent the reluctant disciple Ananias to Saul of Tarsus, informing him that Saul (later known as Paul) was going to be His (God's) "chosen instrument" whom He would send to carry His name "before the Gentiles and kings and the children of Israel" (Acts 9:15).

"You Will Be My Witnesses"

A useful paradigm for how Lutherans understand mission today is the outline that Christ Himself gave to the disciples: "You will be My witnesses in Jerusalem and in all Judea and Samaria, and to the end of the earth" (Acts 1:8). Like a ripple from a stone that is cast into a pond, the Gospel message travels outward in ever-expanding concentric circles. Today, this means that Lutherans recognize that mission begins locally, with individual Christians speaking the Gospel to those around them, especially their friends and neighbors. "Judea and Samaria" today means that Lutherans recognize that there are people who, while they may live nearby geographically, are still distant culturally or linguistically.

Lutheran congregations often join together to sponsor mission work to diverse ethnic or linguistic groups. It is not unusual for Lutherans in any given city to get personally involved in or sponsor mission work among, for example, refugees from Myanmar or immigrants from Latin America or Africa. Such mission work would include helping people with their physical and spiritual needs.

"To the ends of the earth" is what happens when Lutherans become a part of mission work around the world. Lutherans commission, send, and support missionaries to go to "all nations" (Matthew 28:19). Some of those missionaries are ordained ministers who proclaim the Gospel and help to establish worshiping communities. Their evangelistic work is often carried out together with others, such as doctors, dentists, and nurses who are involved in medical work; agronomists who work in agricultural development; and linguists who specialize in translating the Bible into one of the thousands of living languages that do not yet have the Word of God in their language.

FROM THE BIBLE

"Go therefore and make disciples of all nations, baptizing them in the name of the Father and of the Son and of the Holy Spirit." (Matthew 28:19)

Because they affirm, as the apostle Paul did, "we also believe, and so we also speak" (2 Corinthians 4:13), Lutheran churches all around world send their emissaries to locations near and far to announce the Good News of God's love to a world that is in need of hope and life, to establish new congregations, and to train clergy from the local membership.

EVANGELISM BASICS

While some people are called to go to other countries as missionaries, many people are called to be missionaries right at home among their family, friends, and neighbors. If the idea of preaching on a street corner or moving to the other side of the world scares you, God is probably not calling you to do those things, at least not at this point in your life.

Sharing the Gospel

Know Your Goal

Our goal in evangelism is that people come to know that God loves them and that He sent Jesus to be their Savior from sin. Christianity is not just a religion. Christianity is a relationship with God based on what Jesus has done for us instead of what we should do for ourselves.

Be Prepared to Make the Most of Every Opportunity

See 1 Peter 3:15 and Ephesians 5:15–17

Some ways you can be prepared are to memorize Bible verses, keep some key Bible verses on a card in your wallet, carry a Bible with you, pray, and know where to find answers to questions people might ask.

The Holy Spirit Will Help You

See John 14:26 and Mark 13:11

The Holy Spirit will help you to remember verses and choose the right words when someone is ready to hear about Jesus. As long as what comes to mind fits with what the Bible says, go with the flow.

Be Patient

See 2 Peter 3:9

It can feel discouraging when someone we care about keeps rejecting Jesus despite our best efforts. In the same way that we do not see a seed sprouting until it breaks through the soil's surface, the work that the Holy Spirit is doing on that person's soul might not be evident. Remember that God is in control, and He loves that person even more than you do.

Key Gospel Bible Verses

People are sinful and cannot save themselves.	Romans 3:23–24
The fair punishment for sin is death.	Romans 6:23
Jesus died in our place so we could be forgiven.	Isaiah 53:5
Everyone who believes in Jesus is saved.	John 3:16
There is only one way to be saved: a relationship with Jesus.	Acts 4:12
God chose us.	Romans 5:8
We do good works as a response to the love God first showed us.	Ephesians 2:8–10

Some Low-Pressure Evangelism Ideas

- Pray for people who do not yet know Jesus.
- Read Bible stories to your children or grandchildren.
- Sing with a Christian choir at a retirement home or hospital.
- Teach Sunday School or help with Vacation Bible School.
- Send out Christmas or Easter cards with Bible verses.
- Give Bibles to people as gifts for graduations, weddings, or baby showers.
- Visit with and deliver Bibles to people in nursing homes, shelters, jails, and hospitals.
- Invite a friend or neighbor to church for worship, Bible study, or a special event.
- Send letters and care packages to college students or soldiers.
- Give a Christian tract, invitation to your church, or something of the sort along with the candy you hand out at Halloween.
- Make a habit of mentioning your church activities to friends and co-workers in the same way that you would share whatever else you did over the weekend.
- Attend a seekers or new members class with a friend who has questions.

CHAPTER 34

We Share Our Blessings

In This Chapter

- Stewardship recognizes that all we are and all we have is a gift from God.
- The driving force behind stewardship is love.
- God desires us to give out of love for Him and to bless those around us.

For Lutherans, stewardship is the thankful and faith-full response to all that God is and does for us. It is not a case of the "gottas" but a case of the "can't help its!" What we do with our time, talents, and treasures flows from our relationship with God. A commonly used definition of stewardship is this: "Christian stewardship is the free and joyous activity of the child of God and God's family, the Church, in managing all of life and life's resources for God's purposes." Stewardship recognizes that all we are and all we have is a gift from God that we receive and are called to manage. Stewardship recognizes that God remains the owner. We bring nothing into the world, and we cannot take anything with us when we leave. Ever seen a hearse hauling a U-haul?

NEED TO KNOW

Stewardship: The meaning of the biblical word for stewardship is "the management of a household," usually on behalf of someone else.

Offering Yourself

Stewardship is far more than tossing cash in an offering basket. It involves all the resources in our lives! During the offering time in our services, it would be a far more accurate portrayal of stewardship to pass a laundry basket instead of an offering basket—not for a huge cash offering (though that would be cool with most churches), but so that people could step into the basket. You see, God desires *you*, and your giving is a reflection of your relationship with God!

FROM THE BIBLE

King David on Stewardship: "But who am I, and what is my people, that we should be able thus to offer willingly? For all things come from You, and of Your own have we given You." (1 Chronicles 29:14)

FROM THE BIBLE

Jesus on Stewardship: "Give, and it will be given to you. Good measure, pressed down, shaken together, running over, will be put into your lap. For with the measure you use it will be measured back to you." (Luke 6:38)

Love Gives!

The driving force behind stewardship is love. God so loved us that He gave . . . gave us Jesus to die for us. . . . Jesus gave His life for us and gives us life and all our resources. We respond in love back to Him with our giving. God desires us to give out of love for Him and to bless those around us. Think about it—you can give without loving, but you can never love without giving.

The appropriate question we ask ourselves is not how much do we have to give to God (or the least amount we can get away with!), but given that everything belongs to Him, how much are we going to keep for ourselves and how much are we going to use to fulfill His mission and purposes in and through us?

Remember the U-haul behind the hearse idea? Well, there actually is one thing we can take with us when we go: lives changed in Jesus' name. It is to this end and for God's glory that we give!

Putting It All Together

By Gene Edward Veith Jr.

As a refugee—or casualty—of many different kinds of churches and religions before I became a Lutheran, I find the Lutheran Church uniquely satisfying. It has the good parts of all of the other kinds of Christianity. And its distinctive qualities zero in on what is most essential in the Christian faith.

One of my relatives said, "You Lutherans are just like Catholics." Well, not really, but sort of. Like Catholicism, Lutheranism is sacramental. Lutherans really believe that this material world can convey spiritual reality. In Baptism, physical water effects a spiritual cleansing. In Holy Communion, we really believe that Jesus Christ is there and that when we eat the bread and drink the wine we are receiving His body and His blood. (Yes, that is a mind-blowing concept, and my mind is blown every Sunday, to my great benefit.)

Like Catholicism, Lutheranism is historical, in solidarity with the Christianity that goes back throughout the centuries. This means that Lutherans, like Catholics, tend to worship with some version of the ancient liturgy. We do not have to, strictly speaking, but in my case, once I got used to it, I found it more meaningful and even more emotional than any other kind of worship I had previously experienced. (The words of the liturgy are pretty much all taken from the Word of God, so no wonder.)

Also like Catholics we draw on the rich spiritual heritage of the Church through the ages, including the Church Fathers of ancient Rome and medieval writers such as St. Bernard of Clairvaux. We keep denying that we "broke away" from Rome, insisting that we were just trying to reform things, only to get kicked out! What needed reforming are things like the papacy, ritualism, indulgences, legalism, and extrabiblical add-ons to

Christianity. But Lutherans do not throw out the baby with the holy water.

Yet my Catholic friends consider us Lutherans arch-Protestants. And indeed, Lutherans possess everything distinctive about Protestants also. For example, Lutherans emphasize the Bible as much as any Baptist preacher or evangelical Bible study leader. Orthodox Lutherans believe the Bible is inerrant, the ultimate authority, God's personal revelation to human beings by means of human language. We even ratchet that up: the Word of God is also sacramental, conveying God's grace to those who hear or read it, scaring us to death by the severity of God's Law (bringing us to repentance) and comforting us to life by the love in Christ's Gospel (bringing us to faith).

Speaking of that Gospel—the Good News that Christ died for our sins and offers salvation as a free gift—Lutherans preach it and cling to it, just as Evangelicals do. (The word *Evangelical* comes from the word *evangel*, meaning "good news," which is what *Gospel* means. The term *Evangelical* originally meant "Lutheran.")

Again, as with the Word of God, Lutherans ratchet up the concept. Many Protestant Evangelicals today see the Gospel mainly in terms of their conversion, that is, when they first became Christians. Having accepted the Gospel a long time ago, they now assume the Christian life is about following God's Law. Lutherans, though, see the Gospel as something that we need every day and every moment, so that we are always repenting and experiencing Christ's forgiveness, receiving Christ every time we encounter His Word or receive His body broken for us and His blood poured out for the remission of our sins in Holy Communion. Our response to the Gospel is faith, and the Christian life has to do with growing in faith, which, in turn, bears fruit in good works and love for our neighbors. But Lutherans are, indeed, Protestants (a term also first applied to Lutherans).

We are different, perhaps, in our emphasis on the freedom of the Gospel, so that we do not get hung up on extra-biblical pieties and moralisms that characterize many conservative Protestants. For example, some evangelicals are shocked and scandalized to find that Lutheran congregations may well serve beer at their church dinners! Other Evangelicals find the "Lutheran beverage" refreshing, especially because instead of feeling guilty about it, they can enjoy it as a gift of God.

Lutheranism exhibits the best parts of the different varieties of Protestantism. When I was in college, the Evangelical campus ministries that I fell in with were torn with controversies between Calvinists, Arminians, and charismatics. For me, Lutheranism fulfills them all. Like Calvinists, Lutherans believe that we are saved by grace alone, that God does absolutely everything for our salvation; but whereas Calvinists push that notion into the logical extremes of double predestination and limited atonement, Lutherans, understanding the Word and Sacraments as Means of Grace, believe that potentially anyone can be saved because Christ died for all. Like Arminians, Lutherans emphasize God's love and the universality of Christ's sacrifice; but whereas Arminians focus on the role of the human will in both salvation and in the possibility of moral perfection, Lutherans, with a more radical view of both sin and grace, stress the role of God's will rather than our own. Like charismatics, Lutherans expect a direct experience of the supernatural and direct contact with the Godhead. But finessing the dangers of spiritual subjectivity, Lutherans find God's *charisma* (the Greek word for "gift") in His gifts of the Word—in which the Holy Spirit is present—and the Sacraments, in which Christ is miraculously, supernaturally present.

For me, Lutheranism represents a wholeness of Christianity, embracing the most salient features of Catholicism (including Eastern Orthodoxy) and Protestantism (including its various sects). This, of course, means that Lutheranism will be attacked from all sides (Catholics condemning it for being Protestant; Protestants for being Catholic; Calvinists for being Arminian; Arminians for being Calvinist; charismatics for being dead). And frankly, it means that Lutherans will attack all of the others for what they leave out. Part of the unattractiveness of Lutheranism for some people is its theological combativeness. But it isn't that Lutherans have the only truth, though some may seem to act that way. Lutheranism has actually helped me to appreciate other kinds of Christianity. But the Lutheran synthesis depends on a delicate balance that must be defended at every point.

Lutheranism, of course, has its own distinctives, elements that can pretty much be found only in Lutheran churches. These could be held in other churches, but they usually cannot be found among non-Lutherans, even though they go into the depths of the Christian mysteries.

One is the Lutheran focus on Christology. Martin Luther said that we ought not to think of God apart from His incarnation in Jesus Christ. We often think of God the Father as an abstract idea or as an amorphous being far above the universe who looks down on human suffering. But God has become flesh. Not that Lutherans deny the transcendence of the Father or that we believe in the Son of God only at the expense of the other persons of the Trinity. But God the Father has revealed Himself fully in Jesus. To see the Father, we must see Jesus. As Jesus told Philip, "Whoever has seen Me has seen the Father"

(John 14:9). So our knowledge of God must be mediated by our knowledge of the man Jesus.

One of the main reasons some people do not believe in God at all is the problem of the evil and suffering in the world. How could there be a God who looks down on all of the world's evil and suffering and does nothing about it? Notice the assumption: God is a transcendent being who "looks down." What if God actually enters this world of evil and suffering? What if, somehow, He took all of that evil and suffering into Himself? What if this incarnate God suffered the just penalty for all the world's evil? What if this allows for a cosmic forgiveness?

This, of course, is what all Christians believe that Jesus accomplished on the cross. But few Christians, oddly enough, apply Christology to the problem of suffering. This brings us to another Lutheran distinctive: the theology of glory versus the theology of the cross. We would expect God to come down as a mighty king to be victorious over His enemies, to answer all of our questions, and to solve all of our problems. Instead, God came as a baby to a unmarried mother who laid Him in a cattle trough; He was homeless; He was executed by torture. The incarnate God set aside His rightful glory for a cross. In doing so and by rising from the dead and then ascending to His glory, He redeemed us. By the same token, we want the way of glory— and so we expect all of our questions to be answered and all our problems solved—but we, too, have to bear our crosses. Ironically, in those times of our own weakness, suffering, and need, we find that Christ has taken up our crosses into His.

It has been said that American Christianity has no theology of suffering. Consequently, we assume that suffering is meaningless, and if we suffer we cannot bear it, to the point of thinking we must be outside of God's favor or there must not be a God at all. Lutheranism, to its great credit, has a theology of suffering.

But it also has a theology of everyday life that brings satisfaction and joy. One of the most helpful things I have learned since I became a Lutheran is the doctrine of vocation. To realize that just being a husband, a father, an employee, and a citizen are all callings from God, that the day-to-day tasks that all of these entail are holy before God—that was a revelation to me. Not only that, but God is working through human beings to bestow His gifts: He gives me my daily bread through farmers, bakers, and cooks; He protects me by police officers; He heals me by doctors, nurses, and pharmacists; He proclaims His Word and gives me Christ's body and blood through my pastor. And somehow, He is working through me. He created new life through my wife and I when we had our kids. He has taught young people to write through me in my job as an English professor. All of these vocations have the same purpose: to love and serve the different neighbors whom God brings to us in each of our multiple callings.

I used to think that I served God when I did church work and that everything else was just living or making a living. Now that I am a Lutheran, I know that in church God serves me through His Word and Sacraments and that He sends me out in my different vocations to live out my faith in love and service to my neighbors. He is still present, though, even in the mundane, ordinary routines of life, working through me and serving me through others. That gives my life a purpose and a meaning that I never realized before.

One more distinctive: Lutherans talk about "the chief article," "the doctrine upon which the Church rises or falls." That refers to the teaching of justification by faith, or to be more technical, justification by grace through faith in the work of Christ—in other words, the Gospel, the Good News of salvation through Christ. In Lutheran theology, everything goes back to this. Baptism is Christ saving us. Holy Communion is Christ giving us His broken body and His poured-out blood for the remission of our sins. The Bible conveys God's Law, which brings us to repentance, and His Gospel, which brings us to justifying faith. The Trinity is a unity of three persons, which enables us to say that God is love, and because He loves us, He saves us. Jesus is true God, because only God could bear our sins and save us like He did. In vocation, we are, to use Luther's words, little Christs to our neighbors as we sacrifice ourselves in love and service, just as Christ did for us. This "chief article" holds Lutheran spirituality together. It also holds life together. I never realized that until I became a Lutheran.

APPENDICES

Moving Forward

You may have finished the book, but that doesn't mean your journey is over. This section will help you build on the foundation of the basics in *Lutheranism 101* with some fun facts from the Bible and about Lutheran teaching, practice, and life. Additional resources will help you explore topics that interest you or your family. The glossary brings together words and phrases you might encounter in worship or Bible study.

Christian History Basics

3 BC—AD 100 Apostolic age: Jesus was born around 3 BC. He was crucified and ascended to heaven around AD 33. Fifty days after His ascension, Jesus sent the Holy Spirit to help, comfort, and guide believers. The apostles and many other believers worked tirelessly to spread the Good News about Jesus to as many people and places as they could.

100–312 Early Church: By AD 100, most of the eyewitnesses who had met Jesus had died, but the Church continued to grow both in the number of believers and the area of the world over which the Gospel had spread. Early Christians faced persecution by both Jewish leaders and Roman leaders. Many early Christians refused to deny their faith even when faced with violent deaths.

312 Roman Empire stopped persecuting Christians: When Emperor Constantine converted to Christianity, he ended the Roman Empire's persecution of Christians. He later made Sunday a public holiday.

325 Nicene Creed: In order to counter the false teachings by Arius, three hundred pastors met at the Council of Nicaea and came up with a statement of belief about the Trinity and the two natures of Jesus Christ (both God and man).

380 Roman Empire became Christian: Emperor Theodosius declared that Christianity was the only acceptable religion in the Roman Empire.

400 Vulgate Bible: A single, reliable Latin translation of the Bible was made the standard version of the Bible for the Christian Church.

431 and 451 Councils of Ephesus and Chalcedon: Many bishops and pastors met to counter false teachings about the nature of Jesus. The councils reaffirmed that the Nicene Creed accurately summarized the Christian understanding of God the Father, Jesus the Son, and the Holy Spirit. These councils also emphasized that Jesus has two natures (divine and human) in one person.

1054 Great Schism: The one Christian Church split into the western Roman Catholic and Eastern Orthodox branches because of disagreements about how the Trinity is represented in the Nicene Creed and whether priests should be allowed to marry.

1095–1261 Crusades: Many Christians in Europe felt that going on a pilgrimage to Jerusalem would prove their faith and make God pleased with them. When Islamic Turks took control of Jerusalem, many in the Christian lands believed they should fight a holy war to regain Jerusalem for Christians.

1184–1860 Inquisitions: Reacting to religious teachings that did not agree with the Church's doctrine and traditions, church courts were created to root out and punish heretics. There were several inquisitions at different times and in different places.

1517–1648 The Reformation: Martin Luther came to realize that several teachings of the Roman Catholic Church did not fit with what he read in the Bible. He tried to start a discussion that would find and fix what had gone wrong. However, the pope and other leaders received Luther's attempts at reform as a threat, and unwilling to listen or change, they declared him to be a heretic. Luther took his reform movement outside of the Roman Catholic Church, and so we now have a Protestant branch of Christianity in addition to the Roman Catholic and Eastern Orthodox branches.

Biblical Events Timeline

Biblical Events	Dates	World Events
	2560 BC	Great Pyramid of Giza completed
Abram is born (Genesis 11)	2166 BC	
God changes Abram's name to Abraham, and he is circumcised	2067 BC	
Jacob and Esau are born	2006 BC	
Moses is born	1526 BC	
First Passover	1446 BC	
David is born (2 Samuel 5:1–5)	1039 BC	
King Solomon reigns	970–931 BC	Egyptian Pharaoh's daughter marries Solomon
Temple built in Jerusalem (1 Kings 6:1)	967–960 BC	
God's people divided into two kingdoms: Israel and Judah	931 BC	
	776 BC	First Olympic Games
Zechariah becomes king of Israel	753 BC	Rome founded
Jeremiah called to be a prophet	628	
Temple in Jerusalem destroyed	587 BC	
	560 BC	Homer's *Iliad* and *Odyssey* written down
	551 BC	Confucius (founder of Confucianism) is born

	508 BC	Democracy in Athens
	438 BC	Parthenon completed
Jesus born	3–2 BC	
Jesus dies, rises again, and ascends to heaven; Holy Spirit sent to believers	AD 32–33	
Paul's conversion to Christianity	AD 36	
	AD 68	Peter and Paul martyred
	AD 70	Jerusalem temple destroyed
	AD 80	Roman Coliseum completed

For more details, see "Biblical Chronology and World History," *TLSB*, pp. xcii–cix.

Numbering of the Ten Commandments

While the Bible says definitively that there are "Ten Commandments," there is nowhere in Scripture that definitively states how the statements are divided. The main issue is whether one regards Exodus 20:4–6 as commentary on the First Commandment. Martin Luther's catechisms, the Roman Catholic Church, and the Lutheran Church see Exodus 20:4–6 as commentary and not as a separate commandment. The Eastern Church and churches in the Reformed tradition, including the Anglican traditions, see Exodus 20:4–6 as a second, distinct, commandment.

	Lutheran	Catholic	Orthodox	Other Christian	Jewish
I am the Lord your God…	close	1	1	preface	1
You shall have no other gods.	1			1	2
You shall not make for yourself an idol.			2	2	2
You shall not misuse the name of the Lord your God.	2	2	3	3	3
Remember the Sabbath day by keeping it holy.	3	3	4	4	4
Honor your father and your mother.	4	4	5	5	5
You shall not murder.	5	5	6	6	6
You shall not commit adultery.	6	6	7	7	7
You shall not steal.	7	7	8	8	8

You shall not give false testimony against your neighbor.	8	8	9	9	9
You shall not covet your neighbor's house.	9	9	10	10	10
You shall not covet . . . anything that belongs to your neighbor.	10	10			

Bible Buddies

David and Jonathan: Jonathan stayed loyal and protected his friend David when King Saul (Jonathan's father) wanted to kill David (1 Samuel 18:1–4; 23:15–18).

Job and his friends Eliphaz, Bildad, and Zophar: When Job's friends heard about all the terrible things that had happened to him, they went to Job and sat with him for seven days and nights without saying a word (Job 2:11–13). After that week, they tried their best to talk through the problem with Job.

Daniel, Shadrach, Meshach, and Abednego: These four friends stuck together, encouraged one another, and tried to protect one another through their exile to Babylon (Book of Daniel).

Jesus and Lazarus, Mary, and Martha: Lazarus had been dead for several days, and Jesus knew He could bring him back to life, but Jesus was so moved that He cried before raising Lazarus from the dead (John 11:1–44). Lazarus's sisters, Mary and Martha, were also close to Jesus (Luke 10:38–42).

Jesus, Peter, James, and John: Among the twelve disciples, Jesus had three friends with whom He was especially close. At important times like the transfiguration (Mark 9:2–13) and when Jesus was praying before He was arrested (Mark 14:32–42), Peter, James, and John were the only ones with Him. John is sometimes referred to as "the disciple whom Jesus loved," which may mean that John was Jesus' best friend. When Jesus was about to die on the cross, He gave His mother, Mary, over to John to take care of as his own mother (John 19:26–27).

King Herod and Pontius Pilate: They became friends the day Jesus was on trial and crucified. Before that they had been enemies (Luke 23:12).

Weird and Wonderful Bible Facts

About the Bible

The first book to be printed on Gutenberg's printing press was the Bible in 1455. Before then, copies of the Bible were handwritten.

Five books of the Bible are so short that they do not even have chapters. Obadiah, Philemon, 2 John, 3 John, and Jude only have verses.

Shortest book of the Bible	2 John has the fewest number of verses, and 3 John has the fewest number of words
Longest book of the Bible	Psalms
Number of verses in the Bible	31,173
Shortest Bible verse	"Jesus wept." (John 11:35)
Longest Bible verse	Esther 8:9 (more than 70 words)

People in the Bible

Oldest man	Methuselah lived to be 969 years old. (Genesis 5:27)
Oldest woman to give birth	Eve was 130 when she gave birth to Seth. Her husband Adam was also 130 years old. (Genesis 5:3)
Youngest king	Joash became king at 7 years old; Josiah became king at 8 years old. (2 Chronicles 24:1; 34:1)
Tallest person	Goliath was over 9 feet tall. (1 Samuel 17:4)
Wisest person	God told King Solomon that he could ask for whatever he wanted, and Solomon chose to ask God for wisdom so that he could be a good king. (1 Kings 3:12; 4:29–34)
Two people who never died	Enoch and Elijah (Genesis 5:22–24; 2 Kings 2:1–12)

Messiah Prophecies

Did you know that the Old Testament tells us a lot about Jesus long before He was even born?

Old Testament Reference	Prophecy	New Testament Fulfillment
Micah 5:2–4	Born in Bethlehem	Matthew 2:1–6
Isaiah 7:14	Born of a virgin	Matthew 1:18–23
Jeremiah 31:15	Herod killing the babies after Jesus' birth	Matthew 2:16–18
Zechariah 9:9	Riding into Jerusalem on a donkey (Palm Sunday)	John 12:13–15
Psalm 41:9	Betrayed by a friend who ate bread with Him	John 13:18–30
Isaiah 53:7	Silent before His accusers	Matthew 26:62–63
Isaiah 50:6	Being hit and spat on	Mark 14:65
Psalm 22:16	Hands and feet pierced	John 20:27
Psalm 22:6–8	People hurl insults, shaking their heads	Matthew 27:39–43
Psalm 69:21	Given gall and vinegar	Matthew 27:34
Psalm 22:18	People cast lots for His clothing	Mark 15:24
Isaiah 53:9	Buried with the rich	Matthew 27:57–60
Psalm 16:10	He doesn't stay dead	Matthew 28:1–10

When Jesus was born, the Jews were waiting for a Messiah descended from King David to come and save them. Many of them expected the Messiah to be a powerful king or military leader who would free them from the Romans. The name *Jesus* means "the Lord saves." Rather than saving the Jews from the Romans, He saved all people from our sins.

The words *Messiah* and *Christ* mean "Anointed One." In Bible times, people were anointed when they were set apart for specific important jobs like becoming a prophet, priest, or king. God set Jesus apart to be our ultimate Prophet, Priest, and King. As our *Prophet*, He teaches us about God. As our *Priest*, He made the sacrifice for our sins and is the mediator between sinful humans and God, who is holy. As our *King*, He is our rightful leader having authority over us but also a responsibility to take care of us.

For a more detailed list and explanation of prophecies about Jesus as our Messiah, see *TLSB*, p. 1245.

Spiritual Gifts

A good starting point to learn about gifts of the Holy Spirit is to read Romans 12:6–8; 1 Corinthians 12 and 14; and Ephesians 4:7–12.

Spiritual gifts are given to believers so that they can build one another up and reach people who do not know Jesus yet. God's plan for His people is that we work together like a body, with each of us serving a different purpose that benefits the whole (Romans 12:4–6).

God lovingly creates each person with a unique set of natural gifts and abilities. Spiritual gifts are additional abilities and tasks the Holy Spirit gives only to Christians. Each Christian receives different gifts based on what God is calling him or her to do (1 Peter 4:10; 1 Corinthians 12:7).

While some people claim that having an ability to speak in tongues proves that a person is a Christian, there is no support for that claim based on the Bible (1 Corinthians 14:1–25).

Gift of the Spirit	Bible Reference
Administration	1 Corinthians 12:28
Being an apostle	1 Corinthians 12:28–29; Ephesians 4:11
Contributing to needs of others / helping others	Romans 12:8; 1 Corinthians 12:28
Distinguishing between spirits	1 Corinthians 12:10
Encouraging	Romans 12:8
Evangelism	Ephesians 4:11
Faith	1 Corinthians 12:9
Healing	1 Corinthians 12:9, 28, 30
Interpretation of tongues	1 Corinthians 12:10, 30
Knowledge	1 Corinthians 12:8
Leadership	Romans 12:8
Miraculous powers / working miracles	1 Corinthians 12:10, 28–29
Being a pastor	Ephesians 4:11
Prophecy	Romans 12:6; 1 Corinthians 12:10, 28–29; 14:1–25; Ephesians 4:11

Serving	Romans 12:7
Showing mercy	Romans 12:8
Speaking in tongues	1 Corinthians 12:10, 28, 30; 14:1–25
Teaching	Romans 12:7; 1 Corinthians 12:28–29; Ephesians 4:11
Wisdom	1 Corinthians 12:8

The Church Year

Sundays and Seasons

The Time of Christmas

Advent Season
First Sunday in Advent B/V
Second Sunday in Advent B/V
Third Sunday in Advent B/V
Fourth Sunday in Advent B/V

Christmas Season
THE NATIVITY OF OUR LORD W
Christmas Eve
Christmas Midnight
Christmas Dawn
Christmas Day
First Sunday after Christmas W
Second Sunday after Christmas W

Epiphany Season
The Epiphany of Our Lord W
First Sunday after the Epiphany W
The Baptism of Our Lord
Second Sunday after the Epiphany G
Third Sunday after the Epiphany G
Fourth Sunday after the Epiphany G
Fifth Sunday after the Epiphany G
Sixth Sunday after the Epiphany G
Seventh Sunday after the Epiphany G ⎤ 3-Year
Eighth Sunday after the Epiphany G ⎦ Lect.
Last Sunday after the Epiphany W
The Transfiguration of Our Lord

The Time of Easter

Pre-Lent Season
Septuagesima G ⎤ 1-Year
Sexagesima G ⎥ Lect.
Quinquagesima G ⎦

Lenten Season
Ash Wednesday BK/V
First Sunday in Lent V
Second Sunday in Lent V
Third Sunday in Lent V

Fourth Sunday in Lent V
Fifth Sunday in Lent V

Holy Week
Palm Sunday S/V
Sunday of the Passion
Monday in Holy Week S/V
Tuesday in Holy Week S/V
Wednesday in Holy Week S/V
Holy (Maundy) Thursday W/S/V
Good Friday BK
Holy Saturday BK

Easter Season
THE RESURRECTION OF OUR LORD W/GO
Vigil of Easter   Easter Tuesday
Easter Sunrise   Easter Wednesday
Easter Day
Easter Evening/Easter Monday
Second Sunday of Easter W
Third Sunday of Easter W
Fourth Sunday of Easter W
Fifth Sunday of Easter W
Sixth Sunday of Easter W
The Ascension of Our Lord W
Seventh Sunday of Easter W

Pentecost R
Pentecost Eve
The Day of Pentecost
Pentecost Evening/Pentecost Monday
Pentecost Tuesday

The Time of the Church

The Season after Pentecost
The Holy Trinity W
Second through Twenty-seventh Sunday
    after Pentecost *(3-Year Lectionary)* G
First through Twenty-sixth Sunday after
    Trinity *(1-Year Lectionary)* G
Last Sunday of the Church Year G

Feasts and Festivals

November
30 St. Andrew, Apostle R

December
21 St. Thomas, Apostle R
26 St. Stephen, Martyr R
27 St. John, Apostle and Evangelist W
28 The Holy Innocents, Martyrs R
31 **Eve of the Circumcision and Name of Jesus W**
     New Year's Eve

January
 1 **Circumcision and Name of Jesus W**
18 The Confession of St. Peter W
24 St. Timothy, Pastor and Confessor W
25 The Conversion of St. Paul W
26 St. Titus, Pastor and Confessor W

February
 2 **The Purification of Mary and the Presentation of Our Lord W**
24 St. Matthias, Apostle R

March
19 St. Joseph, Guardian of Jesus W
25 **The Annunciation of Our Lord W**

April
25 St. Mark, Evangelist R

May
 1 St. Philip and St. James, Apostles R
31 **The Visitation** *(3-Year Lectionary)* W

June
11 St. Barnabas, Apostle R
24 **The Nativity of St. John the Baptist W**
29 St. Peter and St. Paul, Apostles R

July
 2 **The Visitation** *(1-Year Lectionary)* W
22 St. Mary Magdalene W
25 St. James the Elder, Apostle R

August
15 St. Mary, Mother of Our Lord W
24 St. Bartholomew, Apostle R
29 The Martyrdom of St. John the Baptist R

September
14 Holy Cross Day R
21 St. Matthew, Apostle and Evangelist R
29 **St. Michael and All Angels W**

October
18 St. Luke, Evangelist R
23 St. James of Jerusalem, Brother of Jesus and Martyr R
28 St. Simon and St. Jude, Apostles R
31 Reformation Day R

November
 1 **All Saints' Day W**

Occasions

Anniversary of a Congregation R
Mission Observance W
Christian Education Color of Season
Harvest Observance Color of Season

Day of Thanksgiving W
Day of Supplication and Prayer V
Day of National or Local Tragedy V

The observances listed in **boldface** are principal feasts of Christ and are normally observed when they occur on a Sunday. The other festivals may be observed according to local custom and preference.

The letters indicate the suggested colors: B = blue, BK = black, G = green, GO = gold, R = red, S = scarlet, V = violet, W = white.

Commemorations

Our churches teach that the remembrance of the saints is to be commended in order that we may imitate their faith and good works according to our calling.

Augsburg Confession 21

The Lutheran reformers understood that there was great benefit in remembering the saints whom God has given to His Church. The Apology of the Augsburg Confession (Article 21) gives three reasons for such honor. First, we thank God for giving faithful servants to His Church. Second, through such remembrance our faith is strengthened as we see the mercy that God extended to His saints of old. Third, these saints are examples by which we may imitate both their faith and their holy living according to our calling in life. The calendar of commemorations given below lists a number of men and women from both the Old and New Testaments and from the first nineteen centuries of the Church's life. (Other New Testament persons and events are given with the Feasts and Festivals calendar on page xi.) Their defense of the fundamental beliefs of the Christian faith and/or their virtuous living have caused these individuals to stand out over time as persons worthy of recognition.

In every case, the purpose of our remembrance is not that we honor these saints for their own sake, but as examples of those in whom the saving work of Jesus Christ has been made manifest to the glory of His holy name and to the praise of His grace and mercy.

Therefore, since we are surrounded by so great a cloud of witnesses, let us also lay aside every weight, and sin which clings so closely, and let us run with endurance the race that is set before us.

Hebrews 12:1

January
2 J. K. Wilhelm Loehe, *Pastor*
10 Basil the Great of Caesarea, Gregory of Nazianzus, and Gregory of Nyssa, *Pastors and Confessors*
20 Sarah
27 John Chrysostom, *Preacher*

February
5 Jacob (Israel), *Patriarch*
10 Silas, *Fellow Worker of St. Peter and St. Paul*
13 Aquila, Priscilla, Apollos
14 Valentine, *Martyr*
15 Philemon and Onesimus
16 Philipp Melanchthon (birth), *Confessor*
18 Martin Luther, *Doctor and Confessor*
23 Polycarp of Smyrna, *Pastor and Martyr*

March
7 Perpetua and Felicitas, *Martyrs*
17 Patrick, *Missionary to Ireland*
31 Joseph, *Patriarch*

April
6 Lucas Cranach and Albrecht Dürer, *Artists*
20 Johannes Bugenhagen, *Pastor*
21 Anselm of Canterbury, *Theologian*
24 Johann Walter, *Kantor*

May
2 Athanasius of Alexandria, *Pastor and Confessor*
4 Friedrich Wyneken, *Pastor and Missionary*
5 Frederick the Wise, *Christian Ruler*
7 C. F. W. Walther, *Theologian*
9 Job
11 Cyril and Methodius, *Missionaries to the Slavs*

21   Emperor Constantine, *Christian Ruler*, and Helena, *Mother of Constantine*
24   Esther
25   Bede the Venerable, *Theologian*

June
1   Justin, *Martyr*
5   Boniface of Mainz, *Missionary to the Germans*
12   The Ecumenical Council of Nicaea, AD 325
14   Elisha
25   Presentation of the Augsburg Confession
26   Jeremiah
27   Cyril of Alexandria, *Pastor and Confessor*
28   Irenaeus of Lyons, *Pastor*

July
6   Isaiah
16   Ruth
20   Elijah
21   Ezekiel
28   Johann Sebastian Bach, *Kantor*
29   Mary, Martha, and Lazarus of Bethany
30   Robert Barnes, *Confessor and Martyr*
31   Joseph of Arimathea

August
3   Joanna, Mary, and Salome, *Myrrhbearers*
10   Lawrence, *Deacon and Martyr*
16   Isaac
17   Johann Gerhard, *Theologian*
19   Bernard of Clairvaux, *Hymnwriter and Theologian*
20   Samuel
27   Monica, *Mother of Augustine*
28   Augustine of Hippo, *Pastor and Theologian*

September
1   Joshua
2   Hannah
3   Gregory the Great, *Pastor*
4   Moses
5   Zacharias and Elizabeth
16   Cyprian of Carthage, *Pastor and Martyr*
22   Jonah
30   Jerome, *Translator of Holy Scripture*

October
7   Henry Melchior Muhlenberg, *Pastor*
9   Abraham
11   Philip the Deacon
17   Ignatius of Antioch, *Pastor and Martyr*
25   Dorcas (Tabitha), Lydia, and Phoebe, *Faithful Women*
26   Philipp Nicolai, Johann Heermann, and Paul Gerhardt, *Hymnwriters*

November
8   Johannes von Staupitz, *Luther's Father Confessor*
9   Martin Chemnitz (birth), *Pastor and Confessor*
11   Martin of Tours, *Pastor*
14   Emperor Justinian, *Christian Ruler and Confessor of Christ*
19   Elizabeth of Hungary
23   Clement of Rome, *Pastor*
29   Noah

December
4   John of Damascus, *Theologian and Hymnwriter*
6   Nicholas of Myra, *Pastor*
7   Ambrose of Milan, *Pastor and Hymnwriter*
13   Lucia, *Martyr*
17   Daniel the Prophet and the Three Young Men
19   Adam and Eve
20   Katharina von Bora Luther
29   David

Top Ten Documents of Lutheranism in America

10. **First Constitution of "An Evangelical Lutheran Ministerium in North America"** (1781) It represents the first large-scale organization of Lutheran congregations in the United States.

9. **Constitution of the General Council of the Evangelical Lutheran Church in America** (1867) General Synod Lutherans put culture over Scripture and considered rewriting the Augsburg Confession. Charles Porterfield Krauth and others separated from the General Synod to preserve their fidelity to Scripture and the Book of Concord.

8. **Constitution of the German Evangelical Lutheran Synod of Missouri, Ohio, and Other States** (1846) Represented a means of adapting confessional Lutheranism to the American setting without doctrinal concessions or a dominant central authority.

7. **Constitution of the Evangelical Lutheran Synodical Conference** (1871) This group represented the largest fellowship of confessional Lutherans in North America for more than eighty years.

6. **Brief Statement of the Doctrinal Position of the Missouri Synod** (1932) This document restates the positions ratified by the Missouri Synod in 1893 and summarized in 1897.

5. J. M. Reu, **The Augsburg Confession.** Reu's study remains one of the most thorough. It provides an in-depth examination of core Lutheran documents.

4. **The Common Service.** With representation in the majority of hymnals used by Lutheran synods that speak English, this blend of Lutheran liturgy and Anglican influences represented a stately unity in practice that broadly identified American Lutherans for about ninety years.

3. R. C. H. Lenski's **New Testament commentaries.** Lenski's commentaries have been a long-time standard work for Lutheran pastors in America.

2. C. F. W. Walther's lectures available as **Law and Gospel: How to Read and Interpret the Bible.** Walther's lectures help readers to unlock the true meaning of Scripture and apply the Christ-centered message of Law and Gospel.

1. **The Book of Concord.** From 1851 onward, seven English editions of the Lutheran Confessions have appeared, three of these as popular editions.

Lutheran Churches around the World

There are three main groups of Lutheran churches in the world: the Lutheran World Federation (LWF), the International Lutheran Council (ILC), and the Confessional Evangelical Lutheran Conference (CELC). There are also various independent Lutheran churches and smaller groups of churches not listed below.

Africa

Angola	Evangelical Lutheran Church of Angola (LWF)
Botswana	Evangelical Lutheran Church in Botswana (LWF)
	Lutheran Church in Southern Africa (ILC)
Cameroon	Church of the Lutheran Brethren of Cameroon (LWF)
	Evangelical Lutheran Church of Cameroon (LWF)
	The Lutheran Church of Cameroon (CELC)
Central African Republic	Evangelical Lutheran Church of the Central African Republic (LWF)
Congo, Democratic Rep.	Evangelical Lutheran Church in Congo (LWF)
Congo, Republic	Evangelical Lutheran Church of Congo (LWF)
Eritrea	The Evangelical Lutheran Church of Eritrea (LWF)
Ethiopia	The Ethiopian Evangelical Church Mekane Yesus (LWF)
Ghana	Evangelical Lutheran Church of Ghana (ILC & LWF)
Kenya	Evangelical Lutheran Church in Kenya (ILC & LWF)
	Kenya Evangelical Lutheran Church (LWF)
Liberia	Lutheran Church in Liberia (LWF)
Madagascar	Malagasy Lutheran Church (LWF)
Malawi	Evangelical Lutheran Church in Malawi (LWF)
	Lutheran Church of Central Africa (CELC)
Mozambique	Evangelical Lutheran Church in Mozambique (LWF)
Namibia	Evangelical Lutheran Church in Namibia (LWF)
	Evangelical Lutheran Church in the Republic of Namibia (LWF)
	The Evangelical Lutheran Church in Namibia (LWF)
Nigeria	Christ the King Lutheran (CELC)
	The Lutheran Church of Christ in Nigeria (LWF)
	The Lutheran Church of Nigeria (ILC & LWF)
Rwanda	Lutheran Church of Rwanda (LWF)
Senegal	The Lutheran Church of Senegal (LWF)
Sierra Leone	Evangelical Lutheran Church in Sierra Leone (LWF)
South Africa	Evangelical Lutheran Church in Southern Africa (LWF)
	Free Evangelical-Lutheran Synod in South Africa (ILC)
	Lutheran Church in Southern Africa (ILC)
	Moravian Church in South Africa (LWF)
Tanzania	Evangelical Lutheran Church in Tanzania (LWF)

Swaziland	Lutheran Church in Southern Africa (ILC)
Zambia	Evangelical Lutheran Church in Zambia (LWF)
Zambia Conference	Lutheran Church of Central Africa (CELC)
Zimbabwe	Evangelical Lutheran Church in Zimbabwe (LWF)

Asia & Pacific

Australia	Evangelical Lutheran Synod of Australia (CELC)
	Lutheran Church of Australia (LWF)
Bangladesh	Bangladesh Lutheran Church (LWF)
	Bangladesh Northern Evangelical Lutheran Church (LWF)
China	China Evangelical Lutheran Church (ILC)
Georgia	Evangelical Lutheran Church in Russia and Other States (LWF)
Georgia	Evangelical Lutheran Church in Russia and Other States (LWF)
Hong Kong	The Lutheran Church—Hong Kong Synod (ILC)
	Hong Kong and Macau Lutheran Church (LWF)
	The Chinese Rhenish Church Hong Kong Synod (LWF)
	The Evangelical Lutheran Church of Hong Kong (LWF)
	Tsung Tsin Mission of Hong Kong (LWF)
India	India Evangelical Lutheran Church (ILC)
	Andhra Evangelical Lutheran Church (LWF)
	Evangelical Lutheran Church in Madhya Pradesh (LWF)
	Evangelical Lutheran Church in the Himalayan States (LWF)
	Gossner Evangelical Lutheran Church in Chotanagpur and Assam (LWF)
	India Evangelical Lutheran Church (LWF)
	Jeypore Evangelical Lutheran Church (LWF)
	Northern Evangelical Lutheran Church (LWF)
	South Andhra Lutheran Church (LWF)
	The Arcot Lutheran Church (LWF)
	The Tamil Evangelical Lutheran Church (LWF)
Indonesia	Geraja Lutheran (CELC)
	Batak Christian Community Church (LWF)
	Christian Communion of Indonesia Church in Nias [Gereja AMIN] (LWF)
	Christian Protestant Angkola Church (LWF)
	Christian Protestant Church in Indonesia (LWF)
	Indonesian Christian Lutheran Church (LWF)
	Pakpak Dairi Christian Protestant Church (LWF)
	Protestant Christian Batak Church (LWF)
	Protestant Christian Church in Mentawai (LWF)
	Simalungun Protestant Christian Church (LWF)
	The Indonesian Christian Church (LWF)
	The Protestant Christian Church (LWF)

	The United Protestant Church (LWF)
Israel	The Evangelical Lutheran Church in Jordan & the Holy Land (LWF)
Japan	Japan Lutheran Church (ILC and LWF)
	Japan Evangelical Lutheran Church (LWF)
	Kinki Evangelical Lutheran Church (LWF)
	Lutheran Evangelical Christian Church (CELC)
Jordan	The Evangelical Lutheran Church in Jordan & the Holy Land (LWF)
Kazakhstan	Evangelical Lutheran Church in Russia and Other States (LWF)
Korea	Lutheran Church in Korea (ILC)
	Lutheran Church in Korea (LWF)
Kyrgyzstan	Evangelical Lutheran Church in Russia and Other States (LWF)
Malaysia	Basel Christian Church of Malaysia
	Evangelical Lutheran Church in Malaysia
	Lutheran Church in Malaysia and Singapore
	The Protestant Church in Sabah
Myanmar	Evangelical Lutheran Church in Myanmar (LWF)
New Zealand	Lutheran Church of New Zealand
Papua New Guinea	Evangelical Lutheran Church of Papua New Guinea (LWF)
	Gutnius Lutheran Church (ILC)
	Gutnius Lutheran Church—Papua New Guinea (LWF)
Philippines	The Lutheran Church in the Philippines (ILC)
	Lutheran Church in the Philippines (LWF)
Singapore	Lutheran Church in Singapore (LWF)
Sri Lanka	Lanka Lutheran Church (ILC & LWF)
Taiwan	Taiwan Lutheran Church (LWF)
	The Lutheran Church of Taiwan (Republic of China) (LWF)
Thailand	The Evangelical Lutheran Church in Thailand (LWF)
Uzbekistan	Evangelical Lutheran Church in Russia and Other States (LWF)

Europe

Austria	Evangelical Church of the Augsburg Confession in Austria (LWF)
Belarus	Evangelical Lutheran Church in Russia and Other States (LWF)
Belgium	Evangelical Lutheran Church in Belgium (ILC)
	Lutheran Church of Belgium: Arlon and Christian Mission (LWF)
Bulgaria	Bulgarian Lutheran Church (CELC)
Croatia	Evangelical Church in the Republic of Croatia (LWF)

Czech Republic	Czech Evangelical Lutheran Church (CELC)
	Evangelical Church of Czech Brethren (LWF)
	Silesian Evangelical Church of the Augsburg Confession (LWF)
Denmark	Evangelical Lutheran Church in Denmark (LWF)
	Evangelical Lutheran Free Church in Denmark (ILC)
England	The Evangelical Lutheran Church of England (ILC)
Estonia	Estonian Evangelical Lutheran Church (LWF)
Finland	Evangelical Lutheran Church of Finland (LWF)
	Evangelical Lutheran Confessional Church (CELC)
France	Evangelical Lutheran Church—Synod of France (ILC)
	Evangelical Lutheran Church of France (LWF)
	Malagasy Protestant Church in France (LWF)
	Union of Protestant Churches of Alsace and Lorraine (LWF)
Germany	Evangelical Lutheran Free Church (CELC)
	Independent Evangelical—Lutheran Church (ILC)
	Church of Lippe (Lutheran Section) (LWF)
	Evangelical Church in Central Germany (LWF)
	Evangelical Church of Pomerania (LWF)
	Evangelical Lutheran Church in Baden (LWF)
	Evangelical Lutheran Church in Bavaria (LWF)
	Evangelical Lutheran Church in Brunswick (LWF)
	Evangelical Lutheran Church in Oldenburg (LWF)
	Evangelical Lutheran Church in Württemberg (LWF)
	Evangelical Lutheran Church of Hanover (LWF)
	Evangelical Lutheran Church of Mecklenburg (LWF)
	Evangelical Lutheran Church of Saxony (LWF)
	Evangelical Lutheran Church of Schaumburg-Lippe (LWF)
	Latvian Evangelical Lutheran Church Abroad (LWF)
	North Elbian Evangelical Lutheran Church (LWF)
Hungary	The Evangelical Lutheran Church in Hungary (LWF)
Iceland	The Evangelical Lutheran Church of Iceland (LWF)
Ireland	The Lutheran Church in Ireland (LWF)
Italy	Evangelical Lutheran Church in Italy (LWF)
Latvia	Confessional Lutheran Church (CELC)
	Evangelical Lutheran Church of Latvia (LWF)
Lithuania	Consistory of the Evangelical Lutheran Church of Lithuania (ILC)
	Evangelical Lutheran Church of Lithuania (LWF)
Netherlands	Protestant Church in the Netherlands (LWF)
Norway	Church of Norway (LWF)
	The Evangelical Lutheran Free Church of Norway (LWF)
	Lutheran Confessional Church (CELC)
Poland	Evangelical Church of the Augsburg Confession in Poland (LWF)
Portugal	Lutheran Church of Portugal (CELC)
	Portuguese Evangelical Lutheran Church (ILC)

Romania	Evangelical Church of the Augsburg Confession in Romania (LWF)
	Evangelical Lutheran Church in Romania (LWF)
Russia	Evangelical Lutheran Church—"Concord" (CELC)
	Evangelical Lutheran Church of Ingria in Russia (ILC)
Russian Federation	The Evangelical Lutheran Church of Ingria in Russia (LWF)
	Evangelical Lutheran Church in Russia and Other States (LWF)
Serbia	Slovak Evangelical Church of the Augsburg Confession in Serbia (LWF)
Slovak Republic	Evangelical Church of the Augsburg Confession in the Slovak Republic (LWF)
Slovenia	Evangelical Church of the Augsburg Confession in Slovenia (LWF)
Sweden	Church of Sweden (LWF)
	Lutheran Confessional Church (CELC)
Switzerland	Fed. of Evang. Luth. Churches in Switzerland & in the Principality of Liechtenstein (LWF)
Ukraine	Evangelical Lutheran Church in Russia and Other States (LWF)
	Ukrainian Lutheran Church (CELC)
United Kingdom	Lutheran Church in Great Britain (LWF)

North America

Canada	Lutheran Church—Canada (ILC)
	Evangelical Lutheran Church in Canada (LWF)
United States	American Association of Lutheran Churches (ILC)
	Church of the Lutheran Brethren of America (CLBA)
	Evangelical Lutheran Church in America (LWF)
	Evangelical Lutheran Synod (CELC)
	The Lutheran Church—Missouri Synod (ILC)
	Wisconsin Evangelical Lutheran Synod (CELC)

Latin America & Caribbean

Argentina	Evangelical Church of the River Plate (LWF)
	Evangelical Lutheran Church of Argentina (ILC)
	United Evangelical Lutheran Church (LWF)
Bolivia	Bolivian Evangelical Lutheran Church (LWF)
Brazil	Evangelical Lutheran Church of Brazil (ILC)
	Evangelical Church of the Lutheran Confession in Brazil (LWF)
Chile	Confessional Lutheran Church of Chile (ILC)
	Evangelical Lutheran Church in Chile (LWF)
	Lutheran Church in Chile (LWF)

Colombia	Evangelical Lutheran Church of Colombia (LWF)
Costa Rica	Lutheran Costa Rican Church (LWF)
Ecuador	Evangelical Lutheran Church in Ecuador
El Salvador	Salvadoran Lutheran Church (LWF)
Guatemala	Evangelical Lutheran Congregation "La Epifania" (LWF)
	Lutheran Church of Guatemala (ILC)
Guyana	Evangelical Lutheran Church in Guyana (LWF)
Haiti	The Evangelical Lutheran Church of Haiti (ILC)
Honduras	Christian Lutheran Church of Honduras (LWF)
Mexico	Confessional Evangelical Lutheran Church (CELC)
	Lutheran Synod of Mexico (ILC)
	Mexican Lutheran Church (LWF)
Nicaragua	The Nicaraguan Lutheran Church of Faith and Hope (LWF)
Paraguay	The Evangelical Lutheran Church of Paraguay (ILC)
Puerto Rico	Evangelical Lutheran Confessional Church (CELC)
Peru	Evangelical Lutheran Synod (CELC)
	Peruvian Lutheran Evangelical Church (LWF)
Suriname	Evangelical Lutheran Church in Suriname (LWF)
Venezuela	Evangelical Lutheran Church in Venezuela (LWF)
	Lutheran Church of Venezuela (ILC)

Basic Christian Library

Bible: A reliably translated and easy to read version is the English Standard Version (ESV). Study Bibles include added notes that help to explain the Bible. A great ESV study Bible is this one:
> The Lutheran Study Bible (ESV). St. Louis: Concordia, 2009.

Concordance: A concordance is a listing of all the words found in the Bible and where to find them. It is best to have an exhaustive concordance, one that lists every word in the Bible, rather than just the most commonly looked up words. If possible, get a concordance that matches the version of the Bible you most often use.
> The Crossway Comprehensive Concordance of the Holy Bible (ESV). Wheaton, IL: Crossway Books, 2002.

Bible Reference Tools: Because the Bible was written in such a different time and place from our own, it is helpful to have resources like a Bible dictionary and a Bible atlas on hand.
> Beck, John A. The Land of Milk and Honey. St. Louis: Concordia, 2005. A historical and theological introduction to the geography of Israel in Bible times; includes regional maps and full-color photos.

> Vamosh, Miriam Feinberg. Daily Life at the Time of Jesus. Herzlia, Israel: Palphot, 2007.

> Vine's Complete Expository Dictionary of Old and New Testament Words. Nashville: Thomas Nelson Publishers, 1996.

Small Catechism: Martin Luther wrote the Small Catechism almost five hundred years ago as a resource to help parents and pastors teach the basics of faith. Recent English copies include extra explanations that make the catechism even more helpful as a teaching and learning tool.
> Luther's Small Catechism with Explanation. St Louis: Concordia, 1986, 1991. This catechism is available in an NIV version and an ESV version. Choose the one that matches the Bible version you most often use.

Book of Concord: The Book of Concord is a collection of statements of faith written by Lutheran Christians in the sixteenth century when they were risking their lives to stand up for the Bible being the basis of belief and practice in the Church. It was first published in 1580. A great new English version with helpful introductions and explanations is now available.
> Concordia: The Lutheran Confessions. A Reader's Edition of the Book of Concord. 2nd edition. St. Louis: Concordia, 2006.

Hymnal: A hymnal is an excellent resource for worship and prayer at home as well as at church. Take a look in the table of contents of the hymnals at your church and notice all of the resources they contain in addition to settings for worship (Divine Service) and hymns. Having a hymnal at home will also enrich your Sunday worship experience by giving you and your family the opportunity to become more familiar with the contents of the hymnal when you have more time and fewer distractions than we commonly have at church on Sundays. Your pastor is a great resource to help you choose and purchase a hymnal for your home.

> *Lutheran Service Book.* St. Louis: Concordia, 2006.

Resources for Prayer and Devotions

> Luther, Martin. *Reading the Psalms with Luther.* St. Louis: Concordia, 2007.
> > An English translation of *Luther's Summaries of the Psalms*, which was originally written in 1531. Martin Luther explains how the Psalms naturally connect with the Gospel, the Lord's Prayer, and the Ten Commandments.

> Kinnaman, Scot, ed. *Treasury of Daily Prayer.* St. Louis: Concordia, 2008. A collection of Bible readings, prayers, psalms, hymns, and devotional readings from the Church Fathers, designed to be an all-in-one resource for daily devotions for individuals, families, and small groups.

> *Portals of Prayer.* A quarterly devotional booklet with short daily devotions and prayers. Many congregations purchase copies in bulk and have them available at the church. If your congregation does not have copies available, you can order a subscription through Concordia Publishing House.

> Weedon, William, ed. *Starck's Prayer Book: Revised Concordia Edition.* A book of timeless prayers and devotions for the many curcumstances of life.

About Worship

> Just, Arthur A. *Heaven on Earth: The Gifts of Christ in the Divine Service.* St. Louis: Concordia, 2008. Explains the historical background of Christian worship, what liturgy is and why it is still an important part of being a Christian.

> Kinnaman, Scot. *Worshiping with Angels and Archangels: An Introduction to the Divine Service.* St. Louis: Concordia, 2006. Beautifully illustrated, this book walks the reader through a typical Lutheran worship service, explaining terms such as *Invocation, Introit, Kyrie,* and so on.

> Maschke, Timothy H. *Gathered Guests: A Guide to Worship in the Lutheran Church.* 2nd Edition. St. Louis: Concordia, 2009. An in-depth explanation of what happens in Lutheran worship.

Seasons and Symbols of the Church

> Curtis, H. R. *Ordering Our Days in His Peace: An Introduction to the Christian Church Year.* St. Louis: Concordia, 2009. This book explores the Christian

Church Year and why we use certain colors, hymns, and customs.

Nielsen, Pamela. *Behold the Lamb: An Introduction to Christian Symbolism*. St. Louis: Concordia, 2010. This book features beautiful illustrations of various symbols used in the Church and explains what they represent.

Life as a Christian

Kleinig, John. *Grace upon Grace: Spirituality for Today*. St. Louis: Concordia, 2008. The author clarifies that there is no process for becoming spiritual. Instead, God graciously gives to us every spiritual gift that we need, beginning with the very gift of faith in Christ, our Savior. Because God has joined us to Christ, He continually comes to give us life.

Preus, Klemet I. *The Fire and the Staff: Lutheran Theology in Practice*. St. Louis: Concordia, 2004. Engagingly written with great stories and anticdotes, this book applies the basics of Lutheran theology in ways that make sense and are understandable by the average Christian.

Senkbeil, Harold L. *Dying to Live: The Power of Forgiveness*. St. Louis: Concordia, 1994. Describes how God makes people more like Jesus as they hear and read the Bible and participate in the Sacraments (Baptism and Holy Communion).

Veith, Gene Edward, Jr. *God at Work: Your Christian Vocation in All of Life*. Wheaton, IL: Crossway Books, 2002. Explains the concept of vocation: how God is at work in everything we are called to do, not only in our careers but also in our families, hobbies, and every other part of our lives.

Veith, Gene Edward, Jr. *Spirituality of the Cross*. Expanded and revised. St. Louis: Concordia, 2008. Veith explores and presents a true understanding of justification by faith, the Means of Grace, vocation, theology of the cross, the two kingdoms, worship, and the Church.

Milestone Books. St. Louis, Concordia. These easy-to-read books present the gifts that God gives at four of the milestone events in the life of a Christian and connects the event with the worship life and liturgy of the Church:
• *Rooted in the Faith* (2010) gives a summary of the Christian faith and prepares the reader to make a public confession of that faith as part of becoming a member of a Christian congregation.
• *United in Christ* (2010) uses the rite of Holy Matromony to instruct and prepare a couple for Christian marriage.
• *The Baptism of Your Child* (2007) presents parents with the great importance of raising children in the faith received in Holy Baptism. The liturgy of Holy Baptism becomes a wonderful teacher of the great gift God gives through water and the Word.

• *Final Victory* (2010) contemplates the death and funeral of a Christian; truly the final milestone of life in this world. This book is designed for those who have lost or will lose a loved one, as well as those Christians who are preparing for their own death.

Movies

The following movies are great learning tools that help bring history to life. Be aware, though, that they all include violence that would not be appropriate for children.

Luther, MGM, 2003. A biography of Martin Luther, including important events surrounding the Reformation.

The Nativity Story, New Line Home Video, 2007. The story of Jesus' birth.

The Passion of the Christ, 20th Century Fox, 2004. The story of Jesus' trial and crucifixion.

Theology and History

Engelbrecht, Edward, ed. *To All Eternity: The Essential Teachings of Christianity.* St. Louis: Concordia, 2001. A beautifully illustrated devotional edition of Martin Luther's Small Catechism.

Koehler, Edward. *Summary of Christian Doctrine.* Rπevised by A. Koehler. St. Louis: Concordia, 2005. This systematic study of the doctrines of Scripture is presented in a concise, comprehensive manner. It is an excellent text for those interested in going beyond the catechism.

Preus, Robert D. *Getting into the Theology of Concord.* St. Louis: Concordia, 1998. The author highlights the chief doctrinal emphases of the Confessions and shows their continued importance in the modern Church.

Martin Luther

Kittelson, James. *Luther the Reformer: The Story of the Man and His Career.* Minneapolis: Augsburg Fortress, 2003.

Nohl, Frederick. *Luther: Biography of a Reformer.* St. Louis: Concordia, 2003.

Basic Christian Library for Children

Bible Stories

Arch Books. Various titles and authors. St. Louis: Concordia. This series of Bible story books is written in poem form with lively illustrations and is geared for 5- to 9-year-olds.

Engelbrecht, Edward and Gail Pawlitz. *The Story Bible: 130 Stories of God's Love.* St. Louis: Concordia, 2011. This book includes rich, realistic illustrations, easy-to-read stories, discussion helps, prayer summaries, and a glossary of key terms. Ages 3 and up.

Simon, Mary Manz. Hear Me Read Series. St. Louis: Concordia. There are two reading levels in this series of Bible story books designed for beginning readers. Level 1 is for 2- to 6-year-olds and level 2 is for 5- to 9-year olds.

Henley, Karyn. *The Beginner's Bible: Timeless Children's Stories.* Grand Rapids: Zondervan, 2005. This Bible combines colorful, interesting pictures and age-appropriate telling of a large number of important Old and New Testament Bible stories. It is a great introduction to the Bible for 4- to 8-year-olds.

One Hundred Bible Stories. St. Louis: Concordia, 2004. Designed for older children with more grown-up looking illustrations (one per story). After each story, there is a suggested Bible memory verse and a "for reflection" section to help children think about, remember, and apply the story to their own lives—for 8- to 12-year-olds.

Phonetic Bible Story Series. Various titles and authors. St. Louis: Concordia. The books in this series help beginning readers practice phonics while reading interesting Bible stories with colorful pictures—for 2- to 6-year-olds.

Study Bibles

Faith Alive Student Bible. St. Louis: Concordia, 1995, 2006, ESV 2011. Includes age-appropriate study notes and diagrams to help 8- to 14-year-olds understand the Bible and apply it to their lives.

Catechisms

Luther's Small Catechism with Explanation. St Louis: Concordia, 1986, 1991. This catechism is available in an NIV version and an ESV version. Choose the one that matches the Bible version you most often use.

My First Catechism. St. Louis: Concordia, 2004. Written in kid-friendly language with classic pictures and Bible-story examples used to help children ages 6 to 10 learn the basics of faith, including the Ten Commandments, Lord's Prayer, and Apostles' Creed.

Timeless Bible Truths: The Illustrated Small Catechism. St. Louis: Concordia, 2010. This short graphic novel is a fun and easy way for students of all ages to learn basics of faith like the Lord's Prayer and Ten Commandments.

Walker, Joni. Follow and Do Series. St. Louis: Concordia. A set of six picture books that introduce 4- to 7-year-olds to the Six Chief Parts of Luther's Small Catechism. Titles of the books are *The Apostles' Creed, Confession, Holy Baptism, The Lord's Supper, God's Ten Commandments*, and *The Lord's Prayer*.

Other Books

Bergt, Carolyn. *The Adventures of Martin Luther*. St. Louis: Concordia, 1999. A picture book telling the story of Martin Luther at a level appropriate for 5- to 13-year-olds.

Groth, Jeanette L. *Prayer: Learning How to Talk to God*. St. Louis: Concordia, 2002. Teaches 4- to 7-year-olds about prayer, including what prayer is and different elements of prayer, such as praise, thanking, asking for forgiveness, help, or guidance.

Marxhausen, Joanne. *3 in 1: A Picture of God*. St. Louis: Concordia, 2004. Explains the Trinity (that there is one God in three persons of the Father, Son, and Holy Spirit) at a level that is appropriate for small children 5 years and older.

Wittenback, Janet. *God Makes Me His Child in Baptism*. St. Louis: Concordia, 2007. Children learn about what happens the day a person is baptized and what Baptism means for the rest of a person's life and eternally—3 years and older.

Devotional Magazines: Some congregations order copies of these magazines and distribute them to children in the congregation. If your congregation does not have copies available, you can subscribe to them and have them delivered to your home.

Happy Times. St. Louis: Concordia. A monthly magazine for 3- to 5-year-olds filled with Christian stories, poems, and activities.

My Devotions. St. Louis: Concordia. A quarterly magazine for 8- to 12-year-olds designed to resource parents and to help children develop a habit of daily devotions. There is a Bible verse, devotional message that helps children to apply the verse to their lives, journal suggestion, and a prayer for each day.

Glossary

Agnus Dei. Latin for "Lamb of God" (John 1:29)

Absolution. Literally, "set free." This Latin term was used by theologians as a translation of the biblical word *aphiemi*, meaning "to set free, cancel, or forgive."

absolve. To set free from sin. By virtue of his office, in the name and stead of Christ, a pastor forgives those who have confessed their sins, affirmed their faith in Christ, and promised to amend their lives (Matthew 16:19; 18:18; John 20:19–23).

altar. A stone or wooden structure at the center of the chancel from which the Lord's Supper is celebrated; the sacramental focus from which God gives His gifts; the sacrificial focus of the congregation's worship.

Anabaptism. This is a term that literally means "rebaptism." This was a series of groups that arose during the Reformation that rejected the traditions of the Church, including infant Baptism, insisting on rebaptizing adults. The Mennonites of today are the direct descendants of this movement.

Amen. Hebrew word meaning "it is true; reliable."

amillennialism. The doctrine that the thousand-year reign of Christ mentioned in Revelation 20 should not be taken literally. It symbolizes the reign of Christ from His first appearing to His reappearing at the end of time.

Atonement. From an old French term for being "at one." Reconciliation between parties that were previously divided. One man's life given as a sacrifice and ransom to redeem all others.

Baptism. From the Greek word meaning "to immerse" or "to wash." Many religions have religious washings. But Christian Baptism applies water "in the name of the Father and of the Son and of the Holy Spirit" as described by Jesus (Matthew 28:19). In Baptism, God washes away the person's sins and welcomes that person as a member of His kingdom. Through water joined to God's Word, the Holy Spirit puts to death our sinful nature, connects us to Christ in His death and resurrection, and gives us new spiritual birth as God's children.

Benediction. From the Latin for "[The Lord] bless [you]"; the Aaronic Blessing (Numbers 6:24–26) is commonly used in connection with Holy Communion, while the Apostolic Blessing (2 Corinthians 13:14) is used at other times.

Benedictus. Latin for the first words: "Blessed is he."

canticle. Latin for "little song"; Scripture texts sung as part of the liturgy.

Catholic. (Greek: *katholikos*: "universal" or "general.") A term first applied to the Christian Church as a whole in a letter of Ignatius (ca. AD 110): "Where Christ is, there is the catholic Church." In Lutheran theology (as in early Christendom) the word is often used of the one holy catholic ("Christian") and apostolic Church united to Christ by faith, and transcending time, space, and all other barriers.

Christology. The study of who Jesus is and what He did.

Collect of the Day. A brief, structured prayer.

commemorations. Remembrances of the faithful dead who are set before the Church as an example.

Communion, Holy. To take part in something, to share something. In the Lord's Supper, communicants partake of the body and blood of Christ and are made members of His Body, the Church (1 Corinthians 10:16–17). "Communion" or "participation" translates the Greek word for fellowship, *koinonia.* Another name for the Sacrament of the Altar; *see* Sacrament of the Altar.

concord. The external or public manifestation of agreement in doctrine among Christian churches. It can be seen as the task to promote such external unity through dialogue leading to altar and pulpit fellowship.

confession. The act by which one admits or confesses sin(s) and the guilt of sin.

consecrate. To dedicate to the Lord; to declare holy, as when Jesus' words are spoken over the bread and wine during the celebration of the Lord's Supper.

Council. A solemn meeting of bishops often called to settle doctrinal matters that threaten the unity of the Church.

creed. From the Latin word *credo,* "I believe"; a summary of what the Church believes; refers to any of the three Ecumenical Creeds used in worship: the Apostles' Creed, often used at Baptisms, funerals, and non-Communion services; the Nicene Creed, often used at services with Holy Communion; and the Athanasian Creed, often spoken on Trinity Sunday.

Ecumenics. The field of Christian theology that deals with the study and objectives of unity and fellowship between Christian churches.

Eucharist. From the Greek word that means "to give thanks." The Lord's Supper is a meal offering thanks to God for salvation through the death and resurrection of Jesus (1 Corinthians 10:16). Another name for the Sacrament of the Altar; *see* Sacrament of the Altar.

feasts and festivals. Celebrations in the life of the Church that mark important events and commemorations, such as events in Jesus' life (The Circumcision and Name of Jesus), a celebration of notable people (St. Timothy—January 24, St. Luke—October 18) and great events in the life of the Church (Reformation, Holy Cross Day).

font. Large basin or pool that holds water for Holy Baptism.

Gloria in Excelsis. Latin for "glory in the highest"; the angel's song (Luke 2:14); a Hymn of Praise in the Divine Service.

God's Word. The Holy Scriptures; the inspired revelation of God's plan and record of salvation.

Gospel. The message of Christ's death and resurrection for the forgiveness of sins, eternal life, and salvation. The Holy Spirit works through the Gospel in Word and Sacrament to create and sustain faith and to empower good works. The Gospel is found in both the Old and New Testaments.

Gradual. A portion of a psalm or other Scripture passage that provides a response after the Old Testament Reading.

grace. The unearned and undeserved gift of forgiveness and eternal life received by faith and given to all who believe. Ephesians 2:8–9 shows us that this gift is free to those who receive it but was purchased at great cost by Jesus' life, death on the cross, and resurrection.

hell. Having our own way forever, separated from God.

historical criticism. An approach to studying the Bible in which the Bible is treated as any other historical document. This includes the assumptions that the Bible is historically conditioned, has been adapted over time, and that miracles and other extreme supernatural portions are suspect.

Holy Gospel. A reading from one of the first four books of the New Testament as part of the Service of the Word; always contains the words or deeds of Jesus.

host. Latin for "sacrifice or victim"; the consecrated bread (and thus also Christ's body) of Holy Communion.

Hymn of the Day. Chief hymn of the Divine Service; a hymn specifically selected to reflect the theme of the day, especially the Holy Gospel.

inerrancy. The Bible is the "Holy Scripture" because God the Holy Spirit gave to His chosen writers the thoughts that they expressed and the words that they wrote (verbal inspiration). Because God's Spirit worked through the writers of Scripture, it is God's infallible Word and is completely reliable. There, the Bible is God's own Word and truth, without error (inerrancy).

Introit. The Latin for "enter"; psalm verses sung or spoken at the beginning of the Divine Service.

Invocation. From the Latin for "call upon"; the words "In the name of the Father and of the Son and of the Holy Spirit" spoken at the beginning of the service; serves as a reminder of Holy Baptism.

Kyrie eleison. Greek for "Lord, have mercy." The Kyrie is the first prayer of the congregation in the Divine Service; it is a cry for mercy that our Lord and King will hear us and help us in our needs and troubles.

Lord's Prayer. The model prayer Jesus taught to the disciples (Matthew 6:9–13). Sometimes it is called the Our Father, after the first words of the prayer.

Lord's Supper. Another name for the Sacrament of the Altar; *see* Sacrament of the Altar.

Means of Grace. The means by which God gives us the forgiveness, life, and salvation won by the death and resurrection of Christ: God's Word, Absolution, Baptism, and the Lord's Supper.

Messiah. A Hebrew word meaning "anointed one"—that is, one chosen by God for a special purpose.

office. A specific authority entrusted to specifically chosen people to do specific functions. For example, the Office of the Holy Ministry is the authority to preach, teach, and administer the Sacraments.

Office of the Keys. The authority given to the Church by God to forgive the sins of repentant sinners and to bind sins to unrepentant sinners.

omnipresent. An attribute of God; He is not limited to time or space; He has the ability to fill heaven and earth.

omniscient. An attribute of God; His perfect knowledge of all things.

ordination. The rite through which a man is placed into the Office of the Holy Ministry. According to biblical custom, the "laying on of hands" is associated with this rite, in which pastors place their hands upon the head of the one to be ordained. Ordination formally and publicly places a person in office.

pastor. Latin for "shepherd"; the title for the congregation's public minister who is ordained and called to be the spiritual supervisor of the "flock" that gathers around Word and Sacrament to receive God's good gifts.

Pietism. The movement within Lutheranism that started in the seventeenth century; emphasized personal piety over doctrinal correctness. This movement expected members to refrain from frivolous entertainment and focus purely on personal spiritual improvement. It saw biblical doctrine as less important than "a religion of the heart."

Preface. Proclamation of praise and thanksgiving that begins the Service of the Sacrament; concludes with the Proper Preface.

Proper Preface. A special prayer said before the Lord's Supper that emphasizes the key themes of the feast, occasion, or season of the Church Year.

propers. Parts of the service that change according to the Sunday or festival of the Church Year, for example, the Introit and the Scripture readings.

Rationalism. A philosophical movement that is often hostile to Christianity, especially the Bible's teachings about miracles and faith. Rationalists decide what is true on the basis of human reason rather than Holy Scripture.

regeneration. From a Latin word meaning "rebirth." The Holy Spirit gives new life through Baptism and God's Word.

repentance. The turning away from sin toward faith in Christ and His sacrifice for us.

sacrament. From the Greek word meaning "mystery"; literally, "something sacred." In the Lutheran Church, a Sacrament is a sacred act that (1) was instituted by God, (2) has a visible element, and (3) offers the forgiveness of sins earned by Christ. The Sacraments include Baptism, the Lord's Supper, and also Absolution (if one counts the pastor as the visible element; Large Catechism IV 74; Apology XIII 4–5).

saint. The word *saint* in Scripture refers to believers on earth (Acts 9:32; Romans 1:7) and in heaven (Matthew 27:52). Throughout Church history, it has been used to designate one set apart as especially holy (e.g., St. Paul, St. Francis of Assisi). The Lutheran Reformation rejected prayers and devotions to saints. In Lutheran usage, the title of "saint" is not used for anyone except those who were called such before the Reformation.

Sacrament of the Altar. Sacrament by which the Lord offers His body and blood under the form of consecrated bread and wine for Christians to eat and drink; through such eating and drinking, communicants receive the gifts of the forgiveness of sins and the strengthening of faith; also called Holy Communion, the Eucharist, and the Lord's Supper.

Salutation. Special greeting between pastor and people: "The Lord be with you," followed by the response "And also with you" or "And with your spirit."

sanctification. The spiritual growth that follows justification by grace through faith in Christ. Sanctification is God's work through His Means of Grace: Word and Sacraments.

Sanctus. Latin for "holy"; follows the Preface in the Service of the Sacrament; based on Isaiah 6:3 and Matthew 21:9.

sin. Betraying God; rejecting His will and His ways; any thought, word, or deed that departs from the will of God.

sinful nature. Our human nature, after the fall, is thoroughly corrupted by sin, making us God's enemies and lovers of ourselves.

sola. Latin for "only" or "alone."

stewardship. The meaning of the biblical word for stewardship is "the management of a household," usually on behalf of someone else.

synod. Literally, in Greek, means "to come together" or to "walk together." This is one of the preferred terms by Lutherans to describe a church body or a portion of a church body that is formed of fellow Lutherans who have chosen to "walk together" or work together for their common mission.

testament. A will that establishes the disposition of one's belongings at the time of death, or a covenant established by God between God and man. The Lord's Supper fulfills both definitions: prior to the cross, Jesus leaves Christians His body and blood for the forgiveness of their sins, and this Sacrament is part of His covenant of grace for man.

Time of Christmas. The time of the Church Year that focuses on the Father sending the Son to save the world; includes the seasons of Advent, Christmas, and Epiphany; focuses on the Father sending the Son to save the world.

Time of Easter. The time of the Church Year that focuses on the Son redeeming the world with His life, death, and resurrection; includes the seasons of Lent and Easter; the time from Lent through the week after Ascension (week before Pentecost).

Time of the Church. The time of the Church Year that focuses on the Spirit renewing the Church through Word and Sacrament; includes the Day of Pentecost and extends through the end of the Church Year; sometimes called the nonfestival half of the Church Year.

transubstantiation. The Roman Catholic teaching that in the Lord's Supper the substance or basic reality of bread and wine are changed into the body and blood of Jesus Christ while the outward appearances of bread and wine are not affected.

Trinity, triune. One true God in three persons: Father, Son, and Holy Spirit.

unity. The spiritual bond all Christians share with one another as a gift from God because of their faith in Christ.

Votum. Short prayer based upon a promise from God.

Words of Institution. The words spoken by Christ when He instituted the Sacrament of the Altar (Matthew 26:26–28; Mark 14:22–24; Luke 22:19–20; 1 Corinthians 11:23–25); the pastor speaks these very words of Christ in the Service of the Sacrament at the consecration of the bread and wine.

worship. The service to which God calls and gathers His people to give to them the gifts of life and salvation by means of Word and Sacrament.

Contributors

Rose E. Adle earned a bachelor's degree in Spanish from Valparaiso University and a master's degree in deaconess studies and systematic theology from Concordia Seminary.

Adle interned in Caracas, Venezuela, and later she served as a deaconess at the Center for Hispanic Studies in St. Louis, Missouri, and at Concordia Theological Seminary in Fort Wayne, Indiana.

Now as a pastor's wife and stay-at-home mom, her diaconal background finds expression in loving service to her family. She is also active in their congregation, where she helps with the youth group, sings in the choir, and visits the homebound.

Charles P. Arand graduated from Concordia Seminary and served as pastor of St. John's, New Minden, Illinois, and St. Luke's, Covington, Illinois until 1987. Since 1989 he has served on the faculty at Concordia Seminary, where he holds the Waldemar A. and June Schuette Chair in Systematic Theology and serves as chairman of the Department of Systematic Theology. He translated the Apology of the Augsburg Confession for the Kolb-Wengert edition of the Book of Concord (Fortress) and has written many articles and several books on related topics. Dr. Arand is currently devoting most of his research time and writing to the topic of First Article theology, with a particular emphasis on the stewardship of creation. Much of this has been influenced by his work on Luther's catechisms and a desire to develop Lutheran themes of creation in an American context.

Gary M. Arp earned his bachelor of divinity degree from Concordia Theological Seminary, Springfield, Illinois. Rev. Arp has served at Our Savior Lutheran Church, El Dorado, Arkansas, and St. John Lutheran Church, Crossett, Arkansas; Immanuel Lutheran Church and School, Clarinda, Iowa; and St. John Lutheran Church, Waverly, Iowa. He has also served on the Board of Directors of Iowa District West, and as district president of Iowa District East. In 2003 he was awarded an honorary doctor of divinity degree from Concordia Theological Seminary, Fort Wayne, Indiana.

Ernest Bernet graduated summa cum laude from Concordia, Portland, and received an MDiv from Concordia Seminary and an STM (thesis: *Luther on Sanctification*). He has served as a parish pastor in Seattle, on staff at the library of Concordia Seminary, and is currently serving a parish in Texas. He also serves on the Texas District Commission on Prayer and Spiritual Formation and is currently working toward his doctor of theology degree in Lutheran spirituality at Australian Lutheran College.

Scott A. Bruzek is senior pastor at St. John Lutheran Church, Wheaton, Illinois. He is a graduate of Stanford University, Concordia Seminary (St. Louis), Cambridge University, and Princeton Theological Seminary. While serving two parishes during sixteen years in the ministry, Pastor Bruzek has also taught at colleges and seminaries, served often as a guest lecturer and chaplain, written several articles, done mission work twice in Russia, and supervised more than one hundred interns, many of whom now serve in the Church. Of particular interest to him now is drawing postmodern people into the fullness of the Church's incarnational life using elements of the ancient catechumenate.

David J. Bueltmann is president of the Central Illinois District and has written many articles for district and synodical publications. While serving as district president, he has also started a mission church and serves as the district business manager. In the past he has been a school bus driver, a substitute teacher, the executive director of Ongoing Ambassadors for Christ, and a camp director. His greatest joy is sharing the Good News about Jesus with all with whom he speaks.

Kent J. Burreson is an associate professor of systematic theology and dean of the chapel at Concordia Semi-

nary, St. Louis, Missouri. He teaches courses in systematic theology (doctrine) and liturgy and worship. A graduate of the doctoral program in liturgical studies at the University of Notre Dame, Dr. Burreson wrote a dissertation examining the historical development of Lutheran baptismal rites during the Reformation era. He has a strong interest in the development of liturgical practice in all periods of Church history as well as in the theological meaning of what is said and done in worship. He served on the liturgy committee for the development of *Lutheran Service Book*. Prior to his call to Concordia Seminary, he served as a pastor in Mishawaka, Indiana.

Allan R. Buss is the senior pastor of Immanuel Lutheran Church, Belvidere, Illinois, and first vice president of the Northern Illinois District of the LCMS. He has attended Lutheran schools his whole life, including Concordia University Wisconsin, and Concordia Seminary, Fort Wayne. He considers it a joy and privilege to be a part of what God is doing through His Church. His passions include preaching, leadership, pastoral care, and teaching those who are interested in knowing more about Jesus and life in His Bride, the Church. Some of his greatest joys have come from service to the Church at large, including district and synod.

Paul J Cain is pastor of Immanuel Lutheran Church, Sheridan, Wyoming, and headmaster of Martin Luther Grammar School. He also serves as

Wyoming District Worship chairman and editor of *Liturgy, Hymnody, & Pulpit Quarterly Book Review*. A graduate of Concordia Seminary, St. Louis, Rev. Cain has previously served Emmanuel Lutheran Church, Green River, Wyoming, and Trinity Lutheran Church, Morrill, Nebraska.

Terry Cripe is a graduate of Concordia Theological Seminary, Springfield, Illinois. Desiring further New Testament study, Pastor Cripe attended Princeton Theological Seminary in New Jersey, where he earned his ThM degree. He served St. Peter Lutheran Church in Harbourton, New Jersey, for fourteen years. He then accepted the call to be mission developer of Christ Our Savior Lutheran Church in Defiance, Ohio. He currently serves as president of the Ohio District of the LCMS.

Stewart D. Crown is the pastor of Trinity Evangelical Lutheran Church in Palo Alto, California, where he has served the congregation and worked in campus ministry. He also supervises third-year seminarians in a one-year internship. Having served Christ Evangelical Lutheran Church, Marshfield, Wisconsin, he returned to campus work at Stanford, realizing his concern for student ministry that was formed by campus pastors at Valparaiso University and Concordia University Wisconsin. Rev. Crown attended Concordia Seminary, St. Louis, Missouri, and was granted an MDiv; he went on to earn an STM in Old Testament studies at

Concordia.

H. R. Curtis serves as pastor of Trinity Lutheran Church in Worden, Illinois, and Zion Lutheran Church in Carpenter, Illinois. Pastor Curtis has also served as visiting lecturer in exegetical theology at Concordia Seminary in St. Louis and adjunct professor of theology at Concordia University Chicago. While attending Concordia Seminary in St. Louis, he also gained the master of arts degree in classics from Washington University.

Rebekah Curtis makes food, cleans up messes, and writes sporadically. She vaguely remembers receiving a BS in education from Concordia University Nebraska and an MA from Concordia Seminary. Rebekah reports that she and her husband have five children, all above average.

Randy Duncan is the pastor of Living Word Lutheran Church in Plymouth Township, Michigan. He is a graduate of Concordia, Ann Arbor, and received his MDiv from Concordia Theological Seminary in Fort Wayne, where he majored in missions and systematic theology. He has been a missionary church planter among the Gypsy population of North America and has planted churches in Cote d' Ivoire (Ivory Coast), West Africa, among the Krahn tribe. Randy became the founding missionary of a mission society named POBLO (People of the Book Lutheran Outreach), which is dedicated to communicating the

Gospel and planting Christ-worshiping communities among Muslims in North America and throughout the world.

John G. Fleischmann has been pastor of Christ Lutheran Church, East Moriches, New York, since 1991. He holds a BA in church music (Concordia College, Bronxville) and writes hymns and musical arrangements for use in the parish setting. John has served as an adjunct professor at Suffolk County Community College. He also designed the initial curriculum for the Romans class in the Atlantic District Diaconate Training Program and is still one of the instructors in the program. He presently serves as circuit counselor for the East End of Long Island.

Dan Paul Gilbert serves as president of the Northern Illinois District. He previously served as a parish pastor at St. Paul in Readlyn, Iowa, and Cross in Yorkville, Illinois. His interests include missions (both North American and international), the Spanish language, the new Lutheran Church in Norway, family, reading, and travel. He is a graduate of Concordia Teachers College (now University) in Seward, Nebraska, and Concordia Seminary in St. Louis, Missouri.

Jill Hasstedt, DCE, serves as director of family ministry at Zion Lutheran Church in Belleville, Illinois. She is a recipient of the Master DCE Award from the Lutheran Education Association and currently serves on the LCMS Board for District and Congregational

Services. She is also a KINDLE associate and has worked extensively with LCMS national youth gatherings. Mrs. Hasstedt has a bachelor of science degree from Concordia University Nebraska, and an MA from the University of Illinois, Springfield. She has served congregations in Nebraska, Kansas, Texas, and Illinois. Jill's mission is "to develop, implement, and nurture systems that encourage faith connections with God's people in families so that Jesus becomes the center of every heart and home."

John Hellwege Jr. is the pastor at Emmaus Lutheran Church in St. Louis, Missouri. He previously served the congregations of Grace Lutheran Church in Platte Center, Nebraska, and St. Peter Lutheran Church in Humphrey, Nebraska.. He has served as adjunct faculty at Concordia University Nebraska. He is presently serving as adjunct faculty at Concordia University Wisconsin, St. Louis Center, and Concordia Seminary in St. Louis, Missouri. He has taught classes in both theology and philosophy. Rev. Hellwege has a PhD in historical theology from Concordia Seminary, St. Louis.

Michael L. Keith is a graduate of Concordia University College of Alberta and Concordia Lutheran Seminary in Edmonton, Alberta, Canada. He has served as the pastor of Our Saviour Lutheran Church in Fort Qu'Appelle, Saskatchewan, Canada, since his graduation from the seminary. He serves as a vice president and on the Board of Directors of the Central District of Lutheran Church—Canada. He also serves on the Committee for Missions and Social Ministry Services of Lutheran Church—Canada. Pastor Keith was not born and raised in the Lutheran Church. He became a member of a congregation of Lutheran Church—Canada after studying theology and becoming convinced of the biblical faithfulness of the church body. He rejoices each day in the forgiveness, life, and salvation he has received for the sake of Jesus in Holy Baptism.

Scot A. Kinnaman is a senior editor at Concordia Publishing House. Prior to coming to Concordia, he served as pastor for Lutheran congregations in Illinois and Michigan. He regularly writes on the subjects of worship and Lutheran culture and is author of the book *Worshiping with Angels and Archangels: An Introduction to the Divine Service* (Concordia, 2006).

Shawn L. Kumm attended both public and parochial schools before entering the pre-seminary program and studying literature and biblical languages at Concordia College (University) in St. Paul, Minnesota. Following graduation from Concordia Seminary in St. Louis, Pastor Kumm served as campus pastor to Southern Illinois University at Carbondale, Illinois. He now serves as pastor of Zion Evangelical Lutheran Church in Laramie, Wyoming.

Laura L. Lane has been a member of the editorial team at Concordia Publishing House since 2003. A graduate of Concordia Seminary, St. Louis, she has a masters of theology degree and has worked on numerous titles for the adult consumer and church professional markets, including *The Lutheran Study Bible* (Concordia, 2009).

Naomichi Masaki teaches dogmatics, Lutheran Confessions, Luther studies, and liturgics at Concordia Theological Seminary, Fort Wayne, Indiana, where he also serves as supervisor of the master of sacred theology program. His interests lie in the theology of Martin Luther and the nineteenth-century Confessional Revival in Germany and Sweden. Born in Kobe, Japan, and raised there as a son of a Lutheran pastor and evangelist, Masaki spent one year in Norway attending Rødde Folkehøgskole, studied social work and counseling at Kwansei Gakuin University in Nishinomiya, Japan (BA and MA), and received theological and pastoral training at Concordia Theological Seminary, Ft. Wayne (MDiv and STM), and Concordia Seminary, St. Louis (PhD). Masaki has served the Board for District and Congregational Services and the Liturgy Committee of the Lutheran Hymnal Project of the LCMS.

Benjamin T. G. Mayes, a lifelong Lutheran, grew up in a pastor's family and received God's rich grace in the context of a small congregation. Educated both inside and outside of

LCMS schools, including a year of post-graduate study abroad in Germany, he is now a pastor in the LCMS and has a PhD in historical theology from Calvin Theological Seminary, Grand Rapids, Michigan. Besides serving as an editor for professional and academic books at Concordia Publishing House, he is involved with ministry in the urban setting of St. Louis, Missouri.

Heather Melcher is a certified director of Christian education with a Bachelor of Arts degree majoring in psychology and a master of parish education degree. In addition to staying home full time with her two young sons and occasionally helping her husband on their farm, she writes, presents workshops, and is developing a Christian resource Web site.

Herbert C. Mueller Jr. prepared for the ministry in the LCMS system, graduating from Concordia Seminary, St. Louis. Rev. Mueller has served the Lord as pastor of three parishes in Illinois before being elected Southern Illinois District President February 1994.

President Mueller served on the Synod's Commission on Ministerial Growth and Support from 1998 to 2007 (chairman, 2004–7). In 2004 he began serving on the *Concordia Pulpit Resources* Advisory Committee and has also served in the past on the Synod's Colloquy Committee and the Program Committee for the Council of Presidents. In 2010 Rev. Mueller was elected as First Vice President of the Lutheran Church—Missouri Synod.

Scott R. Murray is interested in missions, having been a mission developer in North America and a teacher in international mission fields. He served as the vice chairman of the Commission on Theology and Church Relations of the LCMS and on the board of the Lutheran Education Association of Houston. He is presently the vice president of the Luther Academy and an editor of *Logia*. He writes a daily e-mail devotion, *Memorial Moment,* that reaches subscribers all over the world, and is the host of the weekly radio program *Dying to Live*. He is the author of numerous journal articles and the book *Law, Life, and the Living God* (Concordia, 2003). In 2010 Dr. Murray was elected as Fifth Vice President of the Lutheran Church—Missouri Synod.

Timothy Pauls currently serves as a pastor at Good Shepherd Lutheran Church, Boise, Idaho. A lifelong Lutheran and resident of the Pacific Northwest, Timothy is the author of several books, devotionals, magazine and journal articles, and especially enjoys writing to communicate the truth of God's Word and demonstrating its significance in daily life.

John T. Pless is assistant professor of pastoral ministry and missions at Concordia Theological Seminary in Fort Wayne, where he also serves as director of field education and editor of the Seminary magazine, *For the Life of* *the World*. Prior to joining the faculty, he served as campus pastor at University Lutheran Chapel at the University of Minnesota in Minneapolis, and prior to that he served on the staff at the Chapel of the Resurrection at Valparaiso University. He is a graduate of Texas Lutheran College, Sequin, Texas (BA), and Trinity Lutheran Seminary, Columbus, Ohio (MDiv). He entered the LCMS by colloquy at Concordia Theological Seminary.

Prof. Pless is the author of *Handling the Word of Truth: Law and Gospel in the Church Today; A Small Catechism on Human Life; Word: God Speaks to Us; Confession: God Gives Us Truth; Luther on the Care for the Sick and the Dying;* and two chapters in *Lutheran Worship: History and Practice*. With Matthew Harrison he is editor of *Women Pastors? The Ordination of Women in Biblical Lutheran Perspective*. He served on the Agenda Committee for *Lutheran Service Book*. He is book review editor for *Logia* and a member of the editorial council of *Lutheran Quarterly*. A regular lecturer at various conferences both in the United States and overseas, Prof. Pless coordinates the seminary's annual "Mercy Mission Expedition to Madagascar" in partnership with the LCMS Board for World Relief and Human Care. He serves as copresident of the International Loehe Society, and he is a member of the LCMS Committee on the Sanctity of Human Life.

Kurt Rolland attended Concordia Seminary, receiving a master of arts in Exegetical Theology. Kurt has a passion and desire to share this lost perspective with fellow Lutherans.

Douglas L. Rutt is a graduate of Bethany Lutheran College (A.A.), Minnesota State University (B.S.), and Concordia Theological Seminary (MDiv and PhD). He has served as a missionary to Guatemala, Central America, where he was involved in church planting and theological education, and as a parish pastor at St. John Evangelical Lutheran Church, St. James, Minnesota, and St. John Evangelical Lutheran Church, Truman, Minnesota. He was also the area secretary for Latin America/Caribbean with LCMS World Mission. He currently serves on the faculty of Concordia Theological Seminary. He has written several articles on mission history and practice and is currently the editor of the *Communicator*, the regular newsletter of the Lutheran Society for Missiology. Dr. Rutt also serves as a consultant and liaison for LCMS World Mission to Latin America. He is called upon regularly to consult and speak on mission issues throughout the United States and Latin America. Currently he is the chairman of the board of Lutheran Bible Translators.

Leopoldo A. Sánchez M. was born in Chile and raised in Panama. He has worked with local churches in Venezuela and San José, California, focusing most of his time on theological education. As a doctoral student, Leopoldo Sánchez was the recipient of a three-year grant from the Hispanic Theological

Initiative of the Pew Charitable Trusts, a program for the development of Hispanic faculty in the fields of theology and religion. He received his Ph.D. from Concordia Seminary, St. Louis, Missouri. Dr. Sánchez has been teaching systematic theology at Concordia Seminary since 2004 and was appointed director of the Center for Hispanic Studies in 2006.

Peter J. Scaer graduated from the Concordia Theological seminary and earned his PhD at Notre Dame. While finishing his graduate work, he served as a parish pastor at Emanuel Lutheran Church in Arcadia, Indiana. He is the author of , *The Lukan Passion and the Praiseworthy Death*, Sheffield Press. In 2000, he was called to teach New Testament at Concordia Theological Seminary in Fort Wayne.

Peter A. Speckhard graduated from Concordia Seminary and worked as a missionary at large before accepting a call to Faith Lutheran Church in Green Bay, where he continues to serve as senior pastor. He also serves as associate editor of *Forum Letter* and has written articles and reviews for *Touchstone*, *First Things*, and the *Journal of Lutheran Ethics*.

Scott Stiegemeyer is a graduate of Concordia Theological Seminary, Fort Wayne, Indiana, Rev. Stiegemeyer's first call was to be an admissions officer for the seminary, which he did for three years. Next he served as pastor to

Concordia Lutheran Church in Pittsburgh, Pennsylvania, and was a circuit counselor for five years of that time. He was cohost for a weekly talk show on Christian radio called *Let's Talk about Jesus*. He returned to the seminary to be the director of admissions. Most recently, he has returned to parish ministry, serving Redeemer Lutheran Church in Elmhurst, Illinois.

Cynda Strong is an English teacher at Lutheran High School in Springfield, Illinois. After years of teaching her students how to write, Cynda started seeking publication of her own work. Her first picture book, *Where Do Angels Sleep?* was published by Concordia in 2007. Her Arch Book, *The Resurrection*, was released in 2010. Cynda has been published in several magazines, Bible studies, *Portals of Prayer*, and anthologies.

William H. Tucker is the senior pastor of Concordia Lutheran Church in San Antonio, where he has served for eight years. Bill attended Concordia University in River Forest, Illinois, where he graduated with a bachelor of arts degree. His major was theological languages (Greek, Hebrew, Latin, German, and French). From there he attended Concordia Theological Seminary in Fort Wayne, Indiana, where he graduated with a master of divinity degree.

Gene Edward Veith Jr. is currently a professor of literature, a college administrator, and a writer. He has written more than a dozen books on Christianity, culture, and the arts. He has a PhD in English literature. He and his wife have three children and live near Washington DC.

Larry M. Vogel has been associate executive director of the Commission on Theology and Church Relations of The Lutheran Church—Missouri Synod. Prior to that he served for twenty-eight years as a parish pastor in Queens, New York City, and in the Camden-Pennsauken, New Jersey area of greater Philadelphia. He loves to think and write about urban and cross-cultural mission and ministry, the evangelical and catholic richness of Lutheran theology, and the church's worship as it creates and sustains faith and spills over into hope and love.

James Wetzstein is associate director of Valparaiso University's Institute of Liturgical Studies, serves as university pastor at Valparaiso University, and has an active liturgical design

consulting practice. He serves on the Lutheran Church Extension Fund (LCEF) Architural Advisory Council, as an advisor to the Center for Liturgical Art at Concordia University Nebraska, and on the Board of Directors of South Shore Arts in Munster, Indiana. **Agnus Day,** the creation of Pastor James Wetzstein, is the only lectionary-based comic strip on the planet. Each week, Rick (the one with the dark nose) and Ted discuss one of the assigned readings from the Common Lectionary. Their conversation drives at a point and sometimes sparks a laugh.

Roland Ziegler teaches systematic theology at Concordia Theological Seminary, Fort Wayne, Indiana. A native of Germany, he came to Fort Wayne in 2000, after being a pastor in Konstanz. His special interests are the Lutheran Confessions, Luther studies, and the topic of prolegomena.

Acknowledgments

Quotations from Luther's Small Catechism are from *Luther's Small Catechism with Explanation*, copyright © 1986, 1991 Concordia Publishing House. All rights reserved.

The quotations from Luther's Works in this publication are from the American Edition: vol. 1 and Companion Vol. © 1958 and 1959, respectively, by Concordia Publishing House. All rights reserved.

The quotations from Luther's Works in this publication are from the American Edition: vols. 31, 32, 34, 35, 36, 41, 49, and 53 © 1957, 1958, 1960, 1960, 1959, 1966, 1972, 1965, respectively, by Augsburg Fortress. Used by permission of the publisher.

The text on pp. 15–17, "Summary of the Christian Faith," and pp. 23 "Common Prayers for Lutherans," is from *Luther's Small Catechism with Explanation*, copyright © 1986, 1991 Concordia Publishing House. All rights reserved.

"Putting It All Together: Confession of Faith" on pp. 179–83 is adapted from the tract "What about . . . Being a Lutheran." Used by permission of the Office of the President, The Lutheran Church—Missouri Synod.

The text on p. 53, "Popular View at Odds with Scripture," was adapted from "The *Left Behind* View Is Out of Left Field," A statement by Dr. A. L. Barry, president of The Lutheran Church—Missouri Synod (December 11, 2000).

Hymn texts with the abbreviation LW are from *Lutheran Worship*, copyright © 1982 by Concordia Publishing House. All rights reserved.

The quotation on p. 29 is from Francis Pieper, *Christian Dogmatics*, vol. 1. St. Louis: Concordia, 1950.

"Prayers for Worship," p. 210, and "The Church Year," pp. 275–78 are from *Lutheran Service Book*, copyright © 2006 Concordia Publishing House. All rights reserved.

The image on p. 221 is from Lee A. Maxwell, *The Altar Guild Manual:* Lutheran Service Book *Edition*. St. Louis: Concordia, 2008.